THE PROPHETS SPEAK ON FORCED MIGRATION

Society of Biblical Literature

Ancient Israel and Its Literature

Thomas C. Römer, General Editor

Editorial Board:
Mark G. Brett
Marc Brettler
Cynthia Edenburg
Konrad Schmid
Gale A. Yee

Number 21

THE PROPHETS SPEAK ON
FORCED MIGRATION

Edited by

Mark J. Boda, Frank Ritchel Ames,
John Ahn, and Mark Leuchter

SBL Press
Atlanta

Copyright © 2015 by SBL Press

All rights reserved. No part of this work may be reproduced or transmitted in any form or by any means, electronic or mechanical, including photocopying and recording, or by means of any information storage or retrieval system, except as may be expressly permitted by the 1976 Copyright Act or in writing from the publisher. Requests for permission should be addressed in writing to the Rights and Permissions Office, SBL Press, 825 Houston Mill Road, Atlanta, GA 30329 USA.

Library of Congress Cataloging-in-Publication Data

The prophets speak on forced migration / edited by Mark J. Boda, Frank Ritchel Ames, John Ahn, and Mark Leuchter.
    p. cm. — (Society of Biblical Literature : Ancient Israel and its literature ; 21)
    Includes bibliographical references and index.
    Summary: "In this collection of essays dealing with the prophetic material in the Hebrew Bible, scholars explore the motifs, effects, and role of forced migration on prophetic literature. Students and scholars interested in current, thorough approaches to the issues and problems associated with the study of geographical displacement, social identity ethics, trauma studies, theological diversification, hermeneutical strategies in relation to the memory, and the effects of various exilic conditions will find a valuable resource with productive avenues for inquiry"— Provided by publisher
    ISBN 978-1-62837-051-5 (paper binding : alk. paper) — ISBN 978-1-62837-052-2 (electronic format) — ISBN 978-1-62837-053-9 (hardcover binding : alk. paper)
    1. Forced migration in rabbinical literature. 2. Bible. Prophets—Criticism, interpretation, etc. I. Boda, Mark J., editor II. Ames, Frank Ritchel, editor. III. Ahn, John J., editor. IV. Leuchter, Mark, editor.
    BM496.9.F67P76 2015
    224'.083408—dc23   2015005716

Printed on acid-free, recycled paper conforming to
ANSI/NISO Z39.48-1992 (R1997) and ISO 9706:1994
standards for paper permanence.

Contents

Preface vii
Abbreviations ix

Introduction
    John Ahn and Frank Ritchel Ames 1

Prophetic Rhetoric and Exile
    David L. Petersen 9

Provenance as a Factor in Interpretation
    Christopher R. Seitz 19

"You are My Witness and My Servant" (Isa 43:10): Exile and
    the Identity of the Servant
    Ulrich Berges 33

Second Isaiah and the Aaronide Response to Judah's Forced
    Migrations
    Stephen L. Cook 47

Nebuchadnezzar, the End of Davidic Rule, and the Exile in
    the Book of Jeremiah
    Konrad Schmid 63

Sacred Space and Communal Legitimacy in Exile: The
    Contribution of Seraiah's Colophon (Jer 51:59–64a)
    Mark Leuchter 77

Ezekiel 15: A משל
    John Ahn 101

The Cultic Dimensions of Prophecy in the Book of Ezekiel
   Corinna Körting 121

Ezekiel as Disaster/Survival Literature: Speaking on Behalf
   of the Losers
   Louis Stulman 133

Forced Migrations and the Visions of Zechariah 1–8
   Frank Ritchel Ames 147

Scat! Exilic Motifs in the Book of Zechariah
   Mark J. Boda 161

Bibliography 181

Contributors 205

Index of Primary Sources 207
Index of Modern Authors 221

Preface

The present volume represents the laborious efforts of many people. First and foremost, we are grateful to the contributors, whose patience and dedication to the publication of this volume is inspiring. The collection of essays here lingered in exile for quite a while before finding a home with the Society of Biblical Literature (SBL)—which is fitting, since they all originated as papers presented at SBL meetings a few years ago (Urzeit is indeed Endzeit, apparently). We are also extremely grateful to Leigh Andersen at SBL, whose understanding and support created a context in which we could complete this project. Sincere thanks and credit must also be given to Meghan Musy, whose copious attention to detail on the copy editing and helpful insights and suggestions for each essay was essential to our production of this volume.

Finally, we wish to thank Tiglath-pileser III, Shalmaneser V, Sargon II, Sennacherib, and Nebuchadnezzar, without whom many writers—biblical and contemporary—would have to find another line of work. Thanks for keeping us employed.

Mark J. Boda
Mark Leuchter

Abbreviations

AB	Anchor Bible
ABD	An*chor Bible Dictionary.* Edited by David Noel Freedman. 6 vols. New York: Doubleday, 1992.
ABIG	Arbeiten zur Bibel und ihrer Geschichte
AfO	Archiv für Orientforschung
AIL	Ancient Israel and Its Literature
AnBib	Analecta Biblica
AOAT	Alter Orient und Altes Testament
ATD	Das Alte Testament Deutsch
AThANT	Abhandlungen zur Theologie des Alten und Neuen Testaments
AUMSR	Andrews University Monographs Studies in Religion
AUSS	*Andrews University Seminary Studies*
BA	*Biblical Archaeologist*
BASOR	*Bulletin of the American Schools of Oriental Research*
BBB	Bonner biblische Beiträge
BETL	Bibliotheca ephemeridum theologicarum lovaniensium
BHRG	*A Biblical Hebrew Reference Grammar.* Christo H. J. van der Merwe, Jackie A. Naudé, and Jan H. Kroeze. Biblical Languages: Hebrew 3. Sheffield: Sheffield Academic, 1999.
BHS	*Biblia Hebraica Stuttgartensia.* Edited by Karl Elliger and Wilhelm Rudolph. Stuttgart: Deutsche Bibelgesellschaft, 1983.
BHT	Beiträge zur historischen Theologie
Bib	*Biblica*
BibOr	*Biblica et orientalia*
BibSem	Biblical Seminar
BJS	Brown Judaic Studies
BK	*Bibel und Kirche*
BKAT	Biblischer Kommentar: Altes Testament

BN	*Biblische Notizen*
BO	Bibliotheca orientalis
BWANT	Beiträge zur Wissenschaft vom Alten und Neuen Testament
BZ	*Biblische Zeitschrift*
BZAW	Beihefte zur ZAW
CahRB	Cahiers de la Revue biblique
CurBR	*Currents in Biblical Research*
DSD	*Dead Sea Discoveries*
EdF	Erträge der Forschung
EncJud	*Encyclopaedia Judaica*. Edited by Cecil Roth and Geoffrey Wigoder. 16 vols. Jerusalem: Keter, 1971–1972.
ETL	*Ephemerides theologicae lovanienses*
ETR	*Etudes théologiques et religieuses*
ETS	Erfurter theologische Studien
EvT	*Evangelische Theologie*
FB	Forschungen zur Bibel
FOTL	Forms of the Old Testament Literature
FRLANT	Forschungen zur Religion und Literatur des Alten und Neuen Testaments
HALOT	*Hebrew and Aramaic Lexicon of the Old Testament*. Edited by Ludwig Koehler, Walter Baumgartner, and Johann Jakob Stamm. Translated and edited under the supervision of M. E. J. Richardson. 5 vols. Leiden: Brill, 1994–2000.
HAR	*Hebrew Annual Review*
HAT	Handbuch zum Alten Testament
HBM	Hebrew Bible Monographs
HBT	*Horizons in Biblical Theology*
HKAT	Handkommentar zum Alten Testament
HSM	Harvard Semitic Monographs
HTKAT	Herders Theologischer Kommentar zum Alten Testament
HUCA	Hebrew Union College Annual
IB	*The Interpreter's Bible*. Edited by George A. Buttrick. 12 vols. New York: Abingdon, 1951–1957.
IBC	Interpretation: A Bible Commentary for Teaching and Preaching
IBHS	Bruce K. Waltke and Michael O'Connor, *An Introduction to Biblical Hebrew Syntax*. Winona Lake, IN: Eisenbrauns, 1990.
ICC	International Critical Commentary

IDB	*The Interpreter's Dictionary of the Bible*. Edited by George A. Buttrick. 4 vols. New York: Abingdon, 1962.
IDBSup	*The Interpreter's Dictionary of the Bible: Supplementary Volume*. Edited by Keith Crim. Nashville: Abingdon, 1976.
IEJ	*Israel Exploration Journal*
Int	*Interpretation*
JANER	*Journal of Ancient Near Eastern Religion*
JBL	*Journal of Biblical Literature*
JETS	*Journal of the Evangelical Theological Society*
JHebS	*Journal of Hebrew Scriptures*
JJS	*Journal of Jewish Studies*
JNES	*Journal of Near Eastern Studies*
JPS	Jewish Publication Society Version
JSJ	*Journal for the Study of Judaism in the Persian, Hellenistic, and Roman Periods*
JSJSup	Journal for the Study of Judaism in the Persian, Hellenistic, and Roman Periods Supplement Series
JSOT	*Journal for the Study of the Old Testament*
JSOTSup	Journal for the Study of the Old Testament Supplement Series
JSS	*Journal of Semitic Studies*
JTS	*Journal of Theological Studies*
KAT	Kommentar zum Alten Testament
KJV	King James Version
KTU	*Die keilalphabetischen Texte aus Ugarit*. Edited by Manfried Dietrich, Oswald Loretz, and Joaquín Sanmartín. Münster: Ugarit-Verlag, 1995.
LHBOTS	Library of Hebrew Bible/Old Testament Studies
MMWR	*Morbidity and Mortality Weekly Report*
NCB	New Century Bible Commentary
NET	New English Translation
NIB	*The New Interpreter's Bible*. Edited by Leander E. Keck. 12 vols. Nashville: Abingdon, 1994–2004.
NICOT	New International Commentary on the Old Testament
NJB	New Jerusalem Bible
NJPS	New Jewish Publication Society Version
NRSV	New Revised Standard Version
NTT	*Norsk Teologisk Tidsskrift*
OBO	Orbis biblicus et orientalis

OBT	Overtures to Biblical Theology
Or	*Orientalia* (Rome)
OTG	Old Testament Guides
OTL	Old Testament Library
OTM	Oxford Theological Monographs
OtSt	*Oudtestamentische Studiën*
RB	*Revue biblique.*
RGG	*Religion in Geschichte und Gegenwart.* Edited by Hans Dieter Betz et al. 4th ed. 9 vols. Tübingen: Mohr Siebeck, 1998–2007.
RSV	Revised Standard Version
SBAB	Stuttgarter biblische Aufsatzbände
SBLDS	Society of Biblical Literature Dissertation Series
SBLMS	Society of Biblical Literature Monograph Series
SBLStBL	Society of Biblical Literature Studies in Biblical Literature
SBT	Studies in Biblical Theology
SHANE	Studies in the History of the Ancient Near East
SHBC	Smyth and Helwys Bible Commentary
SJOT	*Scandinavian Journal of the Old Testament*
STAR	Studies in Theology and Religion
SymS	Symposium Series
ThB	Theologische Bücherei
TLOT	*Theological Lexicon of the Old Testament.* Edited by Ernst Jenni and Claus Westermann. 3 vols. Translated by Mark E. Biddle. Peabody, MA: Hendrickson, 1997
TLZ	*Theologische Literaturzeitung*
TZ	*Theologische Zeitschrift*
VT	*Vetus Testamentum*
VTSup	Supplements to Vetus Testamentum
WBC	Word Biblical Commentary
WMANT	Wissenschaftliche Monographien zum Alten und Neuen Testament
WUNT	Wissenschaftliche Untersuchungen zum Neuen Testament
ZABR	*Zeitschrift für altorientalische und biblische Rechtsgeschichte*
ZAW	*Zeitschrift für die alttestamentliche Wissenschaft*
ZBK	Zürcher Bibelkommentar
ZDPV	*Zeitschrift des Deutschen Palästina-Vereins*

Introduction

John Ahn and Frank Ritchel Ames

Since 2008, the critical study of the exilic period, the sixth century BCE, has been enriched by the Exile-Forced Migrations in Biblical Literature Group of the Society of Biblical Literature (SBL). The great attention this topic has received and the strong support for the group's sessions is an indication of how deeply the topic has affected the spectrum of literature studied in all corners of the guild. The participating panelists in the early years of the group contributed to a much needed conversation on the issue of the Bible's own manifold attempts to categorize and qualify the experience of exile-forced migration, which has led to the publication of important volumes on this matter. The first volume, *By the Irrigation Canals of Babylon: Methods in the Study of the Exile* (2012), highlighted and collectively examined problems on the exile through historical, literary, and sociological lenses by bridging scholars from North America and Europe. This second volume addresses the important subject matter of Exilic Prophetic Gattung in a parallel format. In the 2009 SBL annual meeting, the Exile-Forced Migrations Group (Consultation back then) held four sessions. Three sessions dealt with Exilic Prophetic Gattung: "North American Perspective," "European Perspective," and "From the Minor Prophets to the Mishna Avot." This volume is composed of selected papers from those sessions.

In this short introduction, we note simply that migration is a biological and social fact of life. Migration is found in flora, fauna, and humanity. A seed from China is carried across the Atlanta Ocean through jet streams to break new ground on the west coast of the United States of America. Fish, whales, birds, the Calabooses, among others, all migrate; some returning to their spawning ground after months of an exhaustive journey, only to reproduce and then die. Indeed, death brings life. The story of human beings from the very beginning is one of migration, a forced migration out of Eden (or Africa). Adam and Eve's expulsion from paradise, when read through cultural memory or cultural or social trauma, speaks to the experience of the first-generation Judeans being forced out of their homeland. In the ensuing generation, Cain also experienced forced migration. Even the account of Noah may offer a new perspective on forced migration across or upon the chaos of raging waters. The Primeval History ends (Gen 11) where it began (Gen 1), in Babel or Babylon. In short, in every major section of the Hebrew Bible or, for that matter, even in the New Testament, exile or forced migration takes the center stage of religious life and activities.

Forced migration or exile is no longer viewed as punishment for sin. Complementing such a view is its antithesis—that is, forced migration saves lives. Laden with indescribable pain and hardship in the actual task of migrating, new meaning making is undertaken, old and new values collide in new settings, and hope and new creation are forged for ensuing generations that are the beneficiaries of the selfless first generation. Forced migration sheds new light on the exilic period. For the first time in the history of biblical studies on the exile, forced migration studies has enabled scholars to see and hear real variables that affect peoples on the move. The analysis of migration: Derivative Forced Migration (DFM), Purposive Forced Migration (PFM), Responsive Forced Migration (RFM), and the types of displacement and resettlement imposed on peoples, Development Induced Displaced Persons (DIDPs), Internally Displaced Persons (IDPs), and Refugee Studies (RS) provide a framework to not only demarcate 597, 587, and 582 events but once resettled, generational consciousness provides a new cadre for reexamining redactional literary activity that is reflexive of each generation.[1]

Acculturation or assimilation into the host or dominant culture is a goal of every generation—but not always. The most powerful ideology stems from a desire to transcend and move beyond where one's parents or grandparents started from—not just to mark accomplishment or boast success—but to truly and humbly honor the very first generation that sacrificed and dreamed for a brighter future. Each generation is interconnected, creating a system, a mode for going beyond survival to actualize the desire to "be fruitful and multiply." Such is the mind-set and work ethic

---

1. See further the contribution by John Ahn to the present volume.

of many (im)migrants in modern and possibly ancient times. Each generation is a carrier of the previous generations' memories.

In modern and ancient analysis of forced migration, the framework for migrations is by and large economics, though other factors are taken into consideration. Economists generally agree that calculated and planned immigration policies promote economic development. With this said, the use of mass deportation by the Assyrians, the more local and repeated small waves of forced migration for regional economic development through establishments of ethnic enclaves by the Babylonians, or the use of return migrations to control overpopulation or infrastructure problems during the Persian period all attest to the theory of migration and economics. For many forced migrants, economics is often weighed against religion—not financial gain or resources but God or faith is prescribed as the most important value in life. For people in flight particularly, the driving force in their forced migrations is (paradoxically) God. The prophets of the Hebrew Bible speak to this phenomenon. From a Luhmanian perspective,[2] in a system of religion, religion needs migration.

Broadly speaking, then, after genocide, forced migration is the most pressing humanitarian issue in the twenty-first century. Even the most cursory glance at events regularly reported in the contemporary media reveals the pervasiveness of this theme and the depth of its impact upon local and distant communities and cultures, and the same can be said of the ancient sixth to third centuries BCE. By drawing attention to the prophets on forced migration, a collective voice is heard across time: to be economically viable, socially engaged, culturally relevant, and religiously resolute. To be prophetic is to be conscious and then to speak the divine word, knowing that it is charged with judgment and death but also with redemption and life. The present volume devotes its attention to the recurring motif of exile-forced migration in the prophetic literature in the effort to elucidate and appreciate the intellectual and theological strategies these authors and their audiences deployed while enduring conditions that were viewed as both catastrophic and redemptive at once.

In "Prophetic Rhetoric and Exile," David L. Petersen contrasts the exilic experience and rhetoric of Israel under the Neo-Assyrian Empire with that of Judah under Neo-Babylonian domination. After discussing

---

2. Niklas Luhmann, *Die Religion der Gesellschaft* (Frankfurt am Main: Suhrkamp, 2000); Eng. trans.: *A Systems Theory of Religion,* trans. David A. Brenner with Adrian Hermann, ed. André Kieserling (Stanford: Stanford University Press, 2013).

the importance of defining exile precisely, Petersen differentiates forced migration, voluntary migration, and incarceration; describes the practices of Assyria and Babylon; and examines the rhetoric of exile in Amos, Hosea, Isaiah ben Amoz, Micah, Jeremiah, and Ezekiel. He concludes that exile under Assyria and Babylon differed in the number of captives, effect on identity, and emotional register and that the rhetoric of the prophets in Neo-Babylonian times was shaped not simply by contemporary events but by past Neo-Assyrian experiences. By considering several prophetic books, Petersen surveys the broader conceptual topography of prophetic literature in the context of ancient Mesopotamian imperialism, demonstrating that irrespective of specific nuance, all of these texts contribute to a grammar of perception regarding Israel and Judah's tenuous position on the world stage.

In "Provenance as a Factor in Interpretation," Christopher Seitz considers the exilic/postexilic material embedded within the book of Isaiah in hermeneutical conversation with the material in First Isaiah. Seitz examines how the historical/geographical contexts of these later "Isaiahs" differentiate them from the preexilic material while simultaneously creating a single canonical exhortation that reframes the terms of the exile. The indiscernible within the material of First Isaiah is finally fully expressed by the later material's genetic connection to the earlier oracles. The canonical form of the book relocates material ostensibly originating in Babylon to a Zion-centered context, providing dramatically new meaning for the material. Isaiah, Seitz concludes, emphasizes the comfort of Zion and the far side of judgment, with all nations witnessing the work of the one God who judges and restores Israel.

Continuing the examination of the book of Isaiah are two studies of interpretation within the Isaianic tradition. In his essay, "'You are my witness and my servant' (Isa 43:10): Exile and the Identity of the Servant," Ulrich Berges argues that Isa 40–55 was composed not by an anonymous individual but by members of a group whose identity as descendants of Jacob (Israel) was renewed in exile. Exile forged the group into witnesses of YHWH's universal sovereignty, and these witnesses, who were called to comfort Zion (Jerusalem), as a group constituted Isaiah's Servant (Isa 43:10) and, like David, command all nations not through conquest and domination but by declaring the commandments of YHWH. Stephen Cook highlights the distinctiveness of Second Isaiah's response to the exile over against the very different approaches displayed in the books of Jeremiah and Ezekiel in his essay, "Second Isaiah and the Aaronide Response to Judah's Forced Migrations." Key to Second Isaiah's unique handling of the exile is an impressive sampling of priestly reflections, seen in the close match in orientation and theology between Second Isaiah and the Priestly Torah. While the two writings express themselves with different moods and styles, they share particular themes, motifs, and concerns oriented on a theology of reverence before the numinous otherness of God.

The essays by Berges and Cook point to a growing interdependence between prophetic literature and the texts that would eventually become part of the Pentateuch; this may be a function of exilic conditions that amplified the need to more actively engage ancestral and ritual traditions among communities separated from their ancestral estates and the sacral institutions of the homeland. The Isaiah tradition, steeped in the lore and legacy of Zion and Jerusalem, would be an entirely appropriate forum for the countenancing of these concerns on the literary level, but different approaches are adopted in the other major prophetic texts generated under the hegemony of the Mesopotamian empires.

Turning attention to the book of Jeremiah, Konrad Schmid proposes a solution to an interpretive problem associated with Jer 36:30 in his essay, "Nebuchadnezzar, the end of Davidic Rule, and the Exile in the Book of Jeremiah." As Schmid argues, Jer 36:30 predicts that the Davidic dynasty ends with Jehoiakim in 605 BCE, but the prediction appears to be erroneous because the Davidic dynasty continues under Jehoiakim's successors until 587 BCE. Jeremiah 36:30, however, has a theological rather than documentary purpose and must be read as symbolic. The oracle reveals a shift in the cosmos and sacral history where the center point of divine intention revolved around Babylon and its ruler Nebuchadnezzar, and it offers a powerful theological explanation for foreign dominion over Israel. This explanation, from Schmid's perspective, emerges from a learned scribe involved with the redaction of the book of Jeremiah, for whom the experience of the Babylonian exile forever changed the course of history.

A different issue with respect to geomythology in the Jeremiah tradition is discussed by Mark Leuchter in his essay, "Sacred Space and Communal Legitimacy in Exile: The Contribution of Seraiah's Colophon (Jer 51:59–64a)." Leuchter shows that Seraiah's colophon (Jer 51:59–64a) was part of a scroll that was deposited into the Euphrates and functioned as a foundation inscription, establishing that Mesopotamia, though destined for destruction, was sanctified space, whereas Jerusalem, which eventually would be restored, was unclean. The scroll and colophon, embedded in Jeremiah, gave rise to divergent view of communal identity and sacred space, including rival claims about the relative sanctity of the exiles of 597 and 587 BCE. Leuchter discusses the perspectives of Ezekiel, Jeremiah, and Ezra-Nehemiah, and the persistence, moderation, and irony of this new understanding of sacred space and community identity.

The nexus between the Jeremiah and Ezekiel traditions as containing variant perceptions of the exilic experience (or perhaps better, experiences) is further developed in a series of contributions focusing on the book of Ezekiel. In his essay "Ezekiel 15: A משל," John Ahn examines the design and provenance of Ezek 15, showing how the prophet's puzzling words refer to the exiled communities of 597, 587, and 582 BCE. The prophet's words, Ahn suggests, may explain how changes in the exilic community were accommodated, allowing the exiles of 597 to accept the exiles of 587 through an oracle that blames the exiles of 582 for the desolation of the land. The essay draws attention to what is often overlooked, namely, that the different waves of exile were not rehearsals of the same experience but constituted distinct experienced unto themselves, producing attitudes to which the trustees of the Ezekiel tradition needed to respond.

In her essay, "The Cultic Dimensions of Prophecy in the Book of Ezekiel," Corinna Körting investigates connections between prophecy and the priestly cult in the book of Ezekiel by addressing the relationship between prophetical message and cultic legislation in Ezek 14:1–11. Her search for the function of the combination of different traditions is accompanied by the question of how these traditions supplement each other in the specific historical or constructed historical situation, a time without a temple—the exile. She concludes that there is an enlarged understanding of prophecy that adds priestly tasks to the prophetic office in a context without temple and cult through *Schriftauslegung*. In addition, there is the establishment of a new, clean cultic community within a hostile environment. Körting engages the oft-pondered issue of how a community so defined by its cultic institutions survives an environment where such outlets were no longer accessible; emerging from her study are important implications for the evolution of both the cult and prophecy that extend the current scholarly conversation.

In the final entry on Ezekiel, Louis Stulman considers the effects of exilic trauma on prophetic rhetoric in his essay, "Ezekiel as Disaster/Survival Literature: Speaking on Behalf of the Losers." Stulman examines the oracles of Ezekiel, who speaks on behalf of those who experienced defeat in the conflict between Judah and Babylon and as one who has also suffered and survived the trauma. The mythological paradigms that emerge from dislocation and the struggle to survive emphasize human vulnerability and transience and the traumatization of the divine. Stulman argues that both Ezekiel and YHWH have suffered trauma and that the presence of the divine is experienced not only in triumph and holiness, but through tragedy, destruction, and suffering.

Finally, the volume turns attention to prophetic texts emerging after the period of the Babylonian exile, notably those found in the book of Zechariah. In his essay, "Forced Migrations and the Visions of Zechariah 1–8," Frank Ritchel Ames argues that forced migrations in modern communities diminish resources and security, increase mortality and morbidity, and alter social relationships and identities. Then, applying comparative and literary methods to Zech 1–8, he finds evidence of similar outcomes in Judah's experience of exile, describing how the visions and oracles of Zechariah reflect and address the social realities of Judah's forced migration and later restoration. In "Scat! Exilic Motifs in the Book of Zechariah," Mark J. Boda attends to Zechariah's explicit references to exile as forced migration, a motif that follows the movement of both human and divine characters throughout the book. The book, he observes, uses a variety of images to depict the human experience of exile and the diverse identities of exilic communities as well as exile and return for a Babylonian and Judean deity, linking the human and divine experience of exile and restoration.

Both Boda and Ames unveil rhetorical dimensions of postexilic prophecy that dovetail with contemporary discussions on the degree to which literature from the Persian period and beyond is never far removed from the effects of exile; discourses on restoration and redemption are all predicated upon the inescapability of the more traumatic past. Scholars are realizing with greater frequency the persistence of the social, mythological, and theological ruptures that were brought on by the succession of exilic experience under Assyria and Babylon not only in the self-understanding of those groups who experienced forced migration but also among those who did not.[3] Not coincidentally, both sets of experiences routinely appeal to prophetic tradition as a gauge of cosmic and covenantal legitimacy, and as a hermeneutical lens through which contemporaneous events could be understood (e.g., Dan 9). The present volume

---

3. See recently Dalit Rom-Shiloni, *Inclusive Exclusivity: Identity Conflicts between the Exiles and the People Who Remained (6th–5th Centuries BCE)*, LHBOTS 543 (New York: Bloomsbury T&T Clark, 2013); Mark Leuchter, "Inter-Levitical Polemics in the Late 6th Century B.C.E.: The Evidence from Nehemiah 9," *Bib* 95 (2014): 269–79.

represents another stage in this important scholarly discussion, which is no doubt still in its early stages.

Prophetic Rhetoric and Exile

David L. Petersen

I have, on occasion, been tempted to revise the claim that the exodus was the watershed moment in ancient Israel by suggesting that the exile was at least of equal importance. To make such a case requires that we be clear about what we mean by "exile." Biblical scholars have often used the term *exile* or its adjectival form, *exilic*, (1) to refer to a historical period (vague though the terminus ad quem for that period might be since from 597 BCE on, there were always Yahwists living outside the land), (2) to refer to literature from that period, (3) to refer to practices or behaviors of the Neo-Assyrian and Neo-Babylonian Empires, (4) to characterize various human experiences lived in exile, and (5) to refer to forms of thinking—ideologies or theologies—about exile. I list this roster simply to make the point that the term *exile* means different things to different people. As a result, it is important that we be as precise as possible about what we mean by *exile*.

Definitions and Distinctions

At the outset, I would like to propose that when we review literature in the Hebrew Bible, we can identify at least three different forms of behavior that might be characterized as exile.[1]

First, there is *forced migration*, typically as a part of military and/ or imperial practice. This is probably what first comes to most people's minds. The removal of several thousand Judahites to Mesopotamia in the

---

1. One could add a fourth, banishment (e.g., Neh 7:26), but since banishment often focuses on the individual and is not prominent in prophetic rhetoric, I have not addressed it in this paper.

period 597–582 BCE (Jer 52:28–30) would be a classic example. In Biblical Hebrew, the typical lexeme for this sort of exile is the root *glh*.

Second, one can point to *voluntary migration*. Such movement of groups of people can take place due to natural or political conditions. The tradition of Israel leaving the land and moving to another country during a time of famine would be an instance of the former (Gen 12; 26; 46—all three patriarchs and matriarchs). As for the latter, a group of Judahites, under the leadership of Johanan and Azariah, moved to Egypt to escape a perceived threat from the Neo-Babylonians (Jer 42).

Third, one can point to *incarceration*, taking prisoners and moving them away from their land. This practice is attested in Jer 48:46,[2] referring to the incarceration of certain Moabites.[3] One might, as well, think about the status of Jehoiachin, who was taken to Mesopotamia but who was also, at least according to the Deuteronomistic Historian, imprisoned for a time. The typical diction for incarceration includes *šbh*, its nominal forms (*šibyâ*, *šəbîyâ*; e.g., Jer 48:46), and *bêt hakkəlîʾ* ("prison"; Jer 52:31). In these cases, it is probably appropriate to think of incarceration as a subclass of forced migration.

Ancient Near Eastern Context

Any responsible reflection about this typology must take extrabiblical data into account. Fortunately, there is considerable ancient Near Eastern evidence concerning practices known as "exile." For the purpose of this paper, I will focus on the Neo-Assyrian and Neo-Babylonian evidence.

Bustenay Oded has studied the data from the Neo-Assyrian Empire and construes its movement of populations as "mass deportation."[4] David Vanderhooft refines this notion when emphasizing the practice of cross-deportation, the practice of removing some of population x and replacing it with some of population y.[5] The practice of cross-deportation was consistent with the Neo-Assyrian goal of establishing economically

---

2. Jer 48:45–47 is not in the LXX.

3. The historical agent is unnamed, though the larger literary context presumes the Neo-Babylonians under Nebuchadnezzar.

4. Bustenay Oded, *Mass Deportations and Deportees in the Neo-Assyrian Empire* (Wiesbaden: Reichert, 1979).

5. David Vanderhooft, *The Neo-Babylonian Empire and Babylon in the Latter Prophets*, HSM 59 (Atlanta: Scholars Press, 1999), 110.

productive provinces in the empire. Rather than simply slash and burn, they attempted to regenerate economic activity in provinces that had been conquered.[6]

Neo-Babylonian practices of mass deportation were decidedly different from those of their Neo-Assyrian precursors. There is no evidence that they engaged in cross-deportation. The demographic movement was one way—to the heartland of the Neo-Babylonian Empire. This difference was part of a larger imperial practice, according to which the Neo-Babylonians did not invest time and effort in creating productive provinces throughout the empire. Rather, like the much later Aztecs, they engaged in military campaigns in those regions to secure tribute and to support construction in their urban centers.

Further, the Neo-Babylonians apparently settled deportees en masse in towns that were known by the name of the place where the settlers had lived in their native lands. Vanderhooft has identified urban sites in southern Babylonia with the following names: Ashkelon, Gaza, Neirab, Qedah, Tyre, and, now, Al-Yahudu (or the city of Judah).[7] This last name, which was first known in a cuneiform tablet published by Joannes and Lemaire, has been strikingly confirmed in the so-called TAYN texts (Texts from al-Yahudu and Našar). Roughly thirty texts come from al-Yahudu, a site that Laurie Pearce argues is near Borsippa.[8] In the TAYN corpus, 20 percent of the names include the Yahwistic theophoric ele-

---

6. In accord with this policy, in which conquered territories were redeveloped, the Neo-Assyrians apparently accorded those in exile a certain measure of civil rights. They were not characterized as slaves or as prisoners. To quote Oded, "They lived a family life, had property (land, slaves, silver), were creditors and debtors, had the right to engage in litigation, in commerce and business transactions, and the right to witness contracts and suits, and to maintain their ancestral traditions" (*Mass Deportations*, 87). A recently republished text from Nimrud, which includes the names of two Yahwists, apparently living in Media ca. 730 BCE, corroborates this judgment. See Gershon Galil, "Israelite Exiles in Media: A New Look at ND 2443+," *VT* 59 (2009): 71–79.

7. David Vanderhooft, "New Evidence Pertaining to the Transition from Neo-Babylonian to Achaemenid Administration in Palestine," in *Yahwism after the Exile: Perspectives on Israelite Religion in the Persian Era*, ed. Rainer Albertz and Bob Becking, STAR 5 (Assen: Van Gorcum, 2003).

8. Laurie Pearce, "New Evidence for Judeans in Babylon," in *Judah and the Judeans in the Persian Period*, ed. Oded Lipschits and Manfred Oeming (Winona Lake, IN: Eisenbrauns, 2006), 399–411.

ment. All these highlights point to a group of Judahites who were settled as a group. The book of Ezekiel attests to a comparable community when the book's superscription states that Ezekiel "was among the exiles by the river Chebar" (Ezek 1:1). That these communities retained names reflecting their geographic origins may well help in explaining why these Yahwists were not lost to history, as was the case with their kin exiled from the Northern Kingdom.

Unlike the Neo-Assyrian documentary evidence, the Neo-Babylonian inscriptions do not include many reports about wars and deportations. In fact, when one reads the Babylonian Chronicles, the last year in which the verb *galû* appears is Nabopolassar's fourteenth year, 612 BCE. The term never appears during the Chronicles' reports about Nebuchadnezzar's military exploits. Indeed, there is a striking move away from the taking of prisoners and toward the payment of tribute and the taking of booty during Nebuchadnezzar's campaigns. And that is the way the Babylonian Chronicle 5 describes the conquest of Judah in 597 BCE, "A king of his own choice he appointed in the city and taking the vast tribute he brought it into Babylon."[9] This shift in description during the reign of Nebuchadnezzar should not be underestimated. It may well suggest a moving away from the practice of forced migration under the Neo-Babylonians.[10]

This distinction in the practice of exile by the two Mesopotamian empires can be underscored by attention to the numbers of Yahwists taken into those respective exiles. As for that of Samaria, the Deuteronomistic Historian offers no comment about the number of Israelites taken, other than the hyperbolic statement that "the LORD rejected all the descendants of Israel" (2 Kgs 17:20). Fortunately, Assyrian inscriptions offer greater detail. The so-called Sargon II Display Inscription reports: "I besieged and conquered Samerina. 27,290 people who lived in its midst, I carried away."[11] Another text, the Sargon II Nimrud Prism, puts the figure at 27,280.[12]

---

9. A. K. Grayson, *Assyrian and Babylonian Chronicles* (1975; repr., Winona Lake, IN: Eisenbrauns, 2000), 102.

10. David Vanderhooft, "Babylonian Strategies of Imperial Control in the West," in Lipschits and Oeming, *Judah and the Judeans*, 250. "Even the idea of deportation, for example, which is explicitly referred to in the Assyrian inscriptions in connection with the *šibirru*, is only hinted at in Nebuchadnezzar's inscriptions" (ibid.).

11. Bob Becking, *The Fall of Samaria: An Historical and Archaeological Study*, SHANE 2 (Leiden: Brill, 1992), 26.

12. Ibid., 29.

The textual evidence for the size of the deportations from Judah in the early sixth century BCE is decidedly different. There is nothing comparable to the Sargon inscriptions. The Weidner tablets refer only to members of Judean royalty—Jehoiachin and his five sons along with eight other individuals, presumably of high rank. Biblical texts that report the exile under the Neo-Babylonians offer diverse testimony. In 2 Kgs 24:14, 16, the Deuteronomistic Historian offers two different figures: ten thousand versus eight thousand. The numbers are tellingly round. (Further, the smaller figure is probably a subset of the larger.) The situation in Jer 52:28–30 is very different. That text enumerates exiles taken at three different times: 3,023 in 597 BCE, 832 in 587 BCE, and 745 in 582 BCE, for a grand total of 4,600. Several things can be said. First, Jeremiah offers a much lower total figure for the number of Judahite refugees than does the Deuteronomistic Historian. Second, in opposition to the historian, Jeremiah offers a large number of those taken in 597 BCE. Third, Jeremiah sees the process continuing over a period of fifteen years.[13] Still, the bottom line is this: there is good reason to think that far fewer people were taken into exile by the Neo-Babylonians than were taken by the Neo-Assyrians. It is a commonplace to claim that the Babylonians apparently removed only members of certain specialized or elite classes—royalty, warriors, skilled workers, scribes among them.

In sum, there was no uniform practice of exile in the ancient Near East. What happened in 721 BCE was quite different from that which transpired in the early sixth century BCE. Further, though the symbolic impact of the destruction and depopulation of Jerusalem and its temple was immense, the number of people taken was probably decidedly smaller than those taken from Israel.

Prophetic Rhetoric

At this point, I would like to offer some thumbnail sketches about prophetic rhetoric up to the beginning of the sixth century BCE.[14] I do this

---

13. Since this section is present neither in LXX Jeremiah nor in the corresponding chapter in 2 Kings, one must be wary of overemphasizing this material.

14. See Robert P. Carroll, "Deportation and Diasporic Discourses in the Prophetic Literature," in *Exile: Old Testament, Jewish, and Christian Conceptions*, ed. James Scott, JSJSup 56 (Leiden: Brill, 1997), 63–85. He too surveys individual prophetic books. My overview is primarily literary and historical, whereas Carroll is concerned with the "discourses of diaspora." In addition, he includes analysis of "return," whereas I

because I contend that prophets of the Neo-Babylonian period inherited certain ways of thinking about exile from their prophetic forebears. Neo-Babylonian prophetic rhetoric concerning exile is grounded in experiences of Israel and Judah with the imperial practices of the Neo-Assyrians. Hence, though it might seem natural to highlight Jeremiah, Ezekiel, and prophets who come after them, it is important to assess those prophets who created the rhetoric of exile.

We turn first to the Neo-Assyrian period and Amos.

Amos

The book of Amos knows the practice of exile. He refers to it using perfect verbs. In the oracles against the nations, he indicts both Gaza and Tyre for having handed over entire populations to Edom (1:6, 9). That the smaller Syro-Palestinian states used exile as a military strategy is otherwise unattested, but it does suggest that the practice was not unique to Mesopotamia.

The prophet also anticipates that certain Israelite cities—Gilgal// Bethel (5:5)—will be exiled in the future, as will the Northern Kingdom (5:27; 6:7). That this was a fundamental part of Amos's message may be inferred when Amaziah quotes him as having said, "Israel must go into exile" (7:11). Amos's rhetoric appears to reflect the world of military and imperial practice, particularly when the book refers to Israel being taken into exile beyond Damascus. That is just what an Israelite might have expected the Neo-Assyrians to do.

Hosea

The book of Hosea is much different. It speaks about people leaving the land, for example, "they shall return to Egypt" (8:13), or "they shall not remain in the land of the LORD; but Ephraim shall return to Egypt, and in Assyria they shall eat unclean food" (9:3; cf. 11:5). This language bears the connotations of voluntary migration rather than forced deportation. Hosea claims that Israel's earlier sojourn in Egypt provides the paradigm by means of which Israel's "exile" is to be understood. The time in Egypt

---

focus just on movement away from the land. Finally, he more or less equates the exilic experience of Israel and Judah.

involved enslavement, and enslavement was not a typical status for those in exile under either the Assyrians or the Babylonians.

The prophet does, however, move to other ideas of exile. For example, in 9:17 he claims that "they shall become wanderers among [the verb *ndd* plus *b*] the nations."[15] In only one case does Hosea anticipate an exile that might be wrought by the Neo-Assyrians: "its [Samaria's] idolatrous priests shall wail over it for its glory that has gone into exile away from it" (10:5). For the most part, Hosea constructs the notion of exile out of prior Israelite traditions of voluntary migration rather than referring explicitly to the Neo-Assyrian practice of forced migration.

Isaiah ben Amoz

Isaiah appears to be heavily influenced by the fate of the Northern Kingdom. He refers to an exile that has already taken place. Strikingly, in 5:13, the only text in which the word *glh* occurs, he refers to "my people who have gone [the verb is in the perfect] into exile." And Isaiah anticipates the return of those who were taken to Assyria, "so there shall be a highway from Assyria for the remnant that is left of his people, as there was for Israel when they came up from the land of Egypt" (11:16). Here Isaiah, like Hosea before him, uses older traditions—that of the exodus—to think about exile and its aftermath. Elsewhere, and in prose oracles, Isaiah refers to a remnant of the Northern Kingdom that will, someday, return (10:20–23; 11:11.) Finally, 14:1–2 also focuses on the exile of the Northern Kingdom, though construing it as *captivity*, *šbh*, rather than *exile*. Here Isaiah appeals to exile as incarceration.

Interestingly, only in prose texts are there reference to Judah and exile. In the Deuteronomistic prose of chapters 36–39, we hear about the possibility of exile for Judah. The Rabshakeh announces on behalf of the king of Assyria: "until I come and take you away to a land like your own land" (36:17).

Micah

Micah, like Isaiah, knows about exile, though he does not refer to it often. For him, military destruction rather than removal of a population seems

---

15. The same construction (the verb *ndd* plus the preposition *b*) is used of Cain as a wanderer over the earth.

more important. Nonetheless, the prophet refers to "children who have already gone into exile" (1:16). In this case, the population may well have been Judahite, with Sennacherib as the agent of exile. Moreover, as with the book of Isaiah, the book of Micah anticipates the return for those who have been "driven away" (4:6; cf. 5:3).

In sum, prophetic literature stemming from the Neo-Assyrian period is very familiar with the practices of exile. Amos, Isaiah, and Micah comment about exiles that have already taken place. It has happened to the Northern Kingdom, to Judah, and to other nations. All four prophetic books refer to exile in the future. The books of Micah and Isaiah anticipate the return of a remnant from exile. Interestingly, these prophets attest to the three primary modes of exile: mass deportation, voluntary migration (Hosea), and incarceration (Isaiah).

Neo-Babylonian Period

We turn next to the Neo-Babylonian period. It is difficult to identify the boundary between the Neo-Assyrian and Neo-Babylonian periods. For the sake of this paper, I will simply point to the fall of Nineveh in 612 BCE, though it is clear that Neo-Assyrian power in Syria-Palestine had begun to weaken decades earlier—during the reign of Assurbanipal (668–627 BCE). Prophetic literature purportedly dating to the end of the seventh and the early sixth centuries BCE includes Nahum, Habakkuk, Zephaniah, Jeremiah, and Ezekiel. There is minimal reference to exile in the smaller of these books. Nahum anticipates the future exile of Nineveh (2:7). Neither Habakkuk nor Zephaniah refers explicitly to the exile of anyone, though Zephaniah does anticipate a return of some who are not now in the land: "I will bring you home" (3:20).[16] So I offer two observations about prophetic rhetoric about exile in the late seventh century BCE: (1) It is only minimally present. (2) It is a continuation of prophetic rhetoric that emerged in the Neo-Assyrian period.

---

16. The "you" is now Jerusalem, and the forces that exiled her are presumably the Neo-Babylonians, though that is not stated explicitly. Zephaniah uses a motif present in Isaiah and Micah, namely, a return from exile. Earlier, it had referred to the return of Israel, now it is the return of Jerusalem. The historical agents are different, but the ways of talking about them had been formulated at least one century earlier.

And now for a brief comment about the rhetoric of exile in Jeremiah and Ezekiel, the first prophets who anticipate explicitly an exile wrought by the Neo-Babylonians.

Jeremiah

In the book of Jeremiah, the trope of exile is not particularly prominent when compared with the diction of destruction by the foe from the north. Still, one may discern two different perspectives on exile, one in the poetry, another in the prose. The prose is filled with the classical lexeme for forced migration, the verb *glh*. In poetry the diction is very different: Jer 10:17–18—"I am going to sling out the inhabitants of the land," or 13:24—"I will scatter you like chaff."[17] Jeremianic poetry uses highly figurative language about exile. Yahweh, rather than a human force, is the punitive agent. Captivity rather than forced migration is often in view (13:17; 15:2; 22:22; 30:10.) Nonetheless, Jeremiah's discourse about exile is fundamentally similar to that of his forebears. It will be a disaster, affecting the removal of virtually all the people.[18] The emotional register of this poetry is very high.

Ezekiel

Ezekiel is, of course, the first prophet who could speak at length about Judah's exile in the past tense. But amazingly, he does not. Ezekiel refers to exile, but it is in a vastly different emotional register from Jeremiah. The diction about exile, for example, *glh*, almost always occurs in prose, often in chronological formulae (1:2; 33:21; 40:1). And, with the exception of Ezek 12, the symbolic action report about going into exile, the book always refers to the exile as having taken place. When reading those texts that use the lexemes of *glh* and *šby*, one does not have a sense that Ezekiel is building on the rhetoric of his prophetic predecessors. Strangely, the exile for this prophet is not about Babylon as a place of tears, as we hear in Ps 137. The emotional register is flat, when compared with that of Jeremiah's anticipatory poetry. This prophet's rhetoric has, more than any other prophet to this point, been decisively influenced by the experience of exile.

---

17. The only poetic text that uses the verb *glh* is Jer 13:19: "all Judah is taken into exile, wholly taken into exile."

18. Of course, Jeremiah himself is taken forcibly—by his own countrymen—as they move voluntarily into Egypt.

And his rhetoric has accommodated exile in an almost prosaic way. Life in exile has clearly influenced the Ezekielian rhetoric of exile.

Conclusion

The exile experienced by Judah was in many ways different from the exile of Israel. However, Judahite prophets in the late seventh and early sixth centuries BCE continued to think about exile as had their prophetic forebears. I can only agree with Vanderhooft, when he writes, "the pre-existing Israelite prophetic tradition relating in particular to imperial depredations under Assyria was appropriated in the Babylonian imperial context.... This shows that the prophetic language about empire [I would say exile] was not wholly shaped by the new imperial circumstances, or solely by Babylonian imperial ideas and practices."[19] Rather, the prophets were construing what would happen based on past precedent. Prophetic rhetoric about exile in the Neo-Babylonian period was forged on the anvil of experiences under the Neo-Assyrians. What happened, however, was quite different from that past precedent. Fewer people were taken into exile. Their status and communal identity was higher and stronger. As a result, rhetoric about exile in Ezekiel is muted when compared with his prophetic predecessors. The emotional register rises again with Isa 40–55, probably less due to the circumstances of exile and more to the perceived need to encourage those in exile to return to Israel.

---

19. Vanderhooft, *Neo-Babylonian Empire*, 207. He refers explicitly to Mic 4:10; Isa 14:4b–12; Jer 50:17.

Provenance as a Factor in Interpretation

Christopher R. Seitz

Introductory Remarks

The provision of a setting—for an author and audience—significantly affects the way a biblical book is read and interpreted. To be more precise, one would also have to distinguish between the interpretive effect of a book's own provision of a setting or audience (e.g., Paul's letter to the Galatians) as against the critical recovery of a setting (e.g., the Johannine community; the exilic audience). In the case of a work providing a setting, even here things are not that clear. Linus of Charlie Brown fame said he disapproved of Paul because reading his letters was like reading someone else's mail.[1] This of course makes the point nicely that we read Paul's letters in the context of a canon, on the one hand, and also that the setting (the Galatians) is not so determinative that knowing it (whatever that might mean) is the same as interpreting the letter itself. Paul is writing an epistle, and the notices at the conclusion of some of his letters indicate they are to be passed on to other communities without concern for Linus's remonstrance.[2] Peter commends them and suggests for them a status not unlike the inherited public mail, "the scriptures." So the issue requires further consideration, precisely because the unusual character of biblical writings makes matters like "author" and "setting" far less straightforward.

---

1. See the clever use of this illustration in David Trobisch, *Paul's Letter Collection: Tracing the Origins* (Minneapolis: Fortress, 1994).
2. E.g., Col 4:16. See the discussion in Brevard S. Childs, *New Testament as Canon: An Introduction* (Philadelphia: Fortress, 1984), 48–53, 348; and idem, *The Church's Guide for Reading Paul: The Canonical Shaping of the Pauline Corpus* (Grand Rapids: Eerdmans, 2008), 1–27 (esp. 6), 161. See now Christopher R. Seitz, *Colossians* (Brazos Theological Commentary on the Bible; Grand Rapids: Brazos, 2014), 19–38.

In the case of a critical recovery of an audience, we have the further burden of assessing the success or likelihood of the reconstruction. We must then evaluate the relationship between the reconstruction and the claims the work makes for itself. We may find the precision of dates in the Behistun Inscription remarkable for the way they explain the Persian context of Zechariah, but whether the prophet Zechariah knew anything like this state of affairs in his own context makes the provision of such a setting a matter requiring assessment.[3] Certainly the Zechariah of the night visions appears as anything but a confident historiographer; often he confesses bafflement at what is vouchsafed to him. One could even say that the book must work at securing for Zechariah something like the very status of a prophet, such that he can by chapter 7 stand on his feet and say, "Thus says the LORD," and align himself with agents from the past—the former prophets, who are dead but whose words live on and provide the solid ground upon which his own message stands (not unlike the temple itself and the old foundation stone).[4] So authorship and agency are questions the book foregrounds in the very nature of its presentation.

As for Zechariah, if one wishes to speak of setting and provenance, "postexilic Judah" is a simple answer that works well. The audience can be stipulated more precisely as those attending a rededication ceremony, as the critical reconstruction of the Meyers has it.[5] But such a critical conjecture must work from silence (no mention of the rededication means Haggai and Zech 1–8 were completed before this event); it must blur the canonical distinction of two prophetic works by arguing for a consistent dating scheme covering them both (which is doubtful) and a common concern with the temple (which is a partial view of chs. 1–8); and it must separate the night visions from the oracles in chapters 9–14 if not also

---

3. See the insightful analysis of Al Wolters, "'The Whole World Remains at Rest' (Zechariah 1:11): The Problem and an Intertextual Clue," in *Tradition in Transition: Haggai and Zechariah 1–8 in the Trajectory of Hebrew Theology*, ed. Mark J. Boda and Michael H. Floyd, LHBOTS 475 (New York: T&T Clark, 2008), 128–43.

4. This would be my own view of the logic of Zech 1–8. We witness the gradual reestablishment and recalibration of Israel's offices of king, prophet, and priest, given the sense of a genuine "past" and a new era unfolding. The prophet must, as it were, witness his own divine relegitimization via genuine revelation—an idea fraught with inner tension.

5. Carol L. Meyers and Eric M. Meyers, *Haggai, Zechariah 1–8: A New Translation with Introduction and Commentary*, AB 25B (Garden City, NY: Doubleday, 1987), xliv–xlv.

from the concerns of chapters 7–8.[6] Is this the audience of Zechariah or only a conjecture about a single setting, difficult to prove in the light of the canonical presentation of Zechariah, with the independent works of Haggai on the one side and Malachi on the other[7] (and all three in the Book of the Twelve[8])? Here one sees again how critical it is to make sure the question of provenance is taken up into larger concerns of interpretation, without, at the same time, losing the historical particularity the book seeks and yet on its own terms of presentation.

Exilic Provenance in the Book of Isaiah

In the nineteenth-century work of J. G. Eichhorn, Wilhelm Gesenius, Heinrich Ewald, and Bernhard Duhm, what was being negotiated was the temporal ambition the book of Isaiah undertakes.[9] This was not a matter affecting the latter chapters only, but belonged to Isa 1–39 as well. The

---

6. Mark J. Boda, "From Fasts to Feasts: The Literary Function of Zechariah 7–8," *CBQ* 65 (2003): 390–407; Michael R. Stead, *The Intertextuality of Zechariah 1–8*, LHBOTS 506 (New York: T&T Clark, 2009), 219–47.

7. Here is just a sample of works that read the final three books together: Paul L. Redditt, "Zechariah 9–14, Malachi, and the Redaction of the Book of the Twelve," in *Forming Prophetic Literature: Essays in Honor of John D. W. Watts*, ed. James W. Watts and Paul R. House, JSOTSup 235 (Sheffield: Sheffield Academic, 1996), 245–68; Ronald W. Pierce, "A Thematic Development of the Haggai/Zechariah/Malachi Corpus," *JETS* 27 (1984): 401–11; Mark J. Boda, "Messengers of Hope in Haggai–Malachi," *JSOT* 32 (2007): 113–31; Aaron Schart, "Putting the Eschatological Visions of Zechariah in Their Place: Malachi as a Hermeneutical Guide for the Last Section of the Book of the Twelve," in *Bringing out the Treasure: Inner Biblical Allusion in Zechariah 9–13*, ed. Mark J. Boda and Michael H. Floyd, JSOTSup 370 (London: Sheffield Academic, 2003), 333–43.

8. E.g., James D. Nogalski and Marvin A. Sweeney, eds., *Reading and Hearing the Book of the Twelve*, SymS 15 (Atlanta: Society of Biblical Literature, 2000); Terence Collins, "The Scroll of the Twelve," in *The Mantle of Elijah: The Redaction Criticism of the Prophetic Books*, ed. Terence Collins, BibSem 20 (Sheffield: JSOT Press, 1993), 59–84; James D. Nogalski, *Literary Precursors to the Book of the Twelve*, BZAW 217 (Berlin: de Gruyter, 1993); idem, *Redactional Processes in the Book of the Twelve*, BZAW 218 (Berlin: de Gruyter, 1993); Donald K. Berry, "Malachi's Dual Design: The Close of the Canon and What Comes Afterward," in Watts and House, *Forming Prophetic Literature*, 269–302.

9. Wilhelm Gesenius, *Philologisch-kritischer und historischer Commentar über den Jesaia* (Leipzig: Vogel, 1821); Bernhard Duhm, *Das Buch Jesaja*, HKAT 3.1 (Göttingen: Vandenhoeck & Ruprecht, 1892).

"First Isaiah" was also a properly a "Last Isaiah," in that the Jerusalem Isaiah was joined in the literary presentation of chapters 1–39 by supplementations contemporaneous with or later than chapters 40–66, though the way that was reconstructed by these four interpreters varied.[10] One spoke of an anthology. One likened chapters 36–39 to Jer 52 and called what followed a *pseudepigraph*, maybe even originally attached to Jeremiah but brought over to function under the Isaiah aegis.[11] One likened the entire book to the Book of the Twelve, noting, as did Eichhorn, how often it is appears in lists as its neighbor.[12]

In precritical interpretation, chapters 40–66 of Isaiah were taken to be a spiritual transportation of the prophet Isaiah, who, with his feet planted on the firm historical ground of Jerusalem in chapters 36–39, spoke into a distant future, where he comforted the mourners of Zion.[13] Because the future speech was not speech from prophet to contemporaries in an eighth-century historical context, where he spoke of matters centuries later with the language "now in the latter days," but was rather speech to contemporaries *in that distant time itself*, this was a spiritual transportation all the more wondrous for being so unusual and so ambitious. Only God could bring that about, and so, in the end, the questions of human agency and historical contextualization in chapters 40–66, which would be foregrounded with the rise of the nineteenth-century species of history, were deferred under a view of inspiration centered more on the divine initiative than human agency particularized in time. In the famous fourth edition of Franz Delitzsch's commentary on Isaiah,[14] one can still see, on the other side of the nineteenth-century shift, a creative adaptation of the earlier account.

> Those prophecies originating in post-Isaian times are, in thought and in the expression of thought, more nearly akin to Isaiah than to any other prophet; they are really the homogeneous and simultaneous continua-

---

10. See a fuller discussion in Christopher R. Seitz, "Isaiah, Book of (First Isaiah)," *ABD* 3:472–88.

11. Duhm, *Buch Jesaja*, vii–xiv.

12. J. G. Eichhorn, *Einleitung in das Alte Testament,* 3rd ed., 5 vols. (Leipzig: Weidmann, 1803), 3:101–4.

13. See John Calvin, *Commentary on the Book of the Prophet Isaiah,* trans. William Pringle, 4 vols. (Edinburgh: Constable, 1850).

14. Franz Delitzsch, *Bible Commentary on the Prophecies of Isaiah,* trans. James Kennedy et al., 4th ed., 2 vols. (Edinburgh: T&T Clark, 1889–1910).

tion of Isaian prophecy, the primary stream of which ramifies in them as in branches of a river, and throughout retains its fertilizing power. These later prophets so closely resembled Isaiah in prophetic vision, that posterity might on that account well identify them with him. They belong more or less nearly to those pupils of his to whom he refers, when, in chap. viii. 16, he entreats the Lord, "Seal instruction among my disciples." We know of no other prophet belonging to the kingdom of Judah, like Isaiah, who was surrounded by a band of younger prophets, and, so to speak, formed a school. Viewed in this light, the Book of Isaiah is the work of his creative spirit and the band of followers. These later prophets are Isaian—they are Isaiah's disciples; it is his spirit that continues to operate in them, like the spirit of Elijah in Elisha—nay, we may say, like the spirit of Jesus in the apostles; for the words of Isaiah (viii. 18), "Behold, I and the children whom God hath given me," are employed in the Epistle to the Hebrews (ii. 13) as typical of Jesus Christ.[15]

The point to be stressed is that the temporal particularization of chapters 40–66 did not sever the link with the prophet Isaiah or the chapters of the book of Isaiah that preceded in 1–39, however one in turn dealt with these chapters' diachronic challenge. Efforts to read Isaiah in the modern period bear some resemblance to this concern, even as they have their own history of research intervening in strong fashion in the period between Delitzsch and today. In that intervening period not just the temporal but also the spatial and geographical dimensions of the exilic provenance rose to prominence. The Great Prophet of the Exile was birthed. By this was meant more than the temporal context of Cyrus and the end of the Babylonian exile. The great prophet joined Ezekiel in an exile to a Babylonian setting, popularized in textbook accounts, with notes from the harps of Ps 137 in the background and with the prose sermons of Jeremiah being preached to exiles, as some accounts had it.[16] When Lamentations speak of no comforter or Zechariah describes a heavenly council in which the question of comfort is raised, the link to Isa 40 is not proximate because of the geographical setting argued for the Prophet of the Exile, and so must be explained as influential in some other way. The Pseudo-Isaiah of the nineteenth century was transformed into a flesh-

---

15. Ibid., 1:38.
16. Ernest W. Nicholson, *Preaching to the Exiles: A Study of the Prose Tradition in the Book of Jeremiah* (New York: Schocken, 1971).

and-blood Deutero-Isaiah.[17] It was then a small step to the necessity of Trito-Isaiah, as the Jerusalemite background of chapters 56–66 required a further shift in setting (back to Jerusalem and Judah). One can see in Duhm that the older literary criticism was moving closer to what would be the concerns of form criticism and the prominence this would give to oral speech, original setting, and "situation in life." Rhetorical criticism in the hands of James Muilenburg offered an alternative to the atomizing tendencies of form criticism. If anything, however, his reading enhanced the idea of exilic prominence, as the powerful speeches of the exilic Isaiah soared to their best rhetorical effect in that imagined context.[18]

Thus far, two matters are under consideration: first, the relationship between temporal ambition and historical provenance and the way they are related in the canonical form; second, the effect of chapters 40–55 of Isaiah, existing within the literary presentation of the larger canonical book and a proper assessment of authorship, temporal movement, and literary coherence in light of that. That there was an exile and deportations to Babylon is not in doubt, and the canonical portrayal makes that abundantly clear, with Jeremiah, Ezekiel, Haggai, Zechariah, Ezra, and Nehemiah all providing their respective versions of particularized historical record and theological assessment (we can leave the complexities of Daniel to the side). It appears equally clear in the canonical record that a setting for Lamentations, Haggai, and Zechariah in Judah is part of the canonical presentation and does not require historical speculation for corroboration (arguments for preexilic oracles or recycling in Zech 9–14 notwithstanding).[19]

I should note in passing that objections to a historical setting in Babylon, on literary and historical-critical grounds, were raised right along. On the basis of descriptions of exilic life provided by the prophet Deutero-Isaiah, Duhm conjectured that conditions were not consistent with what we know of the Babylonian exile.[20] Others noted that the orientation

---

17. See, e.g., Seitz, *ABD* 3:473.

18. James Muilenburg, "The Book of Isaiah: Chapters 40–66," *IB* 5:381–773. See the more cautious account of Roy F. Melugin, *The Formation of Isaiah 40–55*, BZAW 141 (Berlin: de Gruyter, 1976), 6–10.

19. E.g., Schart, "Putting the Eschatological Visions."

20. Duhm, *Jesaja*, xviii: "Gelebt hat er gewiss nicht in Babylonien, wahrscheinlich auch nicht in Palästina, vielleicht im nördlichen Phonizien." See Hans M. Barstad, "Lebte Deuterojesaja in Judäa?" *NTT* 83 (1982): 77–87.

of the prophet's proclamation, especially when he speaks of the scattered diaspora of God's judgment, entails all compass points and takes its bearings in relationship to Jerusalem.[21] Others countered that while active in exile, the prophet's imagination continued to center itself on Jerusalem (this begins to reveal the delicate way in which setting and message influence one another in interpretation). Still others saw references to new creation and the upheaval in nature, not as a sign of close links to a single Babylonian return from exile, à la Egypt, but an adaptation of first-exodus typology to reflect a changed situation: exiles north, south, east, west; the return of YHWH to Zion, and *his* way, connected with his sovereign character—not the way back from Babylon—being made straight; and a new creation reflecting the centrality of Zion and the judgment of God being reversed, such that the nations might be brought into mind of God's sovereign purposes.[22] Seeing these factors, and also noting a distinction between chapters 40–48 and 49–55, now widely accepted for other reasons, Jürgen van Oorschot spoke of a movement within Deutero-Isaiah from Babylon to Zion.[23] Klaus Baltzer's highly original Hermeneia commentary, which speaks of a dramatic unity of chapters 40–55, moves the rhetorical setting of Muilenburg into Judah and the context of Persian period political and theological challenge.[24] Joseph Blenkinsopp also notes that the idea of an empty land overstates both the biblical and the

---

21. James D. Smart, *History and Theology in Second Isaiah: A Commentary on Isaiah 35, 40–66* (Philadelphia: Westminster, 1965), 20. He writes, "When we search for evidence of the prophet's residence in Babylon, we are perhaps surprised how hard it is to find any that is convincing. The fact that he addresses himself to exiles does not signify that he was among the Babylonian exiles. His exiles are scattered to the four corners of the earth, north, south, east, and west (chs. 41:9; 42:10–11; 43:5–6; 49:12; 60:9). We have the impression almost everywhere in chs. 40–55 that the prophet is writing to a widely dispersed people rather than speaking to a local community."

22. Klaus Kiesow, *Exodustexte im Jesajabuch: Literarkritische und motivgeschichtlichen Analysen*, OBO 24 (Göttingen: Vandenhoeck & Ruprecht, 1979); Hans M. Barstad, *A Way in the Wilderness: The "Second Exodus" in the Message of Second Isaiah* (Manchester: University of Manchester Press, 1989). Kiesow and Barstad emphasize the metaphorical character of the "way of the LORD" as over against the frequently posited extrapolation, "return from exile" (cf. Isa 35:6–7). See Christopher R. Seitz, "The Book of Isaiah 40–66," NIB 6:335–36.

23. Jürgen van Oorschot, *Von Babel zum Zion*, BZAW 206 (Berlin: de Gruyter, 1993).

24. Klaus Baltzer, *Deutero-Isaiah*, trans. Margaret Kohl, Hermeneia (Minneapolis: Fortress, 2001), 23–25.

ancient Near Eastern historical evidence and so places a question mark against an obvious exilic setting.[25] Hans Barstad had long reiterated that the evidence for a Babylonian setting for Second Isaiah was weak, and he spoke of a tendency to overstate the idea of an empty land as derived from an ideological tendency in the period, unwittingly influencing critical readings of Isa 40–55.[26] A version of this was posited earlier by C. C. Torrey,[27] and a more congenial form of it was popularized in the commentary treatment of James Smart.[28]

What is significant for the purpose of our present inquiry is that this questioning of the Babylonian setting of chapters 40–55 was undertaken on the same terms and from the same starting point of commonly accepted critical methods. The literary, historical, and form-critical evidence did not support such a setting, according to the dissenters. That is, considerations of the form of the book of Isaiah and the place and relationship of chapters 40–55 within it did not figure prominently, if at all. This is also a place where Brevard Childs struggled to understand the canonical form in his *Introduction to the Old Testament as Scripture*. The view of an exilic provenance for Second Isaiah was so prominent in his conceptual framework that, in order to speak of the placement of these chapters in the canonical book of Isaiah, he was forced to speak of removal of historical traces, so as to allow the material to function in a new literary presentation.[29] The ideas that chapters 40–55 were either not composed in Babylon or that the authorship and presentation of the material sensed the burden from the outset of enlarging and continuing a previous Isaiah legacy and

---

25. Joseph Blenkinsopp, *Isaiah 40–55: A New Translation with Introduction and Commentary*, AB 19A (New York: Doubleday, 2002), 102–4.

26. Hans Barstad, *A Way in the Wilderness: The "Second Exodus" in the Message of Second Isaiah* (Manchester: University of Manchester, 1989); *The Babylonian Captivity of the Book of Isaiah: "Exilic" Judah and the Provenance of Isaiah 40–55* (Oslo: Novus: Instituttet for sammenlignende kulturforskning, 1997).

27. C. C. Torrey, *The Second Isaiah: A New Interpretation* (Edinburgh: T&T Clark, 1928).

28. Smart, *History and Theology in Second Isaiah*.

29. Childs, *Introduction to the Old Testament as Scripture* (Philadelphia: Fortress, 1979), 325: "Even though the message was once addressed to real people in a particular historical situation—whether according to the model of Begrich or Muilenburg is indecisive—the canonical editors of this tradition employed the material in such a way as to eliminate almost entirely those concrete features and to subordinate the original message to a new role within the canon."

so of maintaining a Jerusalem orientation were not obvious ones. His later Old Testament Library commentary does not labor under this older conceptual consensus.[30]

It is possible, then, to deal with the historical and literary question of the chapters' most likely provenance as a topic unto itself. But one should also acknowledge that the question can be constrained by a different context of consideration. That is, the interest in provenance may have emerged as decisive because of the methods being employed, without proper attention to the way the material presents itself. The objections to the exilic provenance were lodged on the grounds that the evidence did not support such a view. But one can also ask: What if the canonical form of Isa 40–55 and its literary presentation both deflect us away from a provenance-driven interpretation and suggest that the wider Isaiah context was decisive for the presentation of the material from the outset?

The Second Exodus and Exile

At this juncture, it is important to focus our remarks on the prominence of the "second exodus" motif in chapters 40–55. At one level, "second exodus" is an obvious theme in Deutero-Isaiah, especially in chapters 40–48. At issue is whether one version of its interpretation in these chapters has flattened the creativity of the presentation, leading to a one-to-one correspondence between the former and latter things not warranted by a close reading. On this account, Egypt, wilderness, and conquest provide the types ("former things") for a secondary correspondence of Babylon, physical translation from Babylon, and return to the Promised Land ("latter things"). Because this movement leads into chapters 56–66 and a less than ebullient prosecution of its end notes, an explanation is offered for distinguishing the two prophets from one another but leaving us with an unsatisfactory correspondence between former and latter things, to use the language of the prophet. Third Isaiah looks more like Judges than Joshua.

On the front end of the analogy, moreover, the type "Egypt" has resulted in an undue focus on a single "Babylonian exile" antitype. In chapters 40–55, it would be more appropriate to speak of a diaspora to all com-

---

30. Childs, *Isaiah*, OTL (Louisville: Westminster John Knox, 2001).

pass points and not just Babylon (43:5-7; 49:12).[31] With this observation come two important correlates. Such a depiction is fully consistent with the presentation of judgment in former Isaiah chapters. "The nations" given prominence in the presentation of Deutero-Isaiah, as with First Isaiah, give pride of place to Babylon (the centrality of which is anticipated in ch. 39), but the tableau of chapters 13–23 makes clear that Israel will be dispersed far and wide. The nations who are a drop in the bucket in Deutero-Isaiah (40:15) can without difficulty be correlated with the broader international depiction we see previously in Isaiah, in chapters 13–23, and in the section immediately preceding Deutero-Isaiah (chs. 36–39).[32]

The second correlate points to the problematic nature of the proposed "second exodus" typology at its end point. Second Isaiah's dispersion north, south, east, west—even as the emphasis, here and elsewhere, is on the northland and that particular foe—locates the center of this scattering as emanating from Jerusalem. So it is that the return is not on analogy with the first exodus—from Egypt to wilderness to conquest to promised land—but rather the movement is *straight to Zion* (so chs. 54–55) upon the completion of the work of the servant in chapter 53. Indeed, the Zion of chapter 40 was never all that far from view as we come to chapters 49–55, and its central role is obvious.

We also have no disruption of generations, as in the first exodus. The servants of the Servant pick up seamlessly at the juncture represented by chapters 53 and 54.[33] In the first exodus, a disobedient generation in an act of contrition brings offerings to build the sanctuary, the bank deposit of which was the plunder of the Egyptians. The nations in the land must be defeated. In Isaiah 40–55 the nations are in a different place. They bring offerings to build up Zion, and the promised land is a Zion populated with children, betrothed and not cast off, with barely room for all the newcomers (54:1–17; cf. 49:14–23). The return to Zion is a reversal of the chaos imagery seen in the psalms of Zion, and that is also the source for the language of blooming and fertility that accompanies "the way of the LORD" now being made straight in the desert. It is YHWH returning to love his

---

31. Seitz, *NIB* 6:376; Blenkinsopp, *Isaiah 40–55*, 104; Baltzer, *Deutero-Isaiah*, 24; Barstad, *Way in the Wilderness*, 19–20.

32. Seitz, *NIB* 6:327–32. See also Seitz, *Zion's Final Destiny: The Development of the Book of Isaiah: A Reassessment of Isaiah 36–39* (Minneapolis: Fortress, 1991).

33. Seitz, *NIB* 6:471–74; Willem Beuken, "The Main Theme of Trito-Isaiah, 'The Servants of YHWH,'" *JSOT* 47 (1990): 67–87.

bride Zion, bringing to her children lost, children she did not know she had, and new children yet to be born. The judgment and restoration of God's own people is a spectacle that dethrones the claims of haughty Babylon (chs. 46–47) and sheds a specific kind of light on the nations, who witness in the Suffering Servant and Israel a transformation of Israel, a release from sin and the logic of a former thing and into a new creation out of chaos and death (42:1–9; 49:1–13; 52:13–53:12).

If the idea of a spatial displacement to an exilic provenance is in the foreground, it is difficult to keep such a conceptuality from overwhelming the presentation of the chapters themselves and the "behold I do a *new thing*" use of the former exodus *typos* (48:6–21). The typology that is constructed involves transformation of the former thing, such that the latter is there to point to it, but, also, it is new and different—"created now, not long before" (48:7). That difference also keeps the chapters functioning much more efficiently within the larger Isaiah presentation, where Zion, the nations, a plan, and hope for a new generation of sighted and hearing Israel, only a remnant in Isaiah's own day, belong now to an extended temporal presentation.[34] What could not have been seen before, but which was capable of coordination in God's own sovereign design as analogous to a first exodus, is now grasped in its continuity and newness both.[35]

The new thing represented by the return to Zion, the work of the Servant and the servants to follow, is focused on Israel as a light to the nations. As in Zechariah, the return entails, of course, a focus on the temple and its reestablishment, but this is to a larger purpose involving the nations: both their conformity to plans established in respect of their overreach as God's agents as well as their enclosure in God's plans (see Zech 8:20–23). Even the movement of Jonah conforms to this same pattern, with the prophet descending into the מצולה of judgment and watery exile and vomited out in prophetic vocation to the nations—which happens, as we see with the sailors in chapter 1, as effectively in disobedience as in obedience, whether Jonah likes it or not, sleeping below deck or marching through Nineveh.

The problem presented by an exilic-provenance reading of Isaiah is in reproportioning this amalgam of carefully combined themes, such that physical return from a single Babylonian context ends up overwhelming the

---

34. See the helpful essay of Ronald E. Clements, "Beyond Tradition-History: Deutero-Isaianic Development of First Isaiah's Themes," *JSOT* 31 (1985): 95–113.

35. See the fuller discussion of the treatment of the movement of chs. 40–48 in Seitz, *NIB* 6:327–422.

portrayal of the book itself—if not also leading to a kind of disappointing finale in Isa 56–66 or in a Zechariah now principally linked to rededication as an explanation of its original form.[36]

Restoring the canonical Isaiah might also help us distinguish between the influence of Isaiah on New Testament formulations as against Second Temple history-of-religion reconstructions, where return from exile is said to weigh heavily in the formation of the New Testament narrative world.[37] The canonical Isaiah can "speak over" the more proximate history of religion and should not be confused or conflated with it. Canonical Isaiah has, in the scholarly consensus, both former and latter Isaiah sections. Historical research of the past two hundred years has properly called attention to this dimension. What it has not always been handled with subtlety is the relationship between the canonical form and ostensive reference, that is, the historical context said to be generating the text or the events to which the text refers as the primary location of significance.

In my view, the canonical form assesses the temporal dimension without foregrounding any spatial movement to Babylon (in Calvin's precritical reading, the prophet still comforts "the mourners of Zion"; cf. Sir 48:24). In consequence, the Zion orientation of former Isaiah is maintained throughout the length of the book, with the latter Isaiah bringing forward a new emphasis on the servant and Israel as light to the nations, in the context of God's comfort of Zion, on the far side of judgment. Exile and return are subsidiary features of this more central concern and serve to give it prominence. Isaiah's former and latter word focuses on Zion and the way in which the nations will witness the work of the one God, through the judgment and restoration of his people, through the furnace of affliction and dispersion to every compass point. Indeed, Zion itself descends into a chaos depth like the former waters of Noah (54:9–17). But the LORD makes a way through the desert of sin and chaos and remains true to his promises to Abraham, bringing to fruition the new thing of redemption of the nations by the work of the Servant. One kind of overemphasis on an authorial provenance in Babylon—itself far from obvious—split the book into thirds in too precise a fashion and, in so doing, frustrated our ability

---

36. See n. 5 above.

37. I have in mind here the centrality of "exile" in the published work of N. T. Wright. See my response, in the life of Isa 1–66, "Reconciliation and the Plain Sense Witness of Scripture," in *The Redemption: An Interdisciplinary Symposium on Christ as Redeemer*, ed. Stephen T. Davis et al. (Oxford: Oxford University Press, 2004), 25–42.

to hear former and latter things as emanating from a single divine council of authorial inspiration, grounded in the one overtaking and accomplishing word of God (Isa 55:11). The book of Isaiah has taken up the various provenances of its compositional life and put them to the service of this accomplishing word as we now undertake to receive it in the canonical form of the sixty-six-chapter vision.

"You Are My Witnesses and My Servant" (Isa 43:10): Exile and the Identity Of The Servant

Ulrich Berges

Authorship and Formation of Isaiah 40–55

Before one can discuss the function of the Servant in Isaiah 40–55, one has to clarify the most contested issue of these chapters: the identity of this Servant. I believe that the best angle of approach is to assume a "literary construction of the Servant in the exile." In my German commentary on Isa 40–48 and in the published version of an English-language main paper held at the International Organization for the Study of the Old Testament conference in Ljubljana, I abandoned the concept of an anonymous, exilic, prophetic author called "Deutero-Isaiah," a popular exegetical construct since Bernhard Duhm (1892).[1] I rejected this concept of an individual author in favor of an authorial group close to deported Jerusalem temple singers. When they began to write their drama of renewed hope on Babylonian soil, their primary goal did not consist in continuing the prophetic work of Isaiah ben Amoz, even though they had a certain acquaintance with some of his formulations (especially "the Holy One of Israel"). This group was responsible for the first edition of this prophetic script (40:1–52:10*), using the so-called hymns as structuring elements (42:10–12; 44:23; 45:8; 48:20–21; 52:9–10). This prophetic writing was near completion once the group returned to Jerusalem in the aftermath of Darius's violent oppression of the Gaumata revolt (ca. 520 BCE), but it originated in the Babylonian exile as an attempt to empower the exilic

---

1. Ulrich Berges, *Jesaja 40–48*, HTKAT (Freiburg: Herder, 2008); idem, "Farewell to Deutero-Isaiah or Prophecy without a Prophet," in *Congress Volume Ljubljana 2007*, ed. André Lemaire, VTSup 133 (Leiden: Brill, 2010), 575–95; idem, "The Literary Construction of the Servant in Isaiah 40–55," *SJOT* 24 (2010): 28–38.

community with renewed strength in YHWH. The primary goal, however, did not consist in convincing others but rather in encouraging the prophetic singers themselves to remain faithful to their vocation of being the offspring of Jacob/Israel.

The writers and composers of Isa 40–55 used the hymnic tradition of the Jerusalem temple cult (cf. Pss 96 and 98) to structure their literary drama of renewed hope in the almighty God of Israel. If the dependence had been the other way around, then it would be hard to explain why these psalms did not make additional usage of other motifs in Isa 40–55 (like the one of the servant Jacob/Israel). Thus Henk Leene concludes: "It is difficult to imagine that a psalmist who was inspired by Deutero-Isaiah proceeded so selectively. The opposite is more likely: the composers of Isaiah 40–55 borrowed from an existent hymnic tradition for certain pivotal points of their dramatic composition, or even from these very songs passed on to us in Pss 98 and 96."[2]

It is well known that Isa 40–55's sources are not restricted to Psalms alone but include a whole range of important traditions in the Hebrew Bible: the narratives of the patriarchs and the exodus, the prophetic judgment tradition, some elements of the older Jerusalem Isaiah composition ("the Holy One of Israel"), influences from Jeremiah (especially the so-called Confessions; see Jer 31:35 in Isa 51:15) and Ezekiel (profanation of the name in Isa 48:11; cf. Ezek 20:9, 14, 22),[3] Deuteronomistic elements,[4] Jerusalem cult traditions with the central motifs of Zion, the nations, the refashioned David tradition (Isa 55:3–5), and the intimate connection between creation and history, which is also analogous to the Priestly stratum of the Pentateuch. The combination and amalgamation of these traditions cannot simply be explained as a late phenomenon in the development of the prophetic writings ("Spätling in Israels Prophetie"[5]). Rather,

---

2. Henk Leene, "History and Eschatology in Deutero-Isaiah," in *Studies in the Book of Isaiah: Festschrift Willem A. M. Beuken*, ed. Jacques van Ruiten and Marc Vervenne, BETL 132 (Leuven: Leuven University Press, 1997), 246.

3. Dieter Baltzer, *Ezechiel und Deuterojesaja: Berührungen in der Heilserwartung der beiden großen Exilspropheten*, BZAW 121 (Berlin: de Gruyter, 1971).

4. Antje Labahn, *Wort Gottes und Schuld Israels: Untersuchungen zu Motiven deuteronomistischer Theologie im Deuterojesajabuch mit einem Ausblick auf das Verhältnis von Jes 40–55 zum Deuteronomismus*, BWANT 143 (Stuttgart: Kohlhammer, 1999).

5. Hans-Jürgen Hermisson, "Deuterojesaja," *RGG* 2:687.

they are clear evidence that these chapters were composed by a group, not by an individual.

One could object to this thesis by pointing out that even if these chapters were written and edited by a group of literarily skilled singers, it is still possible to postulate the existence of an individual "Deutero-Isaiah" as the *"spiritus rector"* of these singers, as a kind of *"chef du groupe."*[6] This is certainly possible, but one of the central problems of the Deutero-Isaiah hypothesis would remain unresolved, namely his anonymity. If Deutero-Isaiah had been the leading figure of the group, his anonymity would be all the more puzzling: Why did his disciples not preserve his name and identity? If the analogy to the poets of Psalms holds, then one would expect at least the transmission of his name or the fact of his participation in a certain group, such as one finds in the psalms of "Asaph" or "Korah."[7]

It is particularly significant to note that there is not only an absence of a personal name; there are also no references to personal traits. In contrast to the repeated formula in Ezekiel—"the word of YHWH came to me" (6:1; 7:1; 12:1, 8, etc.), no such example can be found in Isa 40–55. There is no individual prophetic first-person-singular speech in these chapters (for 40:6 and 48:16 see the analysis below). The I-speeches in the second and third Servant Songs (49:1–6; 50:4–9) cannot be used to fill this biographical vacuum because these texts are written in a conventional style ("formgebundene Sprache") that permits no insight into a personal biography.[8] The suffering and death of the servant figure in Isa 53 can also not be interpreted as the destiny of an individual. The disapproval of Julius Wellhausen in this respect is still compelling: "It is a hazardous supposition to think of an incomparably great prophet who was martyred in exile, perhaps by his own people—a prophet who then disappeared. The

---

6. See Rainer Albertz, *Israel in Exile: The History and Literature of the Sixth Century B.C.E.*, trans. David Green, Biblical Encyclopedia 7 (Atlanta: Society of Biblical Literature, 2003), 380–81.

7. See Hermisson, "Deutero-Jesaja," 684: "Die intensive Verwendung der Sprach- und Formenwelt der Psalmen legt nahe, dass Dtjes aus den Kreisen der Kultsänger stammte; seine Anonymität entspräche der Namenlosigkeit der Psalmendichter." ("The intensive use of the language and genres of the Psalms suggests that Deutero-Isaiah had his roots in the community of cultic singers; his anonymity is consistent with the anonymity of the psalmic poets.")

8. This is even admitted by Hermisson, who reckons with an individual Deutero-Isaiah; see Hermisson, "Deutero-Jesaja," 684–85.

statement does not fit a real prophet. Such a one does not have the task of converting all the pagans, still less did a real prophet succeed in that task."[9]

The unique characteristic of Isa 40–55 does not consist in these chapters' portrayal of an individual, anonymous prophet but in their skillful combination of a variety of literary genres.[10] They can be considered to be the literary footprints of a community of authorized speakers.[11] It is especially important to bear in mind that individual authorship as this is typically understood in modern times was unknown in the past:

> In ancient civilizations, such as Mesopotamia and Israel, the human person is understood as a character (*personnage*) rather than a personality (*personne*). The individual is indistinguishable from his or her social role and social status. That is why the distinction between the individual and the community he or she belongs to is not as rigid as it seems to be in our modern world. In Mesopotamia and Israel, the author, being a subcategory of the individual, is a particular character or role. The social group the author belongs to and identifies with is that of the scribes.[12]

Considering the milieu of the scribes or, in the case of Isa 40–45, of the prophetic singers, the modern distinction between individual and collective authorship is inappropriate. This is because "authors belonged to a certain social category or class. Any attempt to enter into the minds of

---

9. Julius Wellhausen, *Israelitische und jüdische Geschichte,* 9th ed. (1958; repr., Berlin: de Gruyter, 1981), 152 n. 1 (my trans.).

10. Christoph Levin, *Das Alte Testament,* 2nd ed., Beck'sche Reihe 2160 (Munich: Beck, 2003), 85: "Die eigene Prägung, die Deuterojesaja besitzt, beruht vor allem auf den verwendeten Gattungen. Sie ist keine individuelle Signatur." ("Deutero-Isaiah's particular characteristic trait consists most of all in the genres it utilizes. This gives no information about an individual person.")

11. Erhard S. Gerstenberger, *Israel in der Perserzeit: 5. und 4. Jahrhundert v. Chr.,* Biblische Enzyklopädie 8 (Stuttgart: Kohlhammer, 2005), 248: "In den starken Heilsworten zeichnet sich ein Profil der Gemeinde ab. Es kommen Rufer, Prediger zu Wort, von 'Propheten' ist nicht die Rede. Nur die literarischen Fußspuren der göttlich autorisierten Sprecher sind zu entdecken." ("In the powerful messages of salvation the profile of the community begins to emerge. Heralds and preachers articulate their message, though there is no talk of 'prophets.' Only the literary footprints of the divinely authorized speakers can be discerned.")

12. Karel van der Toorn, *Scribal Culture and the Making of the Hebrew Bible* (Cambridge: Harvard University Press, 2007), 46.

those authors has to be based on knowledge of the class to which they belonged. As an individual, the author was of little consequence."[13]

At some point in the development of Israel's literary tradition the singing and the liturgical music of the sons of Asaph (among others) came to be regarded as a prophetic activity (נבא *niphal*; 1 Chr 25:2, 3). It is very well possible that the seeds for this development had already been sown by the prophetic singers of the Isaiah scroll. This development seems all the more likely since the song of the Asaphites in 1 Chr 16:8–36, itself composed from Pss 105 and 96, contains the main themes found in Isa 40–55, especially the praise of YHWH among all the nations and the devaluation of the foreign gods as nothingness. These prophets and poets were aware of being transmitters of divine words, akin to the works of the sculptors of divine images, and so they created cutting parodies of the production of cult images (cf. Isa 40:18–20; 41:6–7; 44:9–20; 46:5–7).

Despite this, one may still ask whether it is really possible for a collective group to have composed such a beautiful piece of literature as Isa 40–55. The question, however, can be turned around: why should there be an individual prophet behind these chapters if it is already accepted that Isa 56–66 is the work of skilled writers,[14] not to mention an even later composition in the first part of the book, namely, Isa 24–27?[15] Why should one seek an individual author for Isa 40–55 if such an investigation is judged to be unacceptable for the traditions of the Pentateuch or the historical books?

In my view, the old Jerusalem Isaiah tradition was continuously written and rewritten until the first deportation in 597 BCE. This is the reason why Isa 39 mentions only the deportation of the royal family and not the deportation of the population as such.[16] The subsequent merging of this older tradition with the Babylonian script of the returning temple singers

---

13. Ibid., 49.

14. Wolfgang Lau, *Schriftgelehrte Prophetie in Jes 56–66: Eine Untersuchung zu den literarischen Bezügen in den letzten elf Kapiteln des Jesajabuches*, BZAW 225 (Berlin: de Gruyter, 1994); Brooks Schramm, *The Opponents of Third Isaiah: Reconstructing the Cultic History of the Restoration*, JSOTSup 193 (Sheffield: Sheffield Academic, 1995).

15. James T. Hibbard, *Intertextuality in Isaiah 24–27: The Reuse and Evocation of Earlier Texts and Traditions*, FAT 2/16 (Tübingen: Mohr Siebeck, 2006).

16. See Rüdiger Feuerstein, "Weshalb gibt es 'Deuterojesaja'?" in *Ich bewirke das Heil und erschaffe das Unheil (Jesaja 45,7): Studien zur Botschaft der Propheten; Festschrift für Lothar Ruppert zum 65. Geburtstag*, ed. Friedrich Diedrich and Bernd Willmes, FB 88 (Würzburg: Echter, 1998), 132.

resulted in a win-win situation. The Jerusalem Isaiah tradition was helped over the gorge of the exile—see the break between Isa 39 and 40—and the authors of Isa 40–55 could rely on the undisputed authority of the Jerusalem prophet. The authority of the old Jerusalem prophet progressively permeated the whole script, so that at the end of the formation period in the time of Chronicles the scroll was given the title "the vision of Isaiah, son of Amoz" (Isa 1:1). This approach to the question of authorship and literary development cannot be without consequences for the interpretation of the identity of the Servant in these chapters, the subject of the next section.

Collective Identity of the Servant Jacob/ Israel

My analysis of this question will be primarily focused on Isa 41–48, as in these chapters Jacob/Israel is called עבד (Ebed),[17] receiving from YHWH the mission to witness to the fact that he is the only true God. But what is the relationship between the passages in which Jacob/Israel is called "servant" and the so-called Servant Songs in Isa 42, 49, 50, and 53, in which this is not the case (leaving aside the special case of 49:3)? There is a growing consensus that although the Servant Songs are indeed special units (the element of truth in Duhm's position), these texts are not to be seen in isolation from the rest of Isa 40–55 (in contrast to Duhm).

The separation between the "collective interpretation" in the Jacob/Israel–Ebed passages and the "individual interpretation" in the Servant Songs ignores the fact that in a number of verses the plural and singular address are intermingled. Thus, in preparation for the first Ebed Song in 41:27, one reads: "The first shall say to Zion, Behold, behold *them*: and I will give to Jerusalem *one* that brings good tidings" (KJV). The switch in the Masoretic Text from the plural "behold them" to the singular "the one who brings good tidings" has to be respected. The herald (מבשר) will be constituted by those in Jacob/Israel, members of the blind and deaf Servant, who accept the call to bring the message of salvation to Zion/Jerusalem.

That the reference to the herald in 41:27 stands immediately before 42:1–4 is not accidental but points to the first Servant Song (cf. 48:16c before 49:1–6). The ones who are called to accept the task of comforting

---

17. Isa 41:8; 44:1, 2, 21; 45:4; 48:20; (49:5, 6); Jer 30:10; 46:27, 28; Ezek 28:25; 37:25; (Ps 105:6); 1 Chr 16:13.

Jerusalem (40:1–11) are the heralds of good tidings and thus constitute the Servant.[18] This also provides a plausible explanation for the use of the plural form at the end of 42:9 ("I inform you [pl.]"). Nothing is more illuminating in this respect than 43:10, where God says to the addressees: "You are my witnesses, said the LORD, and my servant whom I have chosen: that you may know and believe me, and understand that I am he: before me there was no God formed, neither shall there be after me" (KJV). The alternation between the plural and singular forms is once more to be maintained, contrary to the Septuagint but in accordance with the Vulgate.[19] The same switch from the singular to the plural takes place in 44:26, where YHWH is presented as the one who confirms the word of his servant (sg.) and fulfills the plan of his messengers (pl.).[20]

Just as 41:27 introduced the first Servant Song in 42:1–4, so 48:16b builds a bridge to the second Servant Song in 49:1–6. The sudden change in the speaking subject from God to a human I-figure in the last part of this verse, "And now Adonai YHWH has sent me and his spirit," indicates that this is an editorial addition.[21] In Isa 40–55 such an I-figure is only present in 49:1–6 and 50:4–9, that is, in the context of the prophetic sending. Thus the colon in question is a pointer to these two Servant Songs, a fact that is especially confirmed by the epithet "Adonai YHWH"—otherwise found only in 50:4, 5, 7, 9.

These verses indicate that it is not an anonymous exilic prophet but the servant community, which, having been purified and elected (48:10), now presents itself as the messenger of good tidings for Israel and the nations.[22]

---

18. See Jürgen Werlitz, *Redaktion und Komposition: Zur Rückfrage hinter die Endgestalt von Jes 40–55*, BBB 122 (Bodenheim: Philo, 1999), 288, in view of Isa 41:27: "Die zur Trostbotschaft an Zion Beauftragten sind der Freudenbote und ebenfalls der Knecht." ("Those who are commissioned to herald comfort to Zion are both the herald of good tidings as well as the servant.")

19. "Vos testes mei dicit Dominus et servus meus quem elegi" (Isa 43:10 Vg.).

20. The singular "his servant" is supported by 1QIsa^a, 4QIsa^b, LXX, and Vg. The plural (LXX^A; Tg. "his servants, the righteous") presents a *lectio facilior*, adjusting "his servant" to the plural "his messengers."

21. Cf. Ulrich Berges, "'Ich gebe Jerusalem einen Freudenboten': Synchrone und diachrone Beobachtungen zu Jes 41,27," *Bib* 87 (2006): 319–37.

22. Reinhard G. Kratz, *Kyros im Deuterojesaja-Buch: Redaktionsgeschichtliche Untersuchungen zu Entstehung und Theologie von Jesaja 40–55*, FAT 1 (Tübingen: Mohr Siebeck, 1991), 118, 137; Henk Leene, *De vroegere en de nieuwe dingen bij Deuterojesaja* (Amsterdam: VU Uitgeverij, 1987), 215.

This is the group—after 54:17 we only find "servants" in the plural[23]—that, for the sake of its own identity, created the literary figure of the Servant.[24]

This development is reminiscent of a postexilic literary phenomenon known as "nachexilische Rollen- und Problemdichtung" in German. This is a technique by which theological problems of postexilic times are enclosed in a literary figure. For example, the question of innocent suffering is addressed in the character of Job, endurance under the wrath of God in the suffering person of Lam 3, and the fate of the true prophet in the confessions of the persecuted Jeremiah.[25] These confessions stem from prophetic circles that projected their own situation of distress into the life of Jeremiah, their master, in order to find consolation and justification.[26]

It is interesting to note in this respect that the Servant in the third song (50:4–9) is seen as much more of a prophetic figure than in the previous two. This speaks in favor of a later development: the Servant increasingly evolves into the ideal figure of a genuine prophet suffering on behalf of YHWH and his word.[27]

In the literary drama of Isa 40–55, the faithful Ebed grows out of the blind and deaf servant Jacob/Israel.[28] The authors understood themselves

---

23. Cf. Isa 54:17; 56:6; 63:17; 65:8, 9, 13, 14, 15; 66:14.

24. Sheldon H. Blank, *Prophetic Faith in Isaiah* (Detroit: Wayne State University Press, 1967), 102: "A personification is both a fiction, a figment, a figure of speech, and a reality, a fact. And a writer employing the device of personification may slip intentionally or unintentionally from fiction into fact."

25. Ivo Meyer, "Die Klagelieder," in *Einleitung in das Alte Testament*, ed. Erich Zenger, 7th ed., Studienbücher Theologie 1.1 (Stuttgart: Kohlhammer, 2008), 482: "Klgl 3 gehört ins Umfeld von Rollen- oder Problemträger-Dichtungen wie die sog. Konfessionen Jeremias, Ijob oder die Texte vom leidenden Gerechten im Psalter." ("Lamentations 3 is another example of a poetic exploration of theological issues by means of a literary persona, just like the so-called Confessions of Jeremiah, Job, or the texts of the suffering righteous individual in the Psalms.")

26. Karl-Friedrich Pohlmann, *Die Ferne Gottes: Studien zum Jeremiabuch: Beiträge zu den "Konfessionen" im Jeremiabuch und ein Versuch zur Frage nach den Anfängen der Jeremiatradition*, BZAW 179 (Berlin: de Gruyter, 1989), 38.

27. Werlitz, *Redaktion und Komposition*, 282; see also Blank, *Prophetic Faith in Isaiah*, 77: "the servant is no single person but Israel personified, and personified as prophet."

28. Cf. Hans-Jürgen Hermisson, "Jakob und Zion, Schöpfung und Heil," *Zeichen der Zeit* 44 (1990): 262–68: "Die Gottesknechtslieder reden also von dem prophetischen Anteil an der Knechts- und Zeugenrolle Israels.... Darum demonstrieren die Gottesknechte [sic Plural!] gemeinsam der Welt, daß die Götter nicht retten, daß allein

to be the ideal Israel, tested and called by God in the furnace of exilic affliction (48:10).[29] Their belief in YHWH as the one and only sovereign over history and creation, thereby subordinating even the nations to his rule, breaks with the particularism of preexilic times and broadens the concept of the God of Israel.[30]

The Redefinition of God's People in Exile

There is no doubt that the Old Testament is, for a large part, the product of a search for identity in times of distress and suffering. The Babylonian exile played a major role in this process of "writing against oblivion." The command "do not forget" has its equivalent in the imperative "remember." It is because of this that Israel's "heroes" (e.g., Abraham, Moses, Aaron, David, Solomon, and, not to forget, Jacob/Israel) became increasingly important figures in the construction of its exilic and postexilic identity. It is therefore not by chance that, apart from Gen 25–36, the highest concentration of references to Jacob/Israel in the entire Old Testament is found in Isa 41–48, with seventeen entries in all. That which Meira Polliack has only stated in a footnote must be strongly underlined: "Considering Deutero-Isaiah's audience, the constant naming of Jacob appears deliberate, since he is addressing exiled Judaites as if they were Israelites, thus appropriating to them the full status of Jacob's descendants. In this he provides an answer to the problem that so preoccupied his generation, namely, who is the real Israel?"[31]

Jahwe rettet" ("The Servant Songs, therefore, talk of the prophetic dimension of Israel's function as servant and witness.... This is the reason why altogether the servants of God [sic plural!] demonstrate to the world that it is not the gods who save but YHWH alone") (265).

29. Cf. Othmar Keel, *Die Geschichte Jerusalems und die Entstehung des Monotheismus*, vol. 4 part 2 of *Orte und Landschaften der Bibel: Ein Handbuch und Studien-Reiseführer zum Heiligen Land* (Göttingen: Vandenhoeck & Ruprecht, 2007), 856.

30. Cf. Volker Haarmann, *JHWH—Verehrer der Völker: Die Hinwendung von Nichtisraeliten zum Gott Israels in alttestamentlichen Überlieferungen*, AThANT 91 (Zurich: TVZ, 2008).

31. Meira Polliack, "Deutero-Isaiah's Typological Use of Jacob in the Portrayal of Israel's National Renewal," in *Creation in Jewish and Christian Tradition*, ed. Henning Graf Reventlow and Yair Hoffman, JSOTSup 319 (Sheffield: Sheffield Academic, 2002), 77 n. 13.

What has to be noted and what is commonly overlooked is that "Jacob" in Isa 41–48 is seen as a positive character, as an identity marker of "Israel in exile." The connotation of "Jacob, the betrayer," is not erased, clearly seen in 43:27—"your first ancestor sinned"—or in 48:8—"from birth you were called a rebel,"[32] but this negative image does not stand in the foreground. What stands in the center is the renewed election of Jacob/Israel in exile: the combination of בחר (to elect) with "Jacob/Israel" in one and the same verse occurs especially in 14:1; 41:8; 44:1, 2; and in Ps 135:4, and there is no doubt that the idea originated within those circles that composed the oldest part of the literary drama in Isa 41–44. The chiastic structure "Israel-Jacob//Jacob-Israel" and the mention of Jeshurun in Isa 44:2 (cf. Deut 32:15; 33:5, 26; Sir 37:25) underline the change from "Jacob, the crooked one" (יעקב: uneven, deceitful, sly) to "Jacob, the straight/just one" (ישר).[33]

According to Polliack, four major literary motifs "drive home the eponymous link between the patriarch and his descendants": (1) the journey; (2) God's accompaniment on the journey in face of adversaries; (3) the calling by name; and (4) the creation from the womb.[34]

Given the centrality of the renewal of Jacob's identity, the "calling by name" is the most important element, as is indicated by Isa 43:7: "everyone who is called by my name, whom I created for my glory, whom I formed and made." Each individual member, every single one of the dispersed people of God, is invited to reactualize his or her being "Jacob/Israel." It is not accidental that in the final reference to the election in 44:1 and 2 the motif of "being called by name" returns, once again individualized, as it is seen in 44:5: "This one will say, 'I am the Lord's,' another will be called by the name of Jacob, yet another will write on the hand, 'The Lord's,' and adopt the name of Israel." When God pours water on the dry ground (of exile), that is, his spirit and blessing on the descendants of the eponymous father, they shall spring up among the grass, as willows by the watercourses (44:3–4).

Within these verses there is no reference to the integration of foreigners into the community of God, which means that "Israelites" are the more likely referent: each one of the addressees is called to live up to their

---

32. Cf. Gen 25:24–34; 27:35–36; Hos 12:4; Jer 9:3; Mal 3:6.

33. Berges, *Jesaja 40–48*, 320; Polliack, "Deutero-Isaiah's Typological Use," 94; cf. Isa 40:4.

34. Polliack, "Deutero-Isaiah's Typological Use," 81–99; quotation from 77.

election by God to be Jacob/Israel and to be proud thereof. In this context "to sprout" (צמח) is not only a vegetal metaphor but indicates a special relationship to YHWH. The statement that this sprout will blossom "in the midst of grass" has to be read in connection with the negative declaration of 40:6: all the people are grass, all their חסד, that is, their constancy, is like the flower of the field.³⁵ The ones addressed in these chapters who accept the renewed vocation and election by YHWH constitute Jacob/Israel or, vice versa, Jacob/Israel is constituted by them. Only these will sprout "like willows" (כערבים) by streams of water. Is it pure coincidence that "willows" (ערבים) are mentioned only once more in an exilic setting, in Ps 137:2: "On the willows [of Babel] there we hung up our harps"?³⁶

The Witness of the True Servant Jacob/Israel

The call to the addressees to constitute Jacob/Israel, each of them individually and as a group, has a specific goal. The revitalization of identity embraces a mission, which is to give witness to the only true godhood of YHWH.

It is only after the presentation of the true Ebed in the first Servant Song in Isa 42 that the word and concept of "witness" appears. The faithful Ebed, that is, those in exile who accept their mission to renew their identity as Jacob/Israel, are called to convince the still blind and deaf majority: "Bring forth the people who are blind, yet have eyes, who are deaf, yet have ears!" (43:8). Jacob/Israel in exile as the true Servant of God shall witness to the true deity of the Lord before the foreign gods and their witnesses: "Let them bring their witnesses to justify them, and let them hear and say, 'It is true.' You are my witnesses, says the Lord, and [you are] my servant whom I have chosen" (43:9–10).

The Masoretic Text in 43:10 has to be respected and ought not to be changed according to the Septuagint reading: "become witnesses for me, and I am witness." Those and only those in exile who abandon their deafness and blindness will become witnesses to God's action through Cyrus.³⁷ The Persian sovereign constitutes the political instrument of God's renewed rule, but he himself is called neither king nor servant. Only YHWH alone is king and his servant is Jacob/Israel as his true witness! The realm of

---

35. Berges, *Jesaja 40–48*, 322; cf. Isa 42:9; 43:19; 55:10; 61:11.
36. The other three references: Lev 23:40 (Feast of Booths); Isa 15:7; Job 40:22.
37. See Cees van Leeuwen, "עד ʿēd witness," *TLOT* 2:842.

Cyrus is politics, the duty of Jacob/Israel is religion. The exilic search for identity is not only a journey back in the footprints of Jacob but also an expedition forward into the witness stand for the monotheistic faith in YHWH. This becomes most evident in 44:1–8, where Jacob is addressed twice as "servant" and Israel/Jeshurun as "chosen" (44:1–2). At the end of the trial speech in 44:6–8 it is hopefully stated: "Do not fear, or be afraid; have I not told you from of old and declared it? You are my witnesses! Is there any god besides me? There is no other rock; I know not one" (44:8).

The proximity to 43:10 is obvious (only at these two places are the addressees said to be "witnesses"), but something has changed. While in the former statement the opponents are presented as a legal party in court (cf. 43:9: "Let all the nations gather together … who among them declared this"), in 44:6–8 their presence is reduced to their words ("let them declare"). Thus the adversaries in this legal dispute, the foreign gods and their followers, receive less and less attention. This is all the more true if one also considers the much longer presentation of the adversaries in 41:1–7, 21–29.[38]

The long description of construction of idols in 44:9–20 highlights the function of Jacob/Israel as witness for YHWH because the producers of idols are depicted as powerless: "*their* witnesses neither see nor know" (44:9). The witnesses of YHWH ought not be afraid (44:8), while the others will be afraid and be put to shame (44:11).

Roy Melugin's interpretation of these verses in his significant monograph has to be somewhat modified. He states, "The people Israel are Yahweh's witnesses; as witnesses they can be persuaded and thus open to hear the word of hope."[39] It is not the people of Israel as such who are sustained by this word of hope. Rather only those within Jacob/Israel who open their minds develop into the true servant and grow to become witnesses for YHWH.[40]

It is very interesting to note that while the designation עבד remains in the singular,[41] the "witnesses" are spoken of in the plural (43:10; 44:8).

---

38. Berges, *Jesaja 40–48*, 279–80.

39. Roy F. Melugin, *The Formation of Isaiah 40–55*, BZAW 141 (Berlin: de Gruyter, 1976), 119.

40. See Jim W. Adams, *The Performative Nature and Function of Isaiah 40–55*, LHBOTS 448 (London: T&T Clark, 2006), 115–16: "Those who witness to themselves and confess Yahweh alone will embrace becoming his people, servant Jacob-Israel."

41. Cf. Isa 41:8, 9; 42:1, 19; 44:1, 2, 21, 26; 45:4; 48:20; from 54:17 onward we find only the plural.

Without employing the word עֶבֶד, the same is true in 48:6: "You have heard; now see all this [sg.]; and will you not declare it [pl.]?" The plural refers to each one of the addressees, commanding them to proclaim the renewed activity of YHWH by calling on Cyrus to liberate God's servant Jacob (48:20). Those who are not willing to do that are excluded from the "new things" (42:9; 43:19; 48:6) and also from the new song (42:10).

Contrary to most commentators, Henk Leene in his Dutch dissertation (with an English summary) on the topic of the "new things" has shown that Cyrus represents not the new things but the outcome of the former things. It is not Cyrus but the Servant who facilitates the entrance into the new things: "The new amounts to the fact that the conversion to which Jhwh invites his blind and deaf Servant and for which he marshals all the arguments of history until Cyrus is really provided. The new presents Israel's conversion as Jhwh's own act of creation."[42] What is really new is the role of the formerly deaf and blind servant Jacob, purified and chosen (48:10) in the furnace of adversity: "The purified Israel is this speaking Servant."[43]

The task of being a witness is presented once again in 55:4, at the end of the Zion/Jerusalem chapters 49–55. Like Jacob, the "wanderer" is called to be a witness to YHWH's sovereign rule in history; the same is true for Zion as the aim of the Servant's journey back home—geographically and spiritually. The people of God are thus represented by both personifications: by Jacob, the patriarch on the journey, and by Zion at the end of the journey. Once Jacob arrives at Zion—like deported children who return to their mother—the designation "Jacob" disappears[44] and is replaced by "Zion/Jerusalem." Common to both is their duty to give witness, but the range of witness is very much enlarged in the case of Zion/Jerusalem: all nations are invited to buy wine and milk at no costs, that is, to get Torah from Zion. God's promises to David will be reenacted in those who have adopted the true Jacob identity and have reached Jerusalem as heralds of good tidings (41:27; 52:7): "I will make an everlasting covenant with you [pl.], the sure mercies of David" (55:3).

As a result, Zion does not only function as the royal bride of YHWH, she also receives kingly prerogatives by becoming the embodiment of

---

42. Leene, *Vroegere en de nieuwe dingen*, 328.
43. Ibid., 330. Cf. Jürgen Werlitz, "Vom Gottesknecht der Lieder zum Gottesknecht des Buches," *BK* 61 (2006): 208–11.
44. Only once again in 49:26, i.e., in the epithet "the Strong One of Jacob."

David: "See, I made him a witness to the peoples, a leader and commander for the peoples" (55:4). Zion's role is not focused on herself but stands in analogy to the mission of the Servant: Jacob/Israel in Zion/Jerusalem is God's witness in the world and enters as such in the Davidic covenant and into the functions of David as ruler.[45]

Thus the identity of the people of God as "Jacob/Israel" and as "Zion/David" centers on the call to be witnesses to YHWH as the only true God. This function is made possible because God glorifies himself first in Jacob (44:23) and then in the community of Zion (55:5). This new Zion-David will not be the conqueror of foreign nations but their leader and commander, that is, the one who proclaims the commandments of YHWH.[46] In this manner, the Zion community, conceived as the new David, embodied by the community of the Servants, becomes the Moses of the nations!

---

45. Hermisson, "Jakob und Zion," 264: "Zions königlich-herrschaftliche Rolle ist kein Selbstzweck, sondern steht in Parallele zur königlichen Erwählung des Gottesknechtes Israel: Zion-Israel ist Zeuge Jahwes vor der Welt und tritt so in den Davidbund und in die Funktion des Herrschers David ein (55,3–5)." ("Zion's royal function is not an end in itself, it parallels the royal election of Israel, the Servant of God: Zion-Israel is a witness to YHWH before the whole world and as such enters both the Davidic covenant as well as the David's function as ruler [55:3–5].")

46. Ulrich Berges, *Das Buch Jesaja: Komposition und Endgestalt,* Herders biblische Studien 16 (Freiburg im Breisgau: Herder, 1998), 400; trans. as *The Book of Isaiah: Its Composition and Final Form,* Hebrew Bible Monographs 46 (Sheffield: Sheffield Phoenix, 2012), 374.

Second Isaiah and the Aaronide Response to Judah's Forced Migrations

Stephen L. Cook

The forced migrations of Judah in the sixth century BCE provoked a specific set of theological reflections among the Aaronide tradents of the Priestly Torah (PT).[1] The poetic prophecies of Second Isaiah present us with an impressive sampling of these priestly reflections, revealing their particular themes, motifs, and concerns oriented on a theology of reverence before the numinous otherness of God. In this essay I examine

---

1. Israel Knohl and Jacob Milgrom have identified a PT document within the Pentateuch, which was later joined with Holiness School (HS) writings to form what has hitherto been considered a basically unified P document. See Jacob Milgrom, *Leviticus 1-16: A New Translation with Introduction and Commentary*, AB 3 (New York: Doubleday, 1991), 1-2, 13-42, 48; Israel Knohl, *The Sanctuary of Silence: The Priestly Torah and the Holiness School* (Minneapolis: Fortress, 1995); idem, *The Divine Symphony: The Bible's Many Voices* (Philadelphia: Jewish Publication Society, 2003). Baruch J. Schwartz advances this new understanding of P in "The Priestly Account of the Theophany and the Lawgiving at Sinai," in *Texts, Temples, and Traditions: A Tribute to Menahem Haran*, ed. Michael V. Fox et al. (Winona Lake, IN: Eisenbrauns, 1996), 103-34; idem, *The Holiness Legislation: Studies in the Priestly Code* [Hebrew] (Jerusalem: Magnes, 1999). All three scholars argue that HS is mostly later than PT and has its own emphases, but they disagree on the extent of its polemical disagreement with PT. Schwartz argues ably against Knohl that HS aims not so much to react against PT as to complement and supplement it. For additional discussion, see David P. Wright, "Holiness in Leviticus and Beyond: Differing Perspectives," *Int* 53 (1999): 351-64; Andreas Ruwe, *"Heiligkeitsgesetz" und "Priesterschrift": Literaturgeschichtliche und rechtssystematische Untersuchungen zu Leviticus 17,1-26,2*, FAT 26 (Tübingen: Mohr Siebeck, 1999), 5-35; Jeffrey Stackert, *Rewriting the Torah: Literary Revision in Deuteronomy and the Holiness Legislation*, FAT 52 (Tübingen: Mohr Siebeck, 2007), 194-95; Mark S. Smith, *The Priestly Vision of Genesis 1* (Minneapolis: Augsburg Fortress, 2010), 172-73, 271 n. 41, 291 n. 62.

several of the Aaronide marks characterizing Second Isaiah's unique handling of the exile. I want to highlight the distinctiveness of the Isaiah community's response to the exile over against the very different approach to these forced migrations apparent in the book of Ezekiel and in the book of Jeremiah.

Israel Knohl traces a temporal, sequential relationship between the two component strands of the priestly writings of the Pentateuch, the Holiness School (HS) and the PT. It is better, in my view, to differentiate these priestly schools along social-scientific lines. Specifically, I want to link them respectively with Zadokite and Aaronide circles. In contrast to Knohl, furthermore, I believe that PT's thinking and theology turn up elsewhere in the biblical texts, specifically in Isa 40–66. I have built a case for this in *Conversations with Scripture: 2 Isaiah*.[2]

Throughout Isa 40–66 texts such as 44:28; 45:13; 52:1, 8; 53:10; 56:7; 60:7, 13; 62:9, 12; 64:11; and 66:6 make plain that the Isaianic authors are oriented on ceremonial purity, adherence to priestly instruction, and the temple's system of sacrifices. It is easy to imagine that the communities of Second and Third Isaiah were composed of Israelite priests. But if this is the case, from which of Israel's priestly houses did the Isaiah circle derive?

Ancient Israel's three major priestly houses can be identified as the Aaronides, the Zadokites, and the Levites. As I will argue below, the latter two houses are unlikely to represent the circle behind Second Isaiah, so our attention is drawn to the Aaronides. The thinking and theology of Second Isaiah differs markedly from HS and Ezekiel, which we may confidently identify as Zadokite compositions. Both outline a pyramidal hierarchy of priests with the Zadokites on top, which is unknown in competing priestly traditions.[3] The responses to Judah's forced migrations in Second Isaiah

---

2. Stephen L. Cook, *Conversations with Scripture: 2 Isaiah*, Anglican Association of Biblical Scholars Study Series (Harrisburg, PA: Morehouse, 2008).

3. Deuteronomy 18:1–8 speaks of the whole tribe of Levi as priests, all of whom have a right to attend before God (v. 7; cf. Jer 33:1, 21, 22). Similarly, the PT strand is uninterested in functional distinctions among the priestly lineages of Levi, Aaron, and Zadok (see Knohl, *Sanctuary of Silence*, 66, 85, 192, 209–12). Things are far different in both HS and Ezekiel. Ezekiel 40:44–46 differentiates two types of priests serving within the temple's restricted inner court, where the Levites are not allowed. The text names the descendants of Zadok as the ranking group over against a lower, middle tier of priests. See Stephen L. Cook and Corrine L. Patton, "Introduction: Hierarchical Thinking and Theology in Ezekiel's Book," in *Ezekiel's Hierarchical World: Wrestling with a Tiered Reality*, ed. Stephen L. Cook and Corrine L. Patton, SymS 31 (Atlanta:

also differ markedly from those of Deuteronomy and Jeremiah. These differences indicate that the Isaianic tradents part company not only with the Zadokites but also with the traditions and ideas of the Levites.[4]

Based on the evidence of texts such as Isa 43:22–28, it is apparent that the Isaianic authors consist of a circle oriented on temple, sacrifice, and reverence for God. In Isa 43, God reiterates Israel's culpability in its exile. The people's problem has not been God's disregard of them but their lack of respect for God's radical otherness. Viewing temple rites as laborious

---

Society of Biblical Literature, 2004), 11–13. Cf. Steven Shawn Tuell, *The Law of the Temple in Ezekiel 40–48*, HSM 49 (Atlanta: Scholars Press, 1992), 32 n. 37, 134, 139. The HS shares the position of Ezekiel. It subordinates other priestly lines within Israel to the line of Eleazar, the ancestor of Zadok. Even the Aaronide line of Ithamar, Eleazar's brother, must accept the Zadokites as their superiors. Ithamar's priestly house may well form the mid-ranking tier of priests described in Ezek 40:44–46. The HS places Ithamar, Eleazar's brother, in charge of Levites with lesser duties, while it has Eleazar direct the Levites responsible for the most important items of the tabernacle (Num 3–4). At Num 3:32, HS even calls Eleazar the "chief over the leaders of the Levites." Numbers 25:10–13 (HS) goes farther, narrating God's grant of a covenant of perpetual priesthood specifically to Eleazar's son, Phinehas. God makes no such grant to any other Aaronide priests. See Cook, review of *Missing Priests: The Zadokites in Tradition and History*, by Alice Hunt, *CBQ* 71 (2009): 372–73. Benjamin D. Sommer is certainly on target in his argument that Second Isaiah takes issue with the hierarchical and restrictive vision of priesthood in HS texts such as Num 18 (*Prophet Reads Scripture: Allusion in Isaiah 40–66* [Stanford, CA: Stanford University Press, 1998], 145–47).

4. For the provenance of Deuteronomy and Jeremiah at least partially within Levitical circles, see, e.g., Robert G. Boling, "Levitical History and the Role of Joshua," in *The Word of the Lord Shall God Forth: Essays in Honor of David Noel Freedman in Celebration of His Sixtieth Birthday*, ed. Carol L. Meyers and M. O'Connor (Winona Lake, IN: Eisenbrauns, 1983), 242–44; Richard Elliott Friedman, *Who Wrote the Bible?* 2nd ed. (San Francisco: HarperSanFrancisco, 1997), 120–24; Cook, *The Social Roots of Biblical Yahwism*, SBLStBL 8 (Atlanta: Society of Biblical Literature, 2004), 59–63, including the bibliography at p. 62 n. 39; Mark Leuchter, *The Polemics of Exile in Jeremiah 26–45* (Cambridge: Cambridge University Press, 2008), 174, 265–66 n. 19; and now S. Dean McBride Jr., "Jeremiah and the Levitical Priests of Anathoth," in *Thus Says the Lord: Essays on the Former and Latter Prophets in Honor of Robert R. Wilson*, ed. Stephen L. Cook and John J. Ahn, LHBOTS 502 (New York: T&T Clark, 2009), 187–89. Among other evidence, McBride notes how Jer 33:17–22 unqualifiedly supports God's covenant with the Levites (cf. Mal 2:4). For a good, recent review of Gerhard von Rad's classic, breakthrough arguments that the Levites composed Deuteronomy, see Peter T. Vogt, *Deuteronomic Theology and the Significance of Torah: A Reappraisal* (Winona Lake, IN: Eisenbrauns, 2006), 36–37.

(vv. 22, 23), they performed them as shams without true surrender (cf. 1:10–17). The means of reconciliation with God at the temple has not worked for them, because they enacted the rites without even the minimum of awe and remorse necessary to ritually cleanse God's shrine. In the theology of reverence of PT, God experiences Israel's sin as a tainting, repelling force. It makes continued contact with the people burdensome.[5] Second Isaiah affirms this theology: God announces, "You have burdened me with your sins; you have wearied me with your iniquities" (43:24). The exile occurred because momentous sin radically restricted and alienated God. Yet the text offers hope in verse 25: God is "He who blots out your transgressions."

Unlike Deuteronomically oriented prophets such as Jeremiah, the Isaiah community does not respond to the culpability of God's people with a mere call to "return" or "repent" (שׁוּב). God first intervenes to ransom and redeem, to blot out Israel's transgressions and sins for God's own sake so as to enable return (Isa 43:25; 44:22; 49:5–6; 51:11). More fundamental than Israel's "return" (שׁוּב) is God's provision of "reparation" (אשׁם).

Scouring their priestly traditions, the community of Second Isaiah lands on the theme that the people must have a "ritual reparation" for their iniquities (אשׁם). Specifically, they come to understand that an enigmatic Suffering Servant will become the people's *reparation offering* (53:10), a priestly technical term (cf. PT at Lev 5:14–6:7).

Far from randomly chosen, this unique offering fits the exiles' spiritual situation. The אשׁם is the specific sacrifice one uses when in dire straits due to momentous offenses against God (Lev 5:17–19; Ezra 10:19). It is the appropriate offering if Judah's downfall was due to fatal sacrilege—irreverence before God's burning sanctity (cf. 2 Chr 36:14; Lev 5:15–16).

The call to "return" (שׁוּב) in other prophets often represents a summons to renew Israel's bilateral covenant with God. The prophecies of Ezekiel and Jeremiah are rooted in the theologies of HS and D, respectively, each of which presents Israel with a bilateral covenant that contains stipulations and associated curses for disobedience. As scholars have long rec-

---

5. Current advances in this understanding build on foundational studies by Jacob Milgrom. See, e.g., "Kipper," *EncJud* 10:1039–44; "Day of Atonement," *EncJud* 5:1384–87; "Sin Offering or Purification Offering?" *VT* 21 (1971): 237–39; "Israel's Sanctuary: The Priestly Picture of Dorian Gray," *RB* 83 (1976): 390–99.

ognized, such a bilateral covenant is conspicuously absent from the texts of Second Isaiah.[6]

Neither the Sinai covenant nor Moses, the great prophetic mediator of the Sinai covenant, figures overtly in Isa 40–55. Instead, Second Isaiah echoes the unilateral, unconditional covenant of the PT source. It emphasizes this covenant as a means of dealing with the theological and existential crisis of exile. Despite people's fears, the exile cannot mean that God has abandoned them in any significant manner.

Unlike HS and D, PT shows the form not of a vassal treaty but of an unconditional commitment. Second Isaiah follows suit, affirming God's permanent commitment to Israel. Although its style of expression differs from PT, the Isaiah community echoes its thinking with words such as those in Isa 54:10, "For the mountains may depart and the hills be removed, but my steadfast love shall not depart from you, and my covenant of peace shall not be removed."

Grappling with the exile meant confronting the doomed history of Israel stretching from the giving of the bilateral Sinai covenant to the forced migrations of the people away from the land. On the basis of all that has happened, the exiles worry that God no longer cares about them (Isa 40:27; 49:14; cf. Lam 5:20). The PT presents God's permanent covenants as completely separate from Israel's sad history after exodus and Sinai, moored, as they are, much earlier in the ancestral period. This tradition allows Second Isaiah to discount the significance of the failure of the Sinai covenant. Israel's sad history of disobedience need not preoccupy the exiles. As Isa 43:18 puts it, "Do not remember the former things, or consider the things of old" (cf. 65:17).[7]

---

6. E.g., Isa 51:2 looks back to God's permanent commitment to Abraham and Sarah in Gen 17 (PT). Isaiah's references to the primordial PT *blessing* and to *multiplication* along with the inclusion of *Sarah* make this certain. For discussion, see Carroll Stuhlmueller, *Creative Redemption in Deutero-Isaiah*, AnBib 43 (Rome: Biblical Institute Press, 1970), 148 n. 495; Walter Brueggemann, "The Kerygma of the Priestly Writer," in Walter Brueggemann and Hans Walter Wolff, *The Vitality of Old Testament Traditions*, 2nd ed. (Atlanta: John Knox, 1982), 103; Michael A. Fishbane, *Biblical Interpretation in Ancient Israel* (Oxford: Clarendon, 1985), 375. Note that HS theology would likely object to the thrust of Isa 51:2 (see Ezek 33:24).

7. On the manner in which PT "goes over the head" of the Sinai covenant, asserting that the promises to Abraham trump Israel's whole history under the shadow of Sinai, see Andreas Eitz, *Studien zum Verhältnis von Priesterschrift und Deuterojesaja* (Heidelberg: Evangelisch Theologische Fakultät, 1969), 25, 38, 57, 66, 71; R. E. Cle-

Second Isaiah's assumption of Israel's security is grounded in PT's theology, as expressed in its promises to Abraham. Thus texts such as Isa 41:1-10 repeatedly allude to Gen 17 (PT). As the "offspring of Abraham" (Isa 41:8), the exiles are heirs to specific, eternal promises of God. As an "everlasting covenant," God promised Abraham "to be God to you and to your offspring after you" (Gen 17:7).[8] This perpetual, unilateral commitment of God to God's people lies at the heart of Second Isaiah's theology. In calling Abraham "my friend" in Isa 41:8, God uses a Hebrew idiom identifying him as an eternal covenant partner (cf. 2 Chr 20:7). Isaiah 41:10 affirms the promise, repeating the oath of Gen 17:7 that "I am your God."

In case the audience might still be tempted to dwell on Israel's sad history after Egypt and Sinai, Isa 54:9-10 reminds them that God's more ancient work with Noah is far more relevant to their situation. The text presents God's irrevocable agreement with Noah (Gen 9:8-17 PT) as a fine example of the unconditional and perpetual nature of God's commitment, God's "covenant of peace" with Zion (Isa 54:10; cf. Ps 46:2). Isaiah 54:9 reads, "Just as I swore that the waters of Noah would never again go over the earth, so I have sworn that I will not be angry with you."

The Sinai covenant, like a marriage, might be terminated through "divorce," but not the perpetual covenants of the PT tradition. Based on PT thinking, Isa 50:1-3 has God challenge the exiles to come up with any "bill of divorce" issued to the nation. They cannot, for in this theology, God's commitment to Zion is unilateral and eternal. As Benjamin Sommer has argued well, Isaiah's position stands in some tension with texts such as Jer 3:1-8.[9]

---

ments, *Abraham and David: Genesis XV and Its Meaning for Israelite Tradition*, SBT 2/2 (Naperville, IL: Allenson, 1967), 74–76; Ralph W. Klein, "The Message of P," in *Die Botschaft und die Boten: Festschrift für Hans Walter Wolff zum 70. Geburtstag*, ed. Jörg Jeremias and Lothar Perlitt (Neukirchen-Vluyn: Neukirchener Verlag, 1981), 62–65; Patricia Tull Willey, *Remember the Former Things: The Recollection of Previous Texts in Second Isaiah*, SBLDS 161 (Atlanta: Scholars Press, 1997), 270; Paul R. Williamson, *Abraham, Israel and the Nations: The Patriarchal Promise and Its Covenantal Development in Genesis*, JSOTSup 315 (Sheffield: Sheffield Academic, 2000), 54.

8. On the attribution of Gen 17:7-8 to PT (against Knohl, *Sanctuary of Silence*, 102 n. 145), see the arguments of Christophe Nihan, *From Priestly Torah to Pentateuch*, FAT 2/25 (Tübingen: Mohr Siebeck, 2007), 34–35 n. 72.

9. Sommer, *Prophet Reads Scripture*, 137–38; cf. Willey, *Remember the Former Things*, 200–203.

Jeremiah thinks in terms of a divorce of God from Israel, which, if it occurs, must be permanent, just as Deut 24 stipulates. Second Isaiah, on the other hand, stresses that the exile does not represent a divorce, which is actually inconceivable. Thus there is no impediment to the nation's restoration. Note the careful parallelism within Isa 50:1. Just as God certainly had not exiled Judah in weakness, to satisfy some creditor (see 52:3; cf. 45:13), so also there will never be found any divorce papers signaling God's hatred (see Deut 24:3). God did sell the people, but there is no creditor. God did send their mother away, but there is no divorce. Neither the strength of God's worldly competition nor a feeling of divine animosity stand in the way of God's plans to restore the exiles.

Sin, not some irretrievable termination, had created a separation between husband and wife. As Isa 54 will clarify, the separation is but for a moment, and hardly represents the marriage's dissolution. Israelite tradition insists that family land and family members that are "sold" (מכר) can and should be redeemed (cf. Lev 25:25, 47–49; Ruth 4:3–4; Isa 52:3).

Isaiah 54:4–8 expands the understanding that God is no divorced spouse. The applicable metaphor is that of the husband-redeemer, permanently bonded to Israel, ransoming his estranged wife from servitude. As Carroll Stuhlmueller has observed, the score of references to God as a husband-redeemer (גאל) in Second Isaiah assumes an unconditional covenant.[10] A *redeemer* (vv. 5, 8) is a close kinsperson—a husband or father if possible—who stands up for a relative in trouble. Often, the redeemer ransoms the relative from indentured servitude. Such an act is an obligatory moral duty, deeply incumbent on the kinsperson. If the kinsperson is a husband-redeemer, there is more than kinship bonding and kinship honor at stake. It must often have been deep marital love that compelled the husband to redeem. A husband-redeemer is deeply obligated to his spouse through a permanent bond of love.

---

10. Stuhlmueller, *Creative Redemption*, 107–8, 115, 122; cf. William P. Wood, "The Congregation of Yahweh: A Study of the Theology and Purpose of the Priestly Document" (ThD diss., Union Theological Seminary in Virginia, 1974), 98; Ralph W. Klein, *Israel in Exile: A Theological Interpretation*, OBT (Philadelphia: Fortress, 1979), 139 n. 15; Knohl, *Sanctuary of Silence*, 17 n. 24. Note that texts such as Isa 50:1 and 52:3 show that Second Isaiah's idea of God as a redeemer is a metaphor that cannot be pressed too literally. Babylonia had not paid anything up front for Israel's service and would receive no actual ransom payment from God. Israel was serving time in reparation for its sins against God.

A radical ontological disjunction distinguishes Israel and God within their deeply profound relationship according to both Second Isaiah and the PT strand. The Aaronide view of Israel's perpetual security entails a jarring understanding that the human covenantal recipient is radically diminutive.[11] The powerful privilege of the covenantal people, flowing down from God, is the flipside of a status that is, humanly speaking, that of both "worm" and "insect" (Isa 41:14).

The exiles join the psalmist in crying, "I am a worm [תולעת], and not human; scorned by others, and despised by the people" (Ps 22:6 [MT 7]). Embracing this cry, our dialectical Aaronide theology claims that the exiles' lowliness is a portal to amazing elevation. The "worm" is about to become a "threshing sledge, sharp, new, and having teeth" (Isa 41:15). Second Isaiah here celebrates a paradox in which humanity's frailty is also its strength (cf. 40:8; 49:2; 52:13–15). In this perspective, the forced humiliations of God's people actually set the stage for spiritual triumph.

This theology of PT, taken up by Second Isaiah, provides the perfect response to the theological problem of the temple's destruction. In this way of thinking, the destruction of Jerusalem and the exile of its priests and leaders can in no way have called God's sovereignty into question. God, the high and lofty one who inhabits eternity, whose name is Other, dwells in no earthly house but only "in the high and holy place, and also with those who are contrite and humble in spirit, to revive the spirit of the humble, and to revive the heart of the contrite" (Isa 57:15; cf. 66:2).

The core of PT's theology stresses God's absolute incomparability, before which all humans and idols are dwarfed like bugs. God's glory is numinous, devouring, and towers above everything human or terrestrial (cf. Exod 24:15–18; Lev 9:23–24; 10:2—all PT). Blessing comes to those who realize their human finitude, mortality, and frailty before God, aligning themselves in reverence for, and dependence on, God. Cognizance of the gulf between the divine and the human is essential.

Israel must banish any thought that God or God's glory might dwell on earth and inspire human emulation, as it does in both HS and Ezekiel (e.g., Exod 25:8; 29:45–46; Lev 11:44; 19:1–2; 20:7–8; 22:32; Num 5:3; 35:34—all HS; Ezek 10:18–22; 20:12; 37:27; 43:7, 9). No, the sanctuary is merely a meeting place between Israel and God (Exod 25:22; 30:6, 36

---

11. For discussion, see Cook, *Conversations*, 1–3, 19–37.

PT). God appears only intermittently, speaking from *between* the cherub statues on the ark, not as a humanoid seated above them (e.g., Exod 25:22; 30:6, 36; Lev 16:2—all PT). The PT never uses the phrase "tabernacle of the LORD," implying an ongoing habitation, nor does it ever have God speak of the sanctuary as "my dwelling." Isaiah 50–66 agrees completely (cf., e.g., 40:22; 57:15; 66:1).

Indeed, all anthropological visualization or representation of God is excluded in PT. God's intermittent appearances on earth are marked by opaque clouds and burning flames. There is no visible image involved whatsoever (e.g., Exod 24:17; Lev 9:23–24; 10:2; 16:2—all PT). The PT strand never describes God consuming sacrifices as food (contrast Num 28:2 HS; Ezek 44:7); it prohibits any burnt offerings, grain offerings, or drink offerings inside the tabernacle where God might be thought to eat them (Exod 30:9 PT). The strand insists that the priests must entirely consume the only food allowed inside the shrine, the bread of the Presence (Lev 24:8–9 PT).[12] Sharing this negative view of anthropomorphism, Second Isaiah has God scoff at the idea that the fat of sacrifices might be "filling" (Isa 43:24).[13] By the same token, the Isaianic prophetic texts go so far as to contest the bold anthropomorphism found in the HS strand that pictures God as weary or tired. Isaiah 40:28–29 stridently declares that God "does not faint or grow weary" but rather "gives power to the faint." The declaration appears to

---

12. For discussion of resistance to anthropomorphism within PT and Second Isaiah, see Cook, *Conversations*, 46–48, 117; Knohl, *Sanctuary of Silence*, 132–37.

13. A paucity of sacrifices is unlikely to be the problem condemned here; texts such as Isa 1:11–14; Jer 6:20; 7:21–22; and Mic 6:6–7 complain of a surfeit of cultic activity in preexilic Judah rather than a lack of it (see, e.g., J. Alec Motyer, *The Prophecy of Isaiah: An Introduction and Commentary* [Downers Grove, IL: InterVarsity Press, 1993], 338–39).The verse must represent a sarcastic rejection of the idea that God might be hungry for ritual sacrifices and find them sating. One might paraphrase as follows: "Do not imagine the fat of your sacrifices sated *me*." See Christopher R. North, *The Second Isaiah: Introduction, Translation, and Commentary to Chapters XL-LV* (Oxford: Clarendon, 1964), 127–30; R. N. Whybray, *Isaiah 40–66*, NCB (London: Oliphants, 1975), 91. As John Oswalt correctly notes, the force of Second Isaiah's language is to "place God beyond the realm of our manipulation." "The rituals themselves were not what God wanted" (*The Book of Isaiah: Chapters 40–66*, NICOT [Grand Rapids: Eerdmans, 1998], 159).

be a polemic against Exod 31:17 (HS),[14] which describes God as taking a deep breath after ceasing work on the seventh day of creation.[15]

---

14. Both Knohl and Milgrom identify the Sabbath pericope of Exod 31:12–17 as HS material, but the question of whether vv. 16–17 within this unit might better be attributed to PT has recently been raised by Saul M. Olyan ("Exodus 31:12–17: The Sabbath according to H, or the Sabbath according to P and H?" *JBL* 124 [2005]: 201–9). Olyan is correct that vv. 12–15 of the pericope contain its most telltale HS characteristics, but he overlooks two decisive features of vv. 16–17 that link these verses to HS as well. First, the graphic anthropopathic language at the end of these verses fits HS much better than PT. Second, unlike PT, vv. 16–17 use the language of ברית עולם (eternal covenant) not to describe a unilateral divine grant (PT's understanding of covenant, as argued above) but a perpetual commitment *on the part of Israel*. This is HS diction, also seen in the Holiness Code at Lev 24:8 (NJPS: "a commitment for all time on the part of the Israelites"). At Lev 24:8, as in Exod 31:16–17, one finds language of "covenant" applied to a ritual observance of the people rather than to a relationship with God. In both Exod 31:16 and Lev 24:8 the ritual observance *itself* is the eternal covenant.

15. The Hebrew verb נפש in Exod 31:17 (HS) pictures God catching God's breath, conjuring a very human image of God. Cf. S. R. Driver: God "took breath" (*The Book of Exodus* [Cambridge Bible for Schools and Colleges; Cambridge: Cambridge University Press, 1953], 345); NJB: "he rested and drew breath"; Benjamin Sommer: "He rested and took a deep breath" (*Prophet Reads Scripture*, 144). But does Second Isaiah also polemicize here against Gen 2:2–3 and its presentation of God's Sabbath rest? For this view, see Sommer, *Prophet Reads Scripture*, 142–44; Fishbane, *Biblical Interpretation*, 322–26; both relying directly on Moshe Weinfeld, "God the Creator in Genesis 1 and in the Prophecy of Second Isaiah" [Hebrew], *Tarbiz* 37 (1968): 105–32. The question is significant, since Knohl assigns Gen 2:2–3 to the PT strand (see Knohl, *Sanctuary of Silence*, 104, 125 n. 4; idem, *Divine Symphony*, 120–21, 164–65 n. 16). A serious tension between Second Isaiah and a PT text would weaken my overall thesis. Upon review of the evidence, I do not find convincing Fishbane's and Sommer's argument for a polemic at this particular point. Indeed, none of the points of disagreement between the priestly creation account and Deutero-Isaiah that these authors have outlined appears to me actually to involve a serious contradiction or tension. I discuss below what I understand to be the idea of Gen 1:26—human beings are in the "likeness" of God (an idea that Sommer considers interprets literally and considers at odds with texts such as Isa 40:18, 25; 46:5). As for PT's notion of God's Sabbath in Gen 2:2–3, the Hebrew term there, שבת, need not mean that God rested out of a state of exhaustion. The verb often simply means to "cease" or "stop," so that this verse probably just indicates that God finished creation and then ceased or stopped all work on the seventh day (see NJPS, NET). There is nothing strikingly anthropomorphic here. Interestingly, my disagreement with Fishbane and Sommer at this juncture might be moot in light of some current scholarly suggestions that Gen 1:1–2:4 is actually an HS text rather than a PT one. See Edwin B. Firmage, "Genesis 1 and the Priestly Agenda," *JSOT* 82

The PT's advocacy of miniscule and humble folk, who shrink before God's awful otherness, is apparent throughout the source. It makes clear that Abraham and Sarah struggled through years of infertility and childlessness before Isaac was born (Gen 11:30; 16:3; 17:17; 21:5—all PT). It describes God intervening for the exodus generation only at the point where Egypt had really "made their lives bitter" (Exod 1:14 PT), where they were nearly paralyzed by a "broken spirit" (Exod 6:9 PT). In its manna story in Exod 16, it stressed the necessity within Israel of a spirit of humility, servanthood, and glad dependence on God's provision.

The opposite orientation, leading to self-destruction, is also illustrated in PT's manna account (Exod 16:19–20). Those who assert their autonomy by gathering more than they need end up humiliated. They wake up to worms and a stench the next morning.[16] Numbers 14:6–10 (PT) similarly exposes the folly of the proud and haughty. On the verge of entering the promised land, according to the narrative, the people end up almost ston-

---

(1999): 97–114; Yairah Amit, "Creation and the Calendar of Holiness" [Hebrew], in *Tehillah le-Moshe: Biblical Studies in Honor of Moshe Greenberg*, ed. Michael Cogan et al. (Winona Lake, IN: Eisenbrauns, 1997), 13*–29*, with an English summary on 315–16. On Gen 2:2–3 in particular as containing HS material, see Jacob Milgrom, *Leviticus 17–22: A New Translation with Introduction and Commentary*, AB 3A (New York: Doubleday, 2000), 1344. For Milgrom's subsequent argument that Gen 1:1–2:3 is entirely HS, see his "HR in Leviticus and Elsewhere in the Torah," in *The Book of Leviticus: Composition and Reception*, ed. Rolf Rendtorff and Robert A. Kugler, VTSup 93 (Leiden: Brill, 2003), 33–40. The debate is surveyed in Smith, *Priestly Vision*, 215 n. 7, 292 n. 63. The arguments for this position have problems of their own, however, and for now I continue to assign Gen 1:1–2:4 to PT. (See also Jeffrey Stackert, "Compositional Strata in the Priestly Sabbath: Exodus 31:12–17 and 35:1–3," *Journal of Hebrew Scriptures* 11.15 [2011]: 12.) Note the differences in wording, for example, between Gen 2:2–3 (PT) and Exod 31:13–17; 35:2–3 (both HS). For a rejoinder to Amit's arguments, see Knohl, *Divine Symphony*, 163 n. 16. A powerful and detailed critique of Amit and Milgrom is leveled by Saul Olyan ("Exodus 31:12–17," 203 n. 8). Also see William P. Brown, *The Ethos of the Cosmos: The Genesis of Moral Imagination in the Bible* (Grand Rapids: Eerdmans, 1998), 120 n. 228.

16. For discussion, see Cook, *Conversations*, 73–74; Norbert Lohfink, *Theology of the Pentateuch: Themes of the Priestly Narrative and Deuteronomy*, trans. Linda M. Maloney (Minneapolis: Fortress, 1994), 132–33. Against Knohl, doublets and other evidence within the priestly portions of Exod 16 betray the underlying presence of the PT source. The HS has expanded the account, adding supplements such as v. 8 and vv. 11–12, and developing the provision for the Sabbath in vv. 22–30. Cf. the observations of Lohfink, *Theology of the Pentateuch*, 145; Driver, *Exodus*, 147.

ing to death God's advocates, Joshua and Caleb. God intervenes, confronting the congregation with a display of divine glory at the tent of meeting.[17]

The traditions of PT provided Second Isaiah a powerful resource for grappling with the downfall of the Davidic dynasty at Judah's forced migrations. Isaiah 55:1–5 addresses the problem of David's line directly, proclaiming that God's new servants on Zion will rise up established in David's royal covenant, God's "steadfast, sure love for David" (v. 3). Davidic royalty (v. 3) and, climactically, God's own beauteous splendor (v. 5, פאר) are now coming upon God's entire community of the faithful. The people's beatification is not merely for their own sake, but will provoke a jubilant pilgrimage of nations to Zion (v. 5).

Genesis 17 (PT) anticipates Isa 55's vision of an entire community of royal servants drawing in pilgrims from the nations. It presents Abraham and Sarah as a royal couple, progenitors of kings (v. 6) and mentors to earth's peoples (vv. 4, 5; cf. Ps 47:9). Note particularly how the language of Gen 17:1 turns up elsewhere in Scripture in passages relevant specifically to David's royal line. Thus 1 Kgs 3:6 speaks of King David in the very terms of Gen 17:1, and God addresses King Solomon in 1 Kgs 9:4 in just the same way. Moreover, King Hezekiah in Isa 38:3 assumes that comparable language is relevant to him. Echoing Abraham's traits, the king claims to have "walked" before God "in faithfulness with a whole heart."

Long before David, according to PT, God elevated Abraham to royal status and made all his seed—not just a single dynasty—beneficiaries of an "everlasting covenant" (Gen 17:7 // Isa 55:3). The authors of Second Isaiah had no need to resort to innovation and creativity in proclaiming the royal majesty of the remnant. Their vision is no "democratization" of Davidic royalty, as is commonly asserted, but an ideal already found in their Aaronide traditions as part of God's original saving plan.

Needless to say, this shared theology of PT and Second Isaiah was extremely helpful in dealing with the downfall of the Davidic dynasty at the time of the exile. True, a series of Babylonian conquests and exiles had removed the line of David from power. Nevertheless, it had not touched the roots of God's grant of royal potential to Israel.

At this point, the specifics of the kerygmatic "primal blessing" of God running through the Aaronide corpus are relevant. This blessing, "be fruit-

---

17. Against Knohl, the priestly portions of Num 14 appear to contain material from both PT and HS. See George Buchanan Gray, *A Critical and Exegetical Commentary on Numbers*, ICC (Edinburgh: T&T Clark, 1903), 131–32.

ful and multiply" (Gen 1:22, 28; 8:17; 9:1, 7; 17:2, 6, 20; 28:3; 35:11; 47:27; Exod 1:7—all PT), surfaces clearly in Gen 17:2 and 6, where God promises both to "multiply" Abraham and to make him "fruitful." But beyond this, the blessing also surfaces in Abraham's *royalty*. According to 1:28, the blessing instructs humanity not only to be fruitful but also to "subdue" and "have dominion" over the created order (1:28; cf. 35:11—both PT). Without doubt, the core divine vision of God's blessing includes the royalty of the entire people of God. In anticipation of their royalty, Gen 1 has God create humans "in the image of God" (v. 27).[18]

In Gen 17, PT envisions the small, select circle of Abraham as a royal beacon radiating a magnetic splendor that draws in the nations. God's blessing will make this circle be fruitful and multiply (vv. 2, 6). The blessing will then spread to a mass of nations, who will proclaim Abraham their spiritual "father" (Gen 17:5). Attracted to an *imago Dei* in their midst, earth's peoples will rally around Israel's God (cf. Ps 47:9). Thus, later, for Jacob to become fruitful and multiply, reflecting the primal blessing, is

---

18. I disagree with the arguments of Fishbane and Sommer that Second Isaiah stands in polemical tension with Gen 1 on God's grant of a divine "likeness" (דמות) to humans (see Fishbane, *Biblical Interpretation*, 325; Sommer, *Prophet Reads Scripture*, 143–44). Gen 1:26 has God state, "Let us make humankind in our image, according to our likeness [דמות]; and let them have dominion" (cf. Gen 9:6, also PT). The term "dominion" unlocks the verse's meaning. In the Near East, the expression "image of God" referred to the status of kings as representatives or viceroys of the gods. The Tukulti-Ninurta Epic from thirteenth-century Assyria calls the king "the eternal image of Enlil." A Neo-Assyrian letter calls both King Sennacherib and King Esarhaddon "the very image of Bēl." For PT, the "image" and "likeness" granted to humanity by God is no visual trait, relating to humanity's appearance or form. Ezekiel's sense of the term is not at issue (see Ezek 1:26). Rather, the significance of the *imago Dei* is God's choice of humanity to represent and channel divine majesty. Within Second Isaiah the enigmatic portrait of the Servant of the Lord reveals an *imago*, a royal majesty, granted to the most unlikely of candidates. Isa 52:13 reads, "See, my servant shall prosper; he shall be high and lofty [ירום ונשא]." The language is striking; several cross-references within Isaiah apply the same description directly to God. In 6:1, recalling his commissioning, the prophet states, "I saw the Lord sitting on a throne, high and lofty [רם ונשא]." Likewise, 33:10 and 57:15 use the very same word pair of God. Second Isaiah insists vehemently on God's incomparability, yet its frail Servant of the Lord ends up elevated to divine status (cf. esp. the parallelism at Isa 50:10a). As God's viceroy, the Servant will command global respect (Isa 52:15) and establish justice on earth (Isa 42:4).

specifically for him to create a קהל עמים, a sacral congregation of many peoples (Gen 28:3; 48:4).

Second Isaiah goes to town with these themes. In Isa 44:1–5, for example, God's spirit pours out on descendants, God's blessing on offspring (v. 3). This *offspring* (v. 3) is none other than the "offspring of Abraham," which Gen 17 emphasizes as central to God's perpetual covenant of grant (vv. 7, 8). As in Gen 17, due to the expansive energy of the primal blessing, the offspring multiply in a radically inclusive manner. Just as Abraham becomes the "ancestor of a multitude" (Gen 17:4), Isaiah speaks of new followers of God sprouting up like grass on a prairie—uncultivated, uncontrolled. As God will later declare, "To me *every* knee shall bow, *every* tongue shall swear" (Isa 45:22–23).

The core PT blessing of Gen 17 reappears in Isa 51:1–8, a passage envisioning a comforted Zion, with "waste places" infused with verdant new life. God's ability to shower down this new life is obvious, the passage claims, in the miraculous beginnings of God's people. Verse 2 reminds the reader that all the masses of Israel stemmed from one solitary infertile couple, Abraham and Sarah, whom God "blessed" (see Gen 17:16) and "made many" (see Gen 17:2).

A link between Second Isaiah and PT is unmistakable in this text. Among the sources of the Pentateuch, it is in Gen 17 (PT) that Abraham and Sarah receive the divine promise as a couple, as in Isa 51:1–2. Further, the combination of the verbs "bless" (ברך) and "multiply" (רבה) with a masculine singular object in Isa 51:2 is a characteristic idiom, signaling the primal divine blessing of PT. The Qumran version 1QIsa[a] heard this echo of PT and further strengthened it, substituting "made him fruitful" (ואפרהו) for "blessed him."

The faithful among the exiles, the text argues, have ready grounds for hope, if only they look to the story of their ancestors, Abraham and Sarah. They are of Abraham and Sarah's stock, since the couple represents "the rock from which you were hewn" and "the quarry from which you were dug" (v. 1). The abundance of this rich quarry once supplied the makings of the entire people of Israel. Now, this same fruitfulness ensures a full-scale restoration from Babylonian captivity.

It is noteworthy that Ezekiel, drawing specifically on alternate, HS traditions, shows *antagonism* to an argument rather similar to that in Isa 51.[19]

---

19. Cf. Fishbane, *Biblical Interpretation*, 350 n. 87, 375, 414.

In Ezek 33:23–29, the prophet tells his audience *not* to rely on God's favor revealed in Abraham's story. They have failed to maintain the land in a holy state, which HS theology makes a condition of Israel's continued dwelling there. Abraham's blessing of fruitfulness in the land is subject to forfeiture, Ezekiel argues, based on the curses of the HS covenant, a bilateral, vassal treaty.

Let me sum up the results of this paper. In each of the probes of this study, there was a close match in orientation and theology between Second Isaiah and PT. The two writings express themselves with different moods and styles, but underneath their differing forms of expression lie common lines of thought. I would encourage scholars to undertake further study of Second Isaiah's development of PT's thinking and theology. I believe there are serious insights yet to be gained by pushing ahead with the hypothesis of the Isaiah community's Aaronide identity.

Nebuchadnezzar, the End of Davidic Rule, and the Exile in the Book of Jeremiah

Konrad Schmid

When did the Davidic dynasty end and when did the Babylonian exile begin?[1] The answer generally given to this question is that the two events coincide and are to be dated to the year 587 BCE. The main witness to these events in the Hebrew Bible, the book of Jeremiah, certainly agrees with this historical perspective, but it also develops a theological perspective that somewhat transcends these historical facts and offers a different answer. Some texts in the book of Jeremiah develop a universal understanding of history that remains in the background and is not formulated explicitly, but is instead accessible only through careful study of the text.

The starting point for my reflections is the narrative of Jer 36.[2] Its narrative development is well known: God commissions Jeremiah to write

---

1. Preliminary versions of this paper have been published in French and German as "L'Accession de Nabuchodonosor à l'hégémonie mondiale et la fin de la dynastie davidique: Exégèse intrabiblique et construction de l'histoire universelle dans le livre de Jérémie," *ETR* 81 (2006): 211–27; "Nebukadnezars Antritt der Weltherrschaft und der Abbruch der Davidsdynastie: Innerbiblische Schriftauslegung und universalgeschichtliche Konstruktion im Jeremiabuch," in *Die Textualisierung der Religion,* ed. Joachim Schaper, FAT 62 (Tübingen: Mohr Siebeck, 2009), 150–66.

2. On Jer 36, see especially the contributions by Hermann-Josef Stipp, *Jeremia im Parteienstreit: Studien zur Textentwicklung von Jer 26, 36–43 und 45 als Beitrag zur Geschichte Jeremias, seines Buches und judäischer Parteien im 6. Jahrhundert,* BBB 82 (Frankfurt am Main: Hain, 1992); idem, "Baruchs Erben: Die Schriftprophetie im Spiegel von Jer 36," in *Wer darf hinaufsteigen zum Berg JHWHs? Beiträge zu Prophetie und Poesie des Alten Testaments,* ed. Hubert Irsigler, Arbeiten zu Text und Sprache im Alten Testament 72 (St. Ottilien: EOS, 2002), 145–70; Yair Hoffman, "Aetiology, Redaction and Historicity in Jeremiah XXXVI," *VT* 46 (1996): 179–89; Harald-Martin Wahl, "Die Entstehung der Schriftprophetie nach Jer 36," *ZAW* 110 (1998):

down a judgment prophecy, which he completes with the help of his scribe, Baruch. Baruch later reads the scroll aloud in the temple before the entire people. This event comes to the attention of the nobles, who order Baruch to come and read the scroll to them a second time. Recognizing the explosiveness of the content recited before them, the nobles advise Jeremiah and Baruch to hide while they have the scroll read a third time, this time before King Jehoiakim. After each section of three or four columns is read, the king takes the scroll and burns it. In response to God's subsequent command, Jeremiah dictates a new version of the same scroll to Baruch. Finally, a severe word of judgment goes forth against Jehoiakim and his family, and it is this word of judgment, announcing the end of the Davidic dynasty in advance to Jehoiakim, that I will now investigate in detail. It can be found in Jer 36:30, and it reads as follows:

לָכֵן כֹּה־אָמַר יְהוָה עַל־יְהוֹיָקִים מֶלֶךְ יְהוּדָה לֹא־יִהְיֶה־לּוֹ יוֹשֵׁב עַל־כִּסֵּא דָוִד וְנִבְלָתוֹ תִּהְיֶה מֻשְׁלֶכֶת לַחֹרֶב בַּיּוֹם וְלַקֶּרַח בַּלָּיְלָה:

365–89; Christof Hardmeier, "Zur schriftgestützten Expertentätigkeit Jeremias im Milieu der Jerusalemer Führungseliten (Jeremia 36): Prophetische Literaturbildung und die Neuinterpretation älterer Expertisen in Jeremia 21–23*," in Schaper, *Textualisierung der Religion*, 105–49; Uwe Becker, "Die Entstehung der Schriftprophetie," in *Die unwiderstehliche Wahrheit: Studien zur alttestamentlichen Prophetie: Festschrift für Arndt Meinhold*, ed. Rüdiger Lux and Ernst-Joachim Waschke, ABIG 23 (Leipzig: Evangelische Verlagsanstalt, 2006), 3–20; Johannes Taschner, "Zusammenhalt trotz inhaltlicher Differenzen: Jer 36 als Selbstvergewisserung der Beamten und Schreiber in frühnachexilischer Zeit," *EvT* 69 (2009): 366–81. Jeremiah 36 seems to have been shaped quite clearly as a counternarrative to 2 Kgs 22; see Gunther Wanke, *Jeremia 25,15–52,34*, vol. 2 of *Jeremia*, ZBK 20.2 (Zurich: TVZ, 2003), 338; Konrad Schmid, *Buchgestalten des Jeremiabuches: Untersuchungen zur Redaktions- und Rezeptionsgeschichte von Jer 30–33 im Kontext des Buches*, WMANT 72 (Neukirchen-Vluyn: Neukirchener Verlag, 1996), 245–47 and n. 206 (for bibliography); Thomas Römer, "La conversion du prophète Jérémie à la théologie deutéronomiste," in *The Book of Jeremiah and Its Reception: Le livre de Jérémie et sa réception* (ed. A. H. W. Curtis and Thomas Römer; BETL 128; Leuven: Peeters, 1997), 27–50, esp. 47–48; G. J. Venema, *Reading Scripture in the Old Testament: Deuteronomy 9–10, 31; 2 Kings 22–23; Jeremiah 36; Nehemiah 8*, OtSt 48 (Leiden: Brill, 2004), 125–27; Caetano Minette de Tilesse, "Joiaqim, repoussoir du 'pieux' Josias: Parallélismes entre II Reg 22 et Jer 36," *ZAW* 105 (1993): 353–76; Norbert Lohfink, "Die Gattung der 'Historischen Kurzgeschichte' in den letzten Jahren von Juda und in der Zeit des Babylonischen Exils," *ZAW* 90 (1978): 319–47; repr. in *Studien zum Deuteronomium und zur deuteronomistischen Literatur II*, SBAB 12 (Stuttgart: Katholisches Bibelwerk, 1991), 55–86.

Therefore thus says the LORD concerning Jehoiakim, king of Judah: There shall not be for him one sitting on the throne of David, and his dead body shall be cast out to the heat by day and the frost by night.

This text combines numerous peculiarities. First of all, it is striking that the prophecy *was not fulfilled* from two perspectives: neither did the Davidic dynasty end with Jehoiakim since both his son Jehoiachin (2 Kgs 24:6, 8) and his brother Mattaniah/ Zedekiah (24:17) ruled after him, nor is there evidence that Jehoiakim did not receive regular burial. Verse 6 formulaically announces that he was laid with his fathers, which is the usual expression for burial in the royal tomb:[3]

וַיִּשְׁכַּב יְהוֹיָקִים עִם־אֲבֹתָיו וַיִּמְלֹךְ יְהוֹיָכִין בְּנוֹ תַּחְתָּיו׃

So Jehoiakim slept with his ancestors; then his son Jehoiachin became king in his place.

Even if an explicit declaration concerning Jehoiakim's burial location is absent (cf. 2 Kgs 21:18, 26), it is unlikely that the author of the book of Kings would have suppressed the fulfillment of a prophetic judgment oracle against Jehoiakim if he had somehow heard that Jehoiakim had not been buried in the usual way.[4]

Jeremiah 36:30 is therefore—when evaluated according to historical standards—a false prophecy. It goes unfulfilled twice over: Jehoiakim was neither the last Davidide nor was he buried irregularly. Historians usually

---

3. Cf. Bernardus Alfrink, "L'expression שָׁכַב עִם עֲבוֹתָיו," *OtSt* 2 (1943): 106–18; Stipp, *Jeremia*, 110; for complete discussion of the problem, see Oded Lipschits, "'Jehoiakim Slept with His Fathers' (II Kings 24.6)—Did He?" in *Perspectives on Hebrew Scriptures,* vol. 1: *Comprising the Contents of Journal of Hebrew Scriptures Volumes 1–4,* ed. Ehud Ben Zvi (Piscataway, NJ: Gorgias, 2006), 405–28; Nadav Na'aman, "Death Formulae and the Burial Place of the Kings of the House of David," *Bib* 85 (2004): 245–54. Less convincing is the argument of Alberto R. W. Green, "The Fate of Jehoiakim," *AUSS* 20 (1982): 103–9.

4. In his *Antiquities*, Flavius Josephus allows the threat in Jer 36:30 to become reality when he writes that Nebuchadnezzar killed Jehoiakim during the events of 597 BCE, having his corpse thrown from the city walls and forbiding proper burial (10.97). Josephus, on this point, merely constructs an *eventum e vaticinio.* Cf. Christopher T. Begg, "Jehoahaz, Jehoiakim, and Jehoiachin (10,81–102 + 229–230)," in *Josephus' Story of the Later Monarchy (AJ 9,1–10,185),* BETL 145 (Leuven: Peeters, 2000), 499–534.

exult in such a conclusion because the likelihood that a prophecy was "genuine" increases if it goes unfulfilled.

However, such is not the case here.[5] The narrative of Jer 36 is highly reflective and probably does not stem from the time of Jeremiah himself,[6] but provides a theological rationale for the demise of Judah and Jerusalem on the basis of Jehoiakim's rejection of the prophetic word. The narrative's learned scribal quality can also be seen in its character as counternarrative to 2 Kgs 22: The righteous king Josiah listens to God's word, while the unrighteous king Jehoiakim rejects it. Therefore, a simple determination that the prophecy in Jer 36:30 is false seems to miss the point of the passage. There must be other reasons for the formulation of 36:30.

Before addressing this question, I should point out a second striking feature in Jer 36:30 (in addition to the unfulfilled pronouncement)—it is closely related to two other texts in Jeremiah: (1) the declaration of judgment against Jehoiakim in 22:18–19, which declares that Jehoiakim will not receive a burial or lamentation; and (2) the declaration of judgment of 22:29–30 against his son Jehoiachin, which announces the end of the Davidic dynasty (v. 30).

That 36:30 draws upon 22:18–19 can be recognized clearly on account of its identical content as declaration of judgment to Jehoiakim and the lack of burial in both.[7] Jeremiah 22:18–19 says:

לָכֵן כֹּה־אָמַר יְהוָה אֶל־יְהוֹיָקִים בֶּן־יֹאשִׁיָּהוּ מֶלֶךְ יְהוּדָה
לֹא־יִסְפְּדוּ לוֹ הוֹי אָחִי וְהוֹי אָחוֹת
לֹא־יִסְפְּדוּ לוֹ הוֹי אָדוֹן וְהוֹי הֹדֹה
קְבוּרַת חֲמוֹר יִקָּבֵר סָחוֹב וְהַשְׁלֵךְ מֵהָלְאָה לְשַׁעֲרֵי יְרוּשָׁלָ͏ִם:

> Therefore thus says the Lord to Jehoiakim son of Josiah king of Judah: They shall not lament for him: "Alas, my brother!" or "Alas, sister!" They shall not lament for him: "Alas, lord!" or "Alas, his majesty!" With the burial of a donkey he shall be buried—dragged off and thrown out outside beyond the gates of Jerusalem.

---

5. Contra Stipp, *Jeremia*, 110. See also his "Sprachliche Kennzeichen jeremianischer Autorschaft," in *Prophecy in the Book of Jeremiah*, ed. Hans M. Barstad and Reinhard G. Kratz, BZAW 388 (Berlin: de Gruyter, 2009), 148–86.

6. Cf., e.g., Hoffman, "Aetiology, Redaction and Historicity," 183; Wahl, "Entstehung der Schriftprophetie," 373–75.

7. The concrete formulation in Jer 36:30 appears to be inspired by Jer 14:16 (מֻשְׁלָכִים).

The connection to 22:30 is obvious, too,[8] although 22:30 is addressed to Jehoiachin, not to his father Jehoiakim. Nevertheless, a close intertextual connection can be seen in the use of the expression יֹשֵׁב עַל־כִּסֵּא דָוִד as well as the embedding of the expression in the declaration of the demise of the Davidic dynasty.[9]

כֹּה אָמַר יְהוָה
כִּתְבוּ אֶת־הָאִישׁ הַזֶּה עֲרִירִי
גֶּבֶר לֹא־יִצְלַח בְּיָמָיו
כִּי לֹא יִצְלַח מִזַּרְעוֹ אִישׁ
יֹשֵׁב עַל־כִּסֵּא דָוִד
וּמֹשֵׁל עוֹד בִּיהוּדָה׃

Thus says the Lord:
Record this man as childless,
a man who shall not succeed in his days;
for none of his offspring shall succeed
in sitting on the throne of David,
and ruling again in Judah.

It therefore seems plausible to propose that these two declarations, 22:18–19 and 22:30, have been combined in 36:30 by means of scribal exegesis. The assumption that 36:30 is dependent on 22:18–19 and 22:30 and not the other way around is justified because 36:30 draws these two texts together. In addition, 22:18–19 and 22:30—unlike 36:30—appear to stem from authentic logia of Jeremiah and are therefore older than 36:30.

Neither 22:18 nor 22:30 is plausible as *vaticinium ex eventu*. Jehoiakim was given a regular burial (as we can safely deduce from 2 Kgs 24:6), and Jehoiachin, in all likelihood, had children (1 Chr 3:17–18 lists seven

---

8. Robert P. Carroll, *Jeremiah: A Commentary*, OTL (Philadelphia: Westminster, 1986), 661; William McKane, *Commentary on Jeremiah XXVI–LII*, vol. 2 of *A Critical and Exegetical Commentary on Jeremiah*, ICC (Edinburgh: T&T Clark, 1996), 921. Stipp (*Jeremia*, 92) affirms the similarities, but his dating of 36:30 prior to 598 BCE rules out any genetic connections. For diachronic differentiations within 22:30, see William L. Holladay, *Jeremiah 1: A Commentary on the Prophet Jeremiah, Chapters 1–25*, Hermeneia (Philadelphia: Fortress, 1986), 611; Christl Maier, *Jeremia als Lehrer der Tora: Soziale Gebote des Deuteronomiums in Fortschreibungen des Jeremiabuches*, FRLANT 196 (Göttingen: Vandenhoeck & Ruprecht, 2002), 213 n. 48.

9. For the Hebrew phrase, see also Jer 17:25; 22:2.

sons for Jehoiachin). In addition, it appears quite improbable that Jer 22:30 knows of the appointment of Jehoiachin's grandson Zerubbabel to the position of "governor" over Judah.[10] Would this oracle have been formulated the way it is if it had known of this later event? Therefore, in opposition to Jer 36:30, neither 22:18–19 nor 22:30 reveals any indication that their historically inaccurate statements of a particular fact came *ex post*. They are therefore likely authentic prophecies. If it is plausible to conclude that the judgment oracle against Jehoiakim in 36:30 reworks both older texts (22:18–19 and 22:30) on a textual level, it is still unclear *why* 36:30 takes up 22:30, a text that is addressing *Jehoiachin* instead of Jehoiakim. The combination of 22:18–19 and 22:30 in 36:30 must have a particular purpose. What could that reason be?

Before offering an answer, I think it would be helpful to review what I have argued so far. First, Jer 36:30 speaks contra the historical reality, stating that the Davidic dynasty came to an end with Jehoiakim and that Jehoiakim was the final representative of Davidic rule. This is historically false. That this pronouncement is unfounded and nevertheless continued to be transmitted as part of the tradition demands explanation. While it is valid to explain 22:18–19 as a fixed part of the written tradition before the death of Jehoiakim and the accession of his son Jehoiachin to the throne, this explanation does not work for 36:30. As it stands, Jer 36 is not a coeval text, but is a highly learned scribal product and presupposes Judah and Jerusalem's demise.

Then how did the historically false theory of the end of the Davidic dynasty with Jehoiakim come about? Why might a biblical writer have formulated this idea? Is there a higher theological purpose behind this historically false theory? Answers can be found by considering Jer 36:30 in its context. Decisive for understanding the announcement of the end of the Davidic dynasty in 36:30 are the *literary* datings in Jer 36. The recording of the first scroll in 36:1 is set in the fourth year of Jehoiakim, and the reading in 36:9, 22 is set in the ninth month of the Jehoiakim's fifth year. What is the theological significance of these dates?

The fourth year of Jehoiakim—according to our calculations, the year 605/604 BCE—was both the year in which the Babylonian king Nabo-

---

10. For the status of Judah as a Persian province as early as the time of Zerubbabel, see Joachim Schaper, "Numismatik, Epigraphik, alttestamentliche Exegese und die Frage nach der politischen Verfassung des achämenidischen Juda," *ZDPV* 118 (2002): 150–68.

polassar died and was Nebuchadnezzar's "first year" according to the Hebrew expression (his "ascension year" according to the Babylonian nomenclature).[11] This was known to the biblical writers as can be seen in a passage dated to the same year: Jer 25:1 expressly records the synchronism between the fourth year of Jehoiakim and the first year of Nebuchadnezzar.

הַדָּבָר אֲשֶׁר־הָיָה עַל־יִרְמְיָהוּ עַל־כָּל־עַם יְהוּדָה בַּשָּׁנָה הָרְבִעִית לִיהוֹיָקִים בֶּן־יֹאשִׁיָּהוּ מֶלֶךְ יְהוּדָה הִיא הַשָּׁנָה הָרִאשֹׁנִית לִנְבוּכַדְרֶאצַּר מֶלֶךְ בָּבֶל:

The word that came to Jeremiah concerning all the people of Judah, in the fourth year of Jehoiakim son of Josiah, king of Judah (that was the first year of King Nebuchadrezzar of Babylon).

The passing of the scepter in Babylon from Nabopolassar to Nebuchadnezzar in the year 605 BCE marks a special date in the history of the ancient Near East, because, earlier in the same year,[12] Nebuchadnezzar, then in his capacity as crown prince of Babylon, led the Babylonians to victory over the Egyptians at the battle of Carchemish, establishing Babylon as the new great power in the ancient world. He became the de facto sitting ruler of the world. Still in the very same year, on the first day of the month of Elul (the sixth month),[13] Nebuchadnezzar ascended to the Babylonian throne.

This also appears to be reflected in the book of Jeremiah: according to Jer 25, Nebuchadnezzar is the "servant" (עבד)[14] of YHWH (v. 9), whom the land of Judah and other nations must serve for seventy years (vv. 10–11). By giving Nebuchadnezzar the title of "servant," Jer 25 picks

---

11. Cf. Herbert Donner, *Von der Königszeit bis zu Alexander dem Großen: Mit einem Ausblick auf die Geschichte des Judentums bis Bar Kochba,* part 2 of *Geschichte des Volkes Israel und seiner Nachbarn in Grundzügen,* 2nd ed., ATD Ergänzungsreihe 4/2 (Göttingen: Vandenhoek & Ruprecht, 1995), 405 and n. 22. More concretely for Nebuchadnezar II, see Albert K. Grayson, *Assyrian and Babylonian Chronicles* (1975; repr., Winona Lake, IN: Eisenbrauns, 2000), 100: line 12: MU.SAG "ascension year"; Z.15 MU I^{kám} "1st year."

12. Cf. Udo Worschech, "War Nebukadnezar im Jahre 605 v.Chr. vor Jerusalem?" *BN* 36 (1987): 57–63.

13. Grayson, *Assyrian and Babylonian Chronicles,* 100, line 11.

14. For the text critical and composition critical problem see Schmid, *Buchgestalten,* 232–33, and literature cited there.

up on a corresponding terminology traditionally ascribed to David, the elect king.[15] The argument involved in this "servant" terminology applied to Nebuchadnezzar seems to be the following: in Nebuchadnezzar's ascendance to world domination in 605 BCE, the kingdom of God's grace passed into Nebuchadnezzar's hands. The closest parallel in terms of content in the Hebrew Bible is found in the Deutero-Isaian Cyrus oracle of Isa 45:1–7, which proclaims Cyrus to be the new messiah, probably a position quite similar to the "servant" designations in Jeremiah.

What do these considerations mean for Jer 36? Jeremiah 36:1–3 places the writing of the words of Jeremiah in the very year that Nebuchadnezzar ascends to world domination and interprets the proclamation of judgment that had been percolating since the time of Josiah until the fourth year of Jehoiakim as a possible trigger for the reversal of the Judeans:

וַיְהִי בַּשָּׁנָה הָרְבִיעִת לִיהוֹיָקִים בֶּן־יֹאשִׁיָּהוּ מֶלֶךְ יְהוּדָה הָיָה הַדָּבָר הַזֶּה אֶל־יִרְמְיָהוּ מֵאֵת יְהוָה לֵאמֹר: קַח־לְךָ מְגִלַּת־סֵפֶר וְכָתַבְתָּ אֵלֶיהָ אֵת כָּל־הַדְּבָרִים אֲשֶׁר־דִּבַּרְתִּי אֵלֶיךָ עַל־יִשְׂרָאֵל וְעַל־יְהוּדָה וְעַל־כָּל־הַגּוֹיִם מִיּוֹם דִּבַּרְתִּי אֵלֶיךָ מִימֵי יֹאשִׁיָּהוּ וְעַד הַיּוֹם הַזֶּה: אוּלַי יִשְׁמְעוּ בֵּית יְהוּדָה אֵת כָּל־הָרָעָה אֲשֶׁר אָנֹכִי חֹשֵׁב לַעֲשׂוֹת לָהֶם לְמַעַן יָשׁוּבוּ אִישׁ מִדַּרְכּוֹ הָרָעָה וְסָלַחְתִּי לַעֲוֺנָם וּלְחַטָּאתָם:

In the fourth year of King Jehoiakim son of Josiah of Judah, this word came to Jeremiah from the LORD: Take a scroll and write on it all the words that I have spoken to you against Israel [LXX: Jerusalem] and Judah and all the nations, from the day I spoke to you, from the days of Josiah until today. It may be that when the house of Judah hears of all the disasters that I intend to do to them, all of them may turn from their evil ways, so that I may forgive their iniquity and their sin.

After the events at Carchemish and Nebuchadnezzar's ascension to the throne, a final way out of the impending judgment by the Babylonians through YHWH's forgiveness was set clearly before their eyes. However, also this final chance was gambled away by the king's reaction to the scroll. According to 36:9, the three readings of the scroll, which finally bring it to

---

15. Helmer Ringgren, "עבד, 'ābad," *TDOT* 10:394: "Whenever David is called *'ebed YHWH*, the context almost always involves election and the perpetual continuation of the dynasty."

the ears of the king, take place several months after the battle at Carchemish and Nebuchadnezzar's ascension, now in the *fifth* year of Jehoiakim:

וַיְהִי בַּשָּׁנָה הַחֲמִשִׁית לִיהוֹיָקִים בֶּן־יֹאשִׁיָּהוּ מֶלֶךְ־יְהוּדָה בַּחֹדֶשׁ הַתְּשִׁעִי קָרְאוּ צוֹם לִפְנֵי יְהוָה כָּל־הָעָם בִּירוּשָׁלָ͏ִם וְכָל־הָעָם הַבָּאִים מֵעָרֵי יְהוּדָה בִּירוּשָׁלָ͏ִם׃

In the fifth [LXX: eighth] year of King Jehoiakim son of Josiah of Judah, in the ninth month, all the people in Jerusalem and all the people who came from the towns of Judah to Jerusalem proclaimed a fast before the LORD.

The ninth month of the fifth year of Jehoiakim is a striking date too. This was the exact month when Nebuchadnezzar destroyed Ashkelon. A record in the Neo-Babylonian Chronicle provides specific information regarding this event:

> The first year of Nebuchadnezzar (II., e.g., 604/603 B.C.E.): [...] He marched to [Ashke]llon (*a-na* ^{uru} *x-x-(x)-il-lu-nu illik-ma*) and in the month Kislev (9th month) he captured it, seized its king, plundered [and sac]ked it. He turned the city into a ruin heap. In the month Shebat he marched away and [returned] to Bab[ylon].[16]

In light of the theological importance of the fourth and fifth years of Jehoiakim in Jer 36, which allude to the two important military events of the battle at Carchemish and the destruction of Ashkelon, the announcement of the demise of the Davidic dynasty in 36:30 becomes immediately plausible without further need of explanation. With Nebuchadnezzar's rise to universal hegemony, generally apparent through the battle of Carchemish and for Judah particularly obvious from the destruction of Ashkelon, the Davidic dynasty is *theologically* dismantled. As everyone could see, God was no longer with the Davidic kings. Notably, according to Jer 36 the demise of the Davidic dynasty takes place *prior* to its *historically observable* end; it is dated to the year 605 BCE instead of 587 BCE.

In fact, Jer 36:30 contains one of the strongest and most pointed declarations in the Hebrew Bible of the theological legitimation of a foreign imperial power's dominion over Israel. Nebuchadnezzar's royal authority has a particular quality that can only be understood correctly when one

---

16. Grayson, *Assyrian and Babylonian Chronicles*, 100, lines 15, 18–20.

notes that it follows the Davidic dynasty and replaces it. Jeremiah 36:30, with the aid of inner-biblical exegesis, reveals a notion of universal history that posits the theological end of the Davidic dynasty and the assumption of world dominion by Nebuchadnezzar as coinciding in the fourth and fifth years of Jehoiakim.

The depiction of events in Jer 27 allows for further explication of this theory of universal history in the book of Jeremiah. Jeremiah 27 is dated to the reign of Jehoiakim, and here too the text is clear that Nebuchadnezzar has already been commissioned with world dominion by God. Jeremiah 27:6 states:

וְעַתָּה אָנֹכִי נָתַתִּי אֶת־כָּל־הָאֲרָצוֹת הָאֵלֶּה בְּיַד נְבוּכַדְנֶאצַּר מֶלֶךְ־בָּבֶל עַבְדִּי
וְגַם אֶת־חַיַּת הַשָּׂדֶה נָתַתִּי לוֹ לְעָבְדוֹ׃

> Now I have given all these lands into the hand of King Nebuchadnezzar of Babylon, my servant, and I have given him even the wild animals of the field to serve him.

The verbal form is perfective (נָתַתִּי) in the speech that YHWH now *"has given"* "all these lands" into Nebuchadnezzar's hand. In the reign of Jehoiakim, this is already the case.

Surprisingly, however, Jer 27:6 is not dated to the fourth or fifth year, but to the ascension year of Jehoiakim, which is 609 BCE.

בְּרֵאשִׁית מַמְלֶכֶת יְהוֹיָקִם בֶּן־יֹאושִׁיָּהוּ מֶלֶךְ יְהוּדָה הָיָה הַדָּבָר הַזֶּה אֶל־יִרְמְיָה
מֵאֵת יְהוָה לֵאמֹר׃

> At the beginning of the reign of King Jehoiakim son of Josiah of Judah, this word came to Jeremiah from the LORD. (27:1)

The present structure of Jer 27:1–6 seems difficult, since it claims Nebuchadnezzar's world dominion already began in the year 609 BCE, four years before the battle of Carchemish and Nebuchadnezzar's elevation to the Babylonian throne.

A number of scholars conclude hastily that the date in Jer 27:1 is mistaken because the subsequent narrative takes place under Zedekiah (who is mentioned in 27:3, 12). This was probably also the reason why the Septuagint skipped this verse: it simply does not fit the context. However, 27:1 can easily be understood without emendation within the framework of the conception of universal history that has been described above.[17] Still in need of explanation, however, is the chronological difference between the two dates 609 (27:1) and 605 (25:1). The proposal presented here is that the book of Jeremiah differentiates between the heavenly allocation and actual assumption of world dominion by Nebuchadnezzar. Yet why would this difference be introduced at all? Does this not complicate the situation unnecessarily?

The reason, even the need, for this difference lies in the "seventy years"[18] prophecy of Jer 25:11–12 (cf. 29:10), which in that chapter limits Babylon's dominion—not the exile!—to seventy years. This seventy years is synchronized in 25:1 between the assumption by Nebuchadnezzar of (world) dominion and Jehoiakim's fourth year, that is 605 BCE. Babylon's dominion came to an end in the year 539 BCE with the Persian king Cyrus's bloodless conquest of Babylon. The resulting time frame from 605 BCE to 539 BCE is sixty-six years, four years short of the "seventy years." Counting from the first year of Jehoiakim, 609 BCE, to 539 BCE produces the exact "seventy years."

Apparently, the difference between the heavenly allocation and earthly assumption of world domination by Nebuchadnezzar was introduced in Jer 27 in order to mediate between the theological idea of "seventy years" and the relevant dates of empirical history, which mark a time span that is close to but not exactly seventy years. The "seventy years" was evidently a theological given and therefore could not simply be changed. This conclusion is supported by the Babylonian inscription of Esarhaddon as well as Zech 1:12, which is likely the oldest record of this concept in the Hebrew Bible. Esarhaddon's Babylonian inscription states (Version a):[19]

---

17. Stipp still prefers the traditional "solution" for Jer 27:1 ("Zur aktuellen Diskussion um das Verhältnis der Textformen des Jeremiabuches," in *Die Septuaginta— Texte, Kontexte, Lebenswelten*, ed. Martin Karrer and Wolfgang Kraus, WUNT 219 [Tübingen: Mohr Siebeck, 2008], 642 n. 62).

18. On the redaction-historical priority of Zech 1:12, see Reinhard G. Kratz, *Translatio Imperii*, WMANT 63 (Neukirchen-Vluyn: Neukirchener Verlag, 1991), 261–67; Schmid, *Buchgestalten des Jeremiabuches*, 223.

19. Cited according to Matthias Albani, *Der eine Gott und die himmlischen Heerscharen: Zur Begründung des Monotheismus bei Deuterojesaja im Horizont der Astralisierung des Gottesverständisses im Alten Orient*, ABIG 1 (Leipzig: Evangelische Verlagsanstalt, 2000), 86. See further Mordechai Cogan, "Omens and Ideology in the Babylon Inscription of Esarhaddon," in *History, Historiography, and Interpretation: Studies in Biblical and Cuneiform Literatures*, ed. Hayim Tadmor and Moshe Weinfeld

Although he wrote (on the tablet of destinies) that the period of the exile would be 70 years, merciful Marduk, once his heart had become quiet, transposed the numbers and commanded the reconstruction to begin in the eleventh year.

The background of this declaration is provided by the mirror image cuneiform signs for the numbers "70" and "11": a vertical wedge (before a *Winkelhaken* "60") plus *Winkelhaken* ("10") means "70"; a *Winkelhaken* ("10") before a vertical wedge ("1") stands for "11." This inscription clearly demonstrates that "70 years" was an established duration that could be applied to the destruction of a city. It is probably implicit that after seventy years an entire generation would have completely passed away, so there was no longer anyone alive who had seen the destruction with their own eyes. The use of the phrase as the topos for a fixed duration of destruction appears for the "seventy years" in Zech 1:12 as well:

וַיַּעַן מַלְאַךְ־יְהוָה וַיֹּאמַר יְהוָה צְבָאוֹת עַד־מָתַי אַתָּה לֹא־תְרַחֵם אֶת־יְרוּשָׁלִַם
וְאֵת עָרֵי יְהוּדָה אֲשֶׁר זָעַמְתָּה זֶה שִׁבְעִים שָׁנָה׃

Then the angel of the LORD answered and said, "O LORD of hosts, how long will you withhold mercy from Jerusalem and the cities of Judah, with which you have been angry these seventy years?"

The book of Jeremiah appears to have taken the "seventy years" from Zech 1:12 (and transferred it to the dominion of Babylon),[20] but the authors of the book of Jeremiah could not simply change it, that is, shorten it; therefore, the conception of universal history needed to be modified ad hoc by differentiating between the heavenly allocation and earthly ascension to world dominion. Also in support of the differentiation between the allocation and ascension is the fact that 609 BCE was the year of Josiah's death; after the death of the last pious king of Judah, Josiah, there was no longer a legitimate royal authority in Judah. To sum up, the proclamation of judgment against Jehoiakim in Jer 36:30 was written down for theological rather than documentary reasons. It reworks earlier prophecies against

---

(Jerusalem: Magnes, 1986), 76–87; Mark Leuchter, "Jeremiah's 70-Year Prophecy and the קמי לב/ששך Atbash Codes," *Bib* 85 (2004): 503–22.

20. See n. 18.

Jehoiakim and Jehoiachin from Jer 22:18–19, 30,[21] and pushes forward the demise of the Davidic dynasty to 605/604 BCE, though contrary to historical fact.

This is explicitly stated in Jer 25:1, a verse that marks the beginning of the reign of Nebuchadnezzar, whose power is on display in the victory at Carchemish and destruction of Ashkelon. In this way a complementary system is constructed in the book of Jeremiah for the Davidic dynasty and the Babylonian world hegemony. As long as the Davidic dynasty remains theologically intact, then the great empire cannot do anything against it. However, once Nebuchadnezzar sits on the Babylonian throne and has taken dominion over the world—visible for all through the events at Carchemish and Ashkelon—then there can no longer be a legitimate Davidide. Instead, the kingdom of God's grace is now transferred to the ruler of the empire, first to Nebuchadnezzar, and then to Cyrus, as can be seen in Deutero-Isaiah (Isa 44:28; 45:1).

Historically speaking, this conception of universal history in the book of Jeremiah was probably developed out of the experience of a double *translatio imperii* from the Assyrians to the Neo-Babylonians to the Persians within a century, which may possibly have brought on the initial sparks of such an understanding of universal history.[22] This conception is probably not older than the fifth century, which does not mean that everything reported in Jer 27 or 36 was invented at that time, but rather that the material was shaped in the described way at that time.

As these examples from the Jeremiah tradition show, scribal prophecy[23] was even able to incorporate contradictions to actual historical events when it had a higher historical purpose in view, namely the display of God's control over history. However, these higher purposes were

---

21. It is probable that the words in 22:18–19 and 22:30 were included or remained in the book of Jeremiah through the reinterpretation of 36:30. In any case, 36:30 provides an understanding of history for why the unfulfilled declarations of judgment against Jehoiakim and Jehoiachin from Jer 22 continued to be passed on.

22. See, already, Martin Noth, "Das Geschichtsverständnis der alttestamentlichen Apokalyptik," in *Gesammelte Studien zum Alten Testament*, ThB 6 (Munich: Theologische Bücherei, 1957), 248–73; Eng. trans.: "The Understanding of History in Old Testament Apocalyptic," in *The Laws in the Pentateuch and Other Studies*, trans. D. R. Ap-Thomas (Edinburgh: Oliver & Boyd, 1966), 194–214.

23. See also Martti Nissinen, "How Prophecy Became Literature," *SJOT* 19 (2005): 153–72; Karel van der Toorn, *Scribal Culture and the Making of the Hebrew Bible* (Cambridge: Harvard University Press, 2007), esp. 173–204 for the book of Jeremiah.

not explicit for the audience of the book of Jeremiah, but first arise upon intense study of the book. The truth concerning this world and its history is recognizable not (any longer) in the events themselves, but through the texts that interpret it. This reveals the beginning point of a development in intellectual history that fundamentally influenced later Judaism and Christianity.

Sacred Space and Communal Legitimacy in Exile: The Contribution of Seraiah's Colophon (Jer 51:59–64a)

Mark Leuchter

Shortly after the fall of Jerusalem in 587 BCE, the prophet Ezekiel conveyed an oracle to his audience regarding how they should regard the exiles from Judah joining them in Mesopotamia:

> And, behold, though there be left a remnant therein that shall be brought forth, both sons and daughters; behold, when they come forth unto you, and you see their way and their doings, then you shall be comforted concerning the evil that I have brought upon Jerusalem, even concerning all that I have brought upon it; and they shall comfort you, when you see their way and their doings, and you shall know that I have not done without cause all that I have done in it, says the Lord YHWH. (Ezek 14:22–23)[1]

In Ezekiel's view, these exiles are of a decidedly different ilk than his audience that had been taken captive to Babylon with him in 597 BCE. Ezekiel's audience must distinguish themselves from the suffering of the new group, and this dovetails with Ezekiel's other oracles addressing the historical circumstances between 597 and 587. In these oracles, the community living in the homeland is subject to YHWH's wrath in a manner that could no longer be applied to Ezekiel's own audience. The latter was a privileged group, close to their patron deity, the bearers of covenant tradition, and worthy of eventual restoration. The new arrivals in Babylon, by contrast, were cursed, fit for brutal punishment, distant from YHWH's

---

1. Translations based on JPS with various revisions by me.

good graces.[2] The homeland itself was a wasteland, the residence of foreign cultures that stood beyond YHWH's covenant, and the new exiles in Babylon were sullied by their residence in such an environment for the last decade of Jerusalem's existence. Ezekiel's audience, on the other hand, resided in Babylon, a sanctified region where they could continue to connect to YHWH and where the terms of the covenant could endure.[3]

Judging from the tenor of Ezekiel's oracles, the tables had turned quite dramatically in Israelite concepts of sacred space and communal identity. The vast majority of traditions stemming from the preexilic era presuppose the ancestral homeland as sacred space, with foreign territory taking on a far more liminal and even chaotic character. The oldest textual witness to this idea, the Song of the Sea in Exod 15, casts this binary dynamic in mythopoeic terms: YHWH sweeps the cosmic foe to the margins, then proceeds to plant his people in the landscape, and it is there that they tend to his holy highlands and affirm his reign as divine sovereign through cultic devotion.[4] This ancient hymn draws extensively from much older Canaanite mythology,[5] in which the homeland constitutes sacred terrain where the domestic, familiar deities reside. The territory beyond its boundaries is the realm of chaos, where enemies from the underworld roam and pose existential threats.[6] In monarchic-era narrative tradition, this crossing of earthly parallels to these boundaries provides opportunities for heroes to ritually renew their viability,[7] but it also reveals that the boundaries were permeable—the forces of chaos beyond the homeland could creep in and wreak havoc.

---

2. For a full study of these features of Ezekiel's rhetoric, see Dalit Rom-Shiloni, "Ezekiel as the Voice of the Exiles and Constructor of Exilic Ideology," *HUCA* 76 (2005): 1–45.

3. Ibid.; Joseph Blenkinsopp, *Judaism: The First Phase* (Grand Rapids: Eerdmans, 2009), 157.

4. For a recent examination of this theme in Exod 15, see Mark Leuchter, "Eisodus as Exodus: The Song of the Sea (Exod 15) Reconsidered," *Bib* 93 (2011): 333–46.

5. The classic study in this regard remains that of Frank M. Cross, *Canaanite Myth and Hebrew Epic* (Cambridge: Harvard University Press, 1973), 121–44.

6. Mark S. Smith, *The Origins of Biblical Monotheism* (New York: Oxford University Press, 2001), 27–29.

7. Jeremy M. Hutton, *The Transjordanian Palimpsest: The Overwritten Texts of Personal Exile and Transformation in the Deuteronomistic History*, BZAW 396 (Berlin: de Gruyter, 2009), 44–50.

Jeremiah 9, a composite text containing poetic oracles as well as subsequent exegetical prose, sheds light on how the Judahite literati would have envisioned these forces in the early sixth century BCE. In accounting for the dissolution of domestic security in the face of the Babylonian conquest, Jer 9:20 claims that Death (the cosmic foe of ancient West Semitic myth) has crept into the sacred landscape and its corrosive forces are manifested in Babylon's presence.[8] Whether this verse addresses the actual destructive events of 587 BCE or simply the corruption of the homeland's integrity through the Babylonian presence beginning in 597 is difficult to determine. But in the later prose exegesis redacted into the chapter, the reason for this turn of events is made clear: the abrogation of YHWH's written law has compromised the landscape (Jer 9:11–12), allowing for the threat to take root and fester. This follows upon the late-seventh-century BCE passages in Deuteronomy where the regular reading of the law and its implementation would push such threats beyond the boundaries of the land, ensuring the security and sanctity of life therein:

> And Moses wrote this law, and delivered it to the priests the sons of Levi, who bore the ark of the covenant of YHWH, and to all the elders of Israel. And Moses commanded them, saying: At the end of every seven years,[9] in the set time of the year of release, in the feast of tabernacles, when all Israel appears before YHWH your God in the place which he shall choose, you shall read this law before all Israel in their hearing. Assemble the people, the men and the women and the little ones, and the stranger that is within your gates, that they may hear, and that they may learn, and fear YHWH your God, and observe to do all the words of this law; and that their children, who have not known, may hear, and learn to fear YHWH your God, as long as you live in the land whither you go over the Jordan to possess it. (Deut 31:9–13)[10]

---

8. See the related comment by Ziony Zevit, *The Religions of Ancient Israel: A Synthesis of Parallactic Approaches* (London: Bloomsbury, 2001), 327.

9. One should note that the septennial reading of the law—securing as it does the fear/devotion to YHWH throughout the land (v. 13)—appears to invoke a mythological trope attested in Ugaritic myth, where Mot/Death threatens to encroach upon the landscape on a septennial basis as well (*KTU* 1.6 V 8–25).

10. Karel van der Toorn has argued that this passage dates from an exilic expansion of Deuteronomy (*Scribal Culture and the Making of the Hebrew Bible* [Cambridge: Harvard University Press, 2007], 160–62). However, the role of this passage is consonant with other passages throughout Deuteronomy that focus on the law as an expression of YHWH's hegemony over the land for the sake of residence therein, and pre-

Divine writ, read and preserved in the central sanctuary ("when all Israel appears before YHWH ... in the place which he shall choose," i.e., the Jerusalem temple), is the vehicle for the homeland's holiness, as long as the community lives up to its responsibilities to adhere to its terms. As Jer 9 attests, to do otherwise ensures that the sacred landscape will revert to a chaotic state, as if YHWH had never sanctified it at all.

Both Jeremiah and Ezekiel share a theology in which the homeland could be corrupted and fail to function as a place where YHWH's covenant might persist. Of course, these ideas are woven into the traditions standing behind both prophets' oracles, namely (and respectively), the Deuteronomistic and Priestly traditions, both of which contain key texts where the safety and sanctity of the land are entirely conditional. Failure to live up to these conditions results in expulsion/exile (Deut 28 // Lev 26), and countless studies have noted how both prophets' oracles exegetically develop these concepts into more extensive discourses. If these parent traditions were conceived in the late preexilic period, then they function rhetorically to serve as threats in the same manner as the older Mesopotamian treaty materials that inspired them; if they were penned in the exilic era, then they contribute to a theology explaining how and why the monarchy came to a violent end and the population was either exiled or internally displaced.[11] In neither Deuteronomy nor the Priestly tradition, however, is

---

sumes that the law-reading ceremony is part of a liturgical cycle ensuring that ongoing residence. This suggests a preexilic provenance where the authors and intended audience are still ensconced in the land.

11. The late preexilic origin of Deuteronomy is generally accepted. The Priestly (P) tradition presents a greater problem. A significant chorus of scholarly voices see P and the Holiness (H) materials as deriving from the preexilic era and subsequently expanded during the exile. See, inter alia, Menahem Haran, "Behind the Scenes of History: Determining the Date of the Priestly Source," *JBL* 100 (1981): 321–33; Avi Hurvitz, "The Evidence of Language in Dating the Priestly Code: A Linguistic Study in Technical Idioms and Terminology," *RB* 81 (1974): 24–56; Israel Knohl, *The Sanctuary of Silence: The Priestly Torah and the Holiness School* (Minneapolis: Fortress, 1995). The arguments mounted by these and other scholars do not, in my view, conclusively demonstrate that P or H existed as complete (or nearly complete) literary works in the preexilic period, but they do indicate that major sources (oral and written) were firm fixtures of the priestly circles that eventually produced these works. See further the study of Lauren A. S. Monroe, who shows that H scribal traditions were well in place already by Josiah's reign (*Josiah's Reign and the Dynamics of Defilement: Israelite Rites of Violence and the Making of a Biblical Text* [Oxford: Oxford University Press, 2011], esp. 131–33), as well as the discussion by David M. Carr regarding the exilic-era

there any indication that if the covenant terms were transgressed, Israel's land would revert to a wasteland that was to be the home of YHWH's cosmic foes. Likewise, there is no indication in either of these parent traditions that any land *other* than the ancestral homeland could be sanctified as a sacred landscape or space where covenantal existence could continue subsequent to residence in the homeland.[12]

It would seem, then, that sometime between the formation of these late preexilic parent traditions and the oracles of Ezekiel noted above, the community exiled in 597 BCE was exposed to some sort of ideological innovation that redefined the parameters of traditional Israelite geomythology. Some indication of this is evident in Jer 29, a chapter that preserves a series of oracles directed to the exiles of 597 that utilizes a combination of older motifs—some Deuteronomic and some Akkadian—to identify Mesopotamia as a viable space wherein covenantal life may continue.[13] The famous "letter to the exiles" in Jer 29:5–7 especially constitutes the point of departure for this discourse, as exilic life for the audience is characterized in agrarian terms that, in other contexts, characterize life in the hinterland.[14] While the audience may be away from their ancestral land, this rhetoric implies continuity rather than disruption or a resetting of sociological/ethnographic terms; this is perhaps necessary, given the promise of restoration to the homeland (vv. 10, 14), which thus remains sacred if inaccessible. What commands greater attention, though, is the innovative notice that during the period of exile, Mesopotamia is to be viewed as a sacred space—this is a temporary condition (as attested repeatedly throughout

---

orchestration of preexilic P and H sources (*The Formation of the Hebrew Bible: A New Reconstruction* [Oxford: Oxford University Press, 2011], 295–303).

12. Deuteronomy emphasizes that the people will be scattered off of the land by YHWH's hand (Deut 28:63–64), and the Holiness Code claims that the land will "vomit" the people out of it because of their abominations (Lev 18:25–28) and that they will languish in foreign lands (Lev 26:38–39, 44). Both traditions, however, lack qualifications for the territories where the provisional exiles will be sent.

13. On the Deuteronomic motifs, see Adele Berlin, "Jeremiah 29:5–7: A Deuteornomic Allusion?" *HAR* 8 (1984): 3–11. On the reference to an Akkadian inscription from the reign of Esarhaddon, see Mark Leuchter, *The Polemics of Exile in Jeremiah 26–45* (Cambridge: Cambridge University Press, 2008), 47–48.

14. The audience in this letter are encouraged to cultivate families and land in a manner entirely consistent with preexilic covenant texts and motifs; see Stephen L. Cook, *The Social Roots of Biblical Yahwism*, SBLStBL 8 (Atlanta: Society of Biblical Literature, 2004), 32–33.

Jer 27–29); but, for the duration of its dominance, Babylon is to be the recipient of Israelite prayers for peace and blessed welfare once directed exclusively to Jerusalem (v. 7).[15]

The material in Jer 27–29 seems to have been preserved as a special oracular unit by the 597 BCE community,[16] but it stopped short of the full reversal of geomythology we encounter in Ezekiel's oracles, which establish wholesale separation between the exiles of 597 and other Judahite groups. In Jer 29, the prophets preaching oracles that promise a swift return to sacred Jerusalem are mistaken, and both they and their supporters will receive harsh judgment (vv. 21–32). However, Jerusalem itself is never characterized as a corrupt, foreign, chaotic territory in the manner of the discourse we encounter in Ezek 16 and 23, as well as elsewhere in that prophetic book. As Dalit Rom-Shiloni has demonstrated, Jerusalem is not only devoid of YHWH's presence, it is the antithesis of covenantally legitimate space in Ezekiel's oracles, and its citizens are thus stripped of the privileges of YHWH's patronage.[17]

In short, Ezekiel's rhetoric presumes a radical conceptual shift that places the sacred landscape in Mesopotamia exclusively, bestowing upon Ezekiel's community a covenantal status that no other post-597 Israelite group could claim. For his audience, Mesopotamia was the land of YHWH until the deity saw fit to restore them to the ancestral homeland (e.g., Ezek 34; 36–37); but until that time, the ancestral homeland was accursed. This has points of contact with some motifs within Jer 29; it is possible that Ezekiel has simply adapted the terms of Jer 29 and restricted them to his own audience. But it is also possible that both Ezekiel and Jer 29 presuppose an antecedent event that opened the horizon for viewing Mesopotamia as a sacred space and developed the repercussions of this event in parallel ways—one leading to a view of Mesopotamia in which the later exiles could conceivably share (e.g., the role of Jer 29 within Jer 26–45, which emphasizes this social vision)[18] and the other leading to a more limited view that established a fixed hierarchy of covenantal rank, with Ezekiel's in-group occupying a special and superior position to all others.

---

15. Compare especially to passages such as Jer 6:14 // 8:11, where the prophet critiques a שלום prayer formula current among the residents of Judah.

16. William L. Holladay, *Jeremiah 2: A Commentary on the Book of the Prophet Jeremiah, Chapters 26–52,* Hermeneia (Minneapolis: Fortress, 1989), 137–39.

17. Rom-Shiloni, "Ezekiel as Voice," 40–41, 44.

18. See the conclusion below for further discussion on this point.

Seraiah's Colophon in Rhetorical and Historical Context

An important text currently embedded in the book of Jeremiah—"Seraiah's colophon" (Jer 51:59-64a MT)—provides crucial evidence for just such an antecedent event that gave rise to these divergent views of communal identity and exilic space. Several years ago, Jack R. Lundbom proposed that the two major versions of the Jeremianic corpus, the Masoretic Text and the Septuagint, were originally shaped by the sons of Neriah, Seraiah and Baruch (respectively).[19] Both were important figures in the political world of Judah in the late seventh-early sixth centuries BCE, both were close allies of the prophet Jeremiah, and both appear to have been associated with the Shaphanide scribal school.[20] For Lundbom, each scribe was responsible for organizing a sequence of material that would become one of these major textual versions, and they "signed" their work by closing each collection with an expanded scribal colophon, that is, a catalog of scribal details that formed the backbone of an oracle.[21] The colophon-oracle of Baruch occupies the very last unit of discourse in the Septuagint version of the book (Jer 51 LXX). Seraiah's colophon-oracle serves the same purpose in the Masoretic Text version, affixed to the anti-Babylon oracle of Jer 50-51 that closes the oracles against the nations in the Masoretic Text tradition (Jer 46-51 MT). The colophon leads directly into the closing דברי ירמיהו notice in Jer 51:64b that forms a closing *inclusio* with Jer 1:1, thus pointing to Seraiah's hand in the formation of that text tradition.

Nevertheless, Seraiah's colophon also appears in the Septuagint tradition, affixed to the same oracle (Jer 27-28 LXX). This reveals that even before it was utilized to close the Masoretic Text sequence of the book, the colophon served a more specific purpose in relation to the early version of that anti-Babylon oracle when it was initially conceived.[22] The early anti-

---

19. Jack R. Lundbom, *Jeremiah: A Study in Ancient Hebrew Rhetoric*, SBLDS 18 (Missoula, MT: Scholars Press, 1975), 118-20; idem, "Baruch, Seraiah and Expanded Colophons in the Book of Jeremiah," *JSOT* 36 (1986): 108-9. See also Richard C. Steiner, "The Two Sons of Neriah and the Two Editions of Jeremiah in the Light of Two Atbash Code-Words for Babylon," *VT* 46 (1996): 74-84.

20. Lundbom, "Baruch, Seraiah," 108-9; Leuchter, *Polemics of Exile*, 99-107, 138-41.

21. Lundbom, "Baruch, Seraiah," 99.

22. The oracle, in its current form, is an assortment of smaller oracular units edited together via common leitmotifs and catchwords and includes post-Jeremianic materials. Different units have been identified and proposed: see Wilhelm Rudolph,

Babylon oracle was likely written and entrusted to Seraiah to deliver to Mesopotamia in the context of a political delegation in about 594 BCE, as indicated by the superscription to the colophon in 51:59 and supported by additional information in 29:1–3. Because the delivery of Jeremiah's letter to the exiles of 597 was facilitated by this same delegation,[23] the letter was therefore somehow associated with Jeremiah's directive to Seraiah to go to the Euphrates and submerge a copy of the scroll containing the anti-Babylon oracle (which included a copy of Seraiah's colophon affixed to it). Yet the anti-Babylon oracle (and affixed colophon) appear to be working at cross-purposes to Jeremiah's letter to the exiles of 597: the latter encourages the captives to "seek the welfare" of Babylon (29:7) while the oracle-colophon scroll proclaims its eventual downfall. How could these two oracular collections advise the audience to accept life in Mesopotamia while, in the same breath, advocate for its devastation?

A closer look at Seraiah's colophon, the phenomenology of the act it depicts, and the cultural tropes invoked in this act provide some resolution to the aforementioned question and points to the development of a complex cosmology where Babylon and Mesopotamia, in general, play multiple roles. First and foremost, it is important to recall that the letter to the exiles in 29:5–7 may counsel deference to Babylonian hegemony, but it is part of a unit that repeatedly anticipates that city's demise (27:7, 22; 29:10–11). What will facilitate this fall is not simply divine will but the efficacy of the text expressing it, and this is evident in the rhetorical structure of the colophon:

> 59 The word [הדבר] that Jeremiah the prophet commanded Seraiah ben Neriah. ...
>> 61 And Jeremiah said to Seraiah: "When you come to Babylon [בבל], then see that you read all these words
>>> 62 and say: 'YHWH, you have spoken concerning this place [המקום הזה], to cut it off, that none shall dwell therein, neither man nor beast, but that it shall be desolate forever.'

Jeremia, 4th ed., HAT 1/12 (Tübingen: Mohr, 1968), 297–316; Georg Fohrer, *Studien zu alttestamentlichen Texten und Themen*, BZAW 155 (Berlin: de Gruyter, 1981), 50–52; Lundbom, *Jeremiah 37–52*, AB 21C (New York: Doubleday, 2004), 364–501. Lundbom asserts, however, that the composite sources woven together do find their point or origin in the prophet's actual words and that the early form of Jer 50–51 included genuinely Jeremianic writings (p. 367), as suggested by the superscription to Seraiah's colophon that is attached to the oracle dating it to ca. 594 BCE.

23. Holladay, *Jeremiah 2*, 22–23, 114–19.

> 63 And it shall be, when you have made an end of reading this scroll [הספר הזה], that you shall bind a stone to it, and cast it into the midst of the Euphrates,
> 64a and you shall say: 'Thus shall Babylon [בבל] sink, and shall not rise again because of the evil that I will bring upon her; and they shall be weary. ...'"
> 64b Here end the words [דברי] of Jeremiah.

A chiastic structure informs the entirety of these verses, and the relationship between exilic life and the vehicles of sanctity are clearly delineated: the בבל keyword delimits the geographical context, the titling of Babylon as a sacred place (המקום הזה) presupposes the residence of Judahites therein that Jeremiah had already counseled to build communities in the spirit of piety, and Seraiah's colophon is granted the status of prophetic proclamation via the דבר inclusion in verses 59 and 64b. The identification of Babylon as a sacred space is made not only through the earlier prophetic oracle in 29:5–7 but through the *text* to which Seraiah's colophon was affixed (and of which it was an essential part), as the phrases המקום הזה and הספר הזה form a binary pair at the heart of the colophon (vv. 62–63). Babylon is the interim sacred space for the exiles of 597 addressed in 29:5–7, but Seraiah's colophon makes clear that just as Jerusalem's preeminence had been eclipsed by Babylon, so too would Babylon's dominance be transient (59:64).

Seraiah's Colophon and Mesopotamian Foundation Inscriptions

As noted by virtually every commentator, Seraiah's charge to submerge the scroll containing the Babylonian oracle obviously symbolizes what the oracle proclaims about the changing fortunes of Babylon itself (51:64).[24] For many, this is an apotropaic act not unlike the sign-act of Hananiah in Jer 28 or other prophetic sign-acts. However, there is more than apotropaism at work within this directive. Lundbom notes that Seraiah's act recalls the depositing of texts in a temple, a common practice among priestly-

---

24. For an overview, see Lundbom, *Jeremiah 37–52*, 503–4. The date of the colophon and its avowed purpose suggests that the turning fortunes of Babylon are original to the oracle (*pace* Georg Fohrer, "Vollmacht über Völker und Königreiche (Jer 46–51)," in idem, *Studien zu alttestamentlichen Texten*, 44–52, who sees the turning political tide as a redactional accretion).

scribal circles in antiquity[25] and goes on to cite some precedent of this both within Deuteronomy (31:26) and 2 Kings (22:8). To this list we may also add the depositing of the Decalogue itself into the ark of the covenant in Deut 10:1–5. This act is not, as often thought, a sign of demythologization of the ark but should instead be regarded as the basis for a new Deuteronomic mythotype. The law is established as the very basis of YHWH's function as the divine warrior, a trait long associated with the ark; the metamessage is that the application of the law in the land is an expression of YHWH's victory over mythic chaos.[26] In short, the inscription (the Decalogue), defines the character of the space surrounding it (the ark) and the purpose it serves. It is for this reason that Deut 31:9–13 specifies that the same Levites who bear the ark are the Levites who read the law, and that it is through the reading of the law that YHWH's hegemony over the sacred landscape is affirmed by the people.

In this sense, the parameters of Lundbom's observation should be expanded, for Deut 10:1–5 is not simply an account of the deposition of text in a temple/sanctuary for the purposes of safekeeping or as part of a temple library. Rather, it presents the Decalogue as a type of foundation inscription, a form of ritual text that was deposited in the foundation work of Mesopotamian temple structures during their construction or restoration/rededication. Foundation inscriptions granted these temples a cosmic character, grounding the favor of the deities within the temple and applying it to the king who commissioned the inscription.[27] A foun-

---

25. Lundbom, *Jeremiah 37–52*, 508. See also van der Toorn, *Scribal Culture*, 86–87.

26. See the discussion in Mark Leuchter, "The Fightin' Mushites," *VT* 62 (2012): 479–500.

27. For a full discussion of foundation inscriptions, see Richard S. Ellis, *Foundation Deposits in Ancient Mesopotamia* (New Haven: Yale University Press, 1968); see also Sandra L. Richter, *The Deuteronomistic History and the Name Theology: lešakkēn šemô šām in the Bible and the Ancient Near East*, BZAW 318 (Berlin: de Gruyter, 2002), 144–53. In relation to the foundation inscriptions from Esarhaddon's reign in the early seventh century BCE, see Barbara N. Porter, *Images, Power, and Politics: Figurative Aspects of Esarhaddon's Babylonian Policy* (Philadelphia: American Philosophical Society, 1993), 50–68. Porter identifies several texts as foundation inscriptions, while other texts are identified as being deposited in the sancta of certain temples (p. 68). In either case, foundation inscriptions served ritual as well as political purposes. A more recent discussion of Mesopotamian foundation inscription praxes is given by Jamie Novotny, "Temple Building in Assyria: Evidence from Royal Inscriptions," in *From the*

dation inscription affirmed the royal patron of the temple construction/restoration as the ultimate agent and trustee of divine will, supporting the political interests of the ruler in question and bestowing upon that ruler's policies a divine seal of approval.[28] These inscriptions delineated the purpose of new temples or transformed the purpose of restored temples, declaring that they symbolized and concretized the commissioning ruler's hegemony and the divine sponsorship he enjoyed.[29]

The passages in Deut 10:1–5, 31:26, and 2 Kgs 22:8, all of which emerged at a time when Judahite culture had long been under Assyrian influence, speak to a familiarity with the function of Mesopotamian foundation inscriptions. Following Mesopotamian convention, these Israelite sacred texts create a bridge between heaven and earth, defining the cosmic significance and social function of sacred space—the temple and the landscape surrounding it.[30] The Deuteronomistic redactor of 1 Kgs 6 declares that this was always the intention of the Jerusalem temple by inserting vv. 11–13—a prophetic proclamation to Solomon—into the very heart of the chapter:

> And the word of YHWH came to Solomon, saying: "As for this house which you are building, if you will walk in my statutes, and execute my ordinances, and keep all my commandments to walk in them; then will I establish my word with you, which I spoke to David your father; in that

---

Foundations to the Crenellations: Essays on Temple Building in the Ancient Near East and Hebrew Bible, ed. Mark J. Boda and Jamie Novotny, AOAT 366 (Münster: Ugarit-Verlag, 2010), 115–24.

28. See Victor A. Hurowitz, *I Have Built for You an Exalted House: Temple Building in the Bible in Light of Mesopotamian and Northwest Semitic Writings*, JSOTSup 115 (Sheffield: Sheffield Academic, 1992), 131–310.

29. See further Mark J. Boda, "Legitimizing the Temple: The Chronicler's Temple Building Account," in Boda and Novotny, *From the Foundations*, 310–12, 315–17. The Chronicler's own composition presupposes the conventions of a temple foundation inscription/document, but positions his work as a "rebooting" of the temple's foundation/legitimacy as rooted in traditions predating and even trumping royal prerogatives.

30. In Deut 10:1–5, the Decalogue transforms the ark from war palladium to symbol of YHWH's hegemony via the law. Likewise, in Deut 31:26 the written law deposited in the sanctuary transforms it from the locus of the divine כבוד safeguarded by the elite priests to the center of a covenantal community bound through legal principle, and its discovery in the temple in 2 Kgs 22:8 reaffirms that space as the inheritor of that earlier sanctuary's purpose.

I will dwell therein among the children of Israel, and will not forsake my people Israel." (1 Kgs 6:11–13)

These verses specify that the temple was founded on prophetic principles regarding submission to a law that governed life well beyond the temple. The oracle in which this idea is conveyed becomes a sort of literary foundation inscription in the account of the temple's construction;[31] this, perhaps, co-opts Solomon's hegemonic role in the construction of that sacred space and appropriates it for the ideological circle the scribe represents (one that repeatedly characterizes kings as subordinate to Levites and prophets). But irrespective of factional politics, the passage attests to Israelite scribes' awareness of the social and sacral function of foundation inscriptions in the Mesopotamian world with which they were so thoroughly intertwined and positions Israel's own religious institutions as a parallel or corollary to it.

The Geomythic Role of the Euphrates River

Seraiah's colophon contains many of the same motifs as Mesopotamian foundation inscriptions and the aforementioned Deuteronomistic texts regarding the realignment or qualification of sacred space. Its deposition in the Euphrates may therefore signify that its primary function was not to serve as some apotropaic talisman but rather to serve as a foundation inscription, claiming the Euphrates and the entirety of the land it bounded for YHWH just as other such documents claimed Mesopotamian temples for various other deities. The paramount geographic significance of the Euphrates is reflected in the Persian titling of the satrapy containing the western provinces as עבר נהרה, "Across-the-River"; even for the Achaemenid rulers, the Euphrates was a boundary marker lending cosmic order to their empire. Within the biblical record, it is identified as the נהר הגדול, the "great river" (Gen 15:18; Deut 1:7; Josh 1:4), recalling the old

---

31. Richard Elliott Friedman assigns this accretion to the exilic redaction of the Deuteronomistic History (*The Exile and Biblical Narrative: The Formation of the Deuteronomistic and Priestly Works*, HSM 22 [Missoula, MT: Scholars Press, 1981], 33); it would thus be quite suitable for this accretion to be embedded in the text describing the temple in the absence of the physical temple itself. But it may also be a late preexilic accretion if it arose from a preexilic redaction of sources that sought to subordinate royal and royally sponsored institutions to the law.

mythologies regarding primordial waters demarcating the sacred landscape from the wilderness and, eventually, the underworld.[32] The Euphrates is often recruited as a topos deeply involved in YHWH's mythological domination of the physical world, commonly in conflict with pretenders to that international role,[33] and as a landmark delineating a mythic otherspace where divine punishment could be administered (e.g., 1 Kgs 14:15). In short, the Euphrates represented the geomythic boundary marker for the sociopolitical world in which YHWH affected Israel's fate. It is for this reason that the record of David's exploits gives the impression that he established his kingdom to the shores of the Euphrates,[34] as well as the reason for why Solomon is said to rule over a territory of similar geographical range (1 Kgs 4:21). The implication is that the united monarchy under these kings rivaled the great Mesopotamian kingdoms granted special status by that river.[35]

The role of the Euphrates in Seraiah's colophon may have been informed by the river's rhetorical function in Esarhaddon's foundation inscriptions. Barbara N. Porter draws special attention to the ideology of the contents in these texts, noting that while they served the traditional ritual purposes of infusing temple spaces with cosmic potency, they were also carefully designed to convey propagandistic content via the copies of the texts distributed throughout the empire.[36] Various passages within the book of Jeremiah (especially those clearly composed in the wake of Babylon's success at Carchemish) show specific knowledge of the contents of these Esarhaddon texts.[37] One example, a foundation inscription from the temple of Nabu Ša Hare in Babylon attesting to Esarhaddon's rebuilding of the Esagila temple, is particularly instructive:

---

32. Mark Smith, *Origins of Biblical Monotheism*, 27–29.

33. Esther Eshel, "Isaiah 11:15: A New Interpretation Based on the Genesis Apocryphon," *DSD* 13 (2006): 38–45.

34. Baruch Halpern, *David's Secret Demons: Messiah, Murderer, Traitor, King* (Grand Rapids: Eerdmans, 2001), 187–95.

35. This function of the Euphrates may be a sort of response or adjustment to its role as a mythic foundation of Babylonian temples; Esarhaddon's Black Stone Inscription presupposes the mythic role of this river and the rebuilt Esagila temple in Babylon as a symbol of cosmic order that redirects its potency. See Riekele Borger, *Die Inschriften Asarhaddons Königs von Assyrien*, AfO 9 (Graz: Biblio-Verlag, 1967), 12–19. See also further below regarding the Nabû Ša Ḫare Inscription.

36. Porter, *Images*, 109–10, 112.

37. Leuchter, *Polemics of Exile*, 47–48.

> Before my time the great lord Marduk's heart was enraged against E-sangil and Babylon, and he became angry. His people were answering each other "Yes!" (for) "No!" They were speaking untruths. ...Their deeds were loathsome to Marduk and Zarpanitu, so they ordered that the people be scattered. They made water flow over the city and turned it into waste land. ...
>
> At the beginning of my reign, in the first year of my rule, when I sat solemnly on the throne of kingship, merciful Marduk's heart relented and he became reconciled to the city with which he had been angry. I had E-sangil and Babylon built anew. I renovated the statues of the great gods. In their dwelling places I settled them on everlasting seats. ...
>
> ... In a favourable month, on a propitious day ... I rebuilt that temple completely, from its foundations to its parapets....
>
> May Nabû, the exalted son, look upon [this work] with joy! May he bless my reign in the steadfastness of his heart! May he let my hand grasp a just sceptre that widens my dominion. For Ashurbanipal, the crown prince of Assyria, and Šamaš-šum-ukin, the crown prince of Babylon, the two brothers sprung from my loins, may he determine as their destiny a good destiny, a favorable destiny entailing the extension of the days of their reigns and the protection of the thrones of their stewardships.[38]

In this excerpt, politics, history, and the cosmos are woven together through the deposition of the foundation inscription. Esarhaddon establishes his reign as the basis for the divine turning of Babylon's fortunes and fixes his own dynasty as the governing principle that secures the city's ongoing security as an integral—though subordinate—part of Esarhaddon's greater empire. The rebuilding of the Esagila temple is not simply an act signifying political domination; the foundation inscription expands the cosmic potency of that act, eclipsing the temple's earlier function or symbolic purpose and subordinating it to a new divinely sponsored ruler. It is notable that the scribe behind this inscription highlights the gods' mastery over the primordial waters—a reference, no doubt, to Sennacherib's flooding of Babylon through strategic manipulation of the Euphrates and its tributaries—in punishing the wayward city.[39] The restoration of Esagila and Babylon itself suggests that Esarhaddon's reign reflects the gods' hegemony over the waters of chaos and serves as a sort of cosmic event hori-

---

38. Translation by Nawala al-Mutawalli, "A New Foundation Cylinder from the Temple of Nabû Ša Ḫarê," *Iraq* 61 (1999): 193.

39. D. D. Luckenbill, *The Annals of Sennacherib* (Chicago: Oriental Institute, 1924), 83–84.

zon, ensuring the safety of Babylon from their destructive forces. Under Esarhaddon's reign and expressed through the rhetoric of the inscription, the Euphrates secures the realm and empowers it to conquer rivals. The river, then, is a mythic vehicle for domination over surrounding territory. The inscription does not just describe its purpose; through its language, it determines and licenses the earthly reality manifesting the river's purpose as both the immediate and enduring declaration of the gods.[40]

The content of Seraiah's colophon presumes the same geopolitical and mythological potential for the Euphrates, but it departs from the Esarhaddon inscription in some important ways. First and foremost, Esarhaddon's inscription was embedded in the Nabu Ša Hare temple; but, in Seraiah's colophon, the river itself takes on that role as the locus of the textual deposition. While this departs from the Mesopotamian convention, the depositing of a Yahwistic oracle-inscription within its depths capitalizes on the river's mythic potency: temples within Mesopotamia may be claimed by this or that deity via their respective foundation inscriptions, but the river that defined the exalted status of the entire region is now claimed by YHWH through the oracle-scroll that has sunk into its depths. And the harsh contents of the oracle-scroll make clear what YHWH's intentions are for that region—it will eventually be toppled. As in the Esarhaddon inscription, the Euphrates symbolizes the destiny of the political realm. However, it is now a geomythic symbol under YHWH's control (not Marduk's), mediated through the prophetic word mediated by a scribe that now extends to regions far beyond the ancestral homeland.

Seraiah's Colophon and the Qualifying of Sacred Space

The ceremony surrounding the submergence of Seraiah's oracle-colophon scroll inaugurated a set of sociosacral conditions that now governed life among the exiles. The anti-Babylon oracle claims that Babylon will eventually fall, but the public reading of the oracle and its deposition in the Euphrates marks that river and Mesopotamia as YHWH's territory.[41]

---

40. See esp. van der Toorn, *Scribal Culture*, 217–21, for the shift to written texts not as a record of revelation but as the very substance of revelation; the promulgation of foundation inscriptions in eighth- and seventh-century Mesopotamia presupposes this function of their mytho-textuality and relies on the rhetorical power of this view for propagandistic purposes.

41. Compare the features of Seraiah's colophon to the similar episodes legislated

Through the ceremonial deposition of the oracle-scroll into the river, Mesopotamia became a temporary sacred landscape wherein communion with the deity remained possible, a type of surrogate "sanctuary" by virtue of the Yahwistic foundation inscription resting in its depths. It is not too drastic a conceptual leap to see this event as initiating an ideology that was eventually developed into starker, more exclusive terms in Ezekiel's oracles. Those (like him) living in this new sacred landscape superseded those still residing in the ancestral homeland;[42] the residents of the homeland remained bound to an older sanctuary site that was no longer directly accountable to YHWH but was instead a symbol of a foreign king's dominance over the western periphery of the Babylonian empire bereft of YHWH's presence (Ezek 1; 8–11). Ezekiel's in-group, by contrast, now resided in the very center of that realm, and had been made privy to a ceremony that transformed it into the direct conduit to YHWH himself.

If the allegiance to a Jerusalem-centric ideology within this community indeed persisted (as Jer 27 // 29 claim it did), the development of Seraiah's oracle-colophon scroll ceremony into a theology of exclusion and binary opposition would constitute an effective way to counter the influence of those Jerusalem-allied voices. The adoption of such a view would not only provide a defense against the dissolution of cultural/social identity wrought by the trauma of exile, but it would effectively dissuade members of his audience from accepting the legitimacy of prophets who remained devoted to Jerusalem and its now-vacant temple as a sacred space. The declaration that Ezekiel received his visions "by the Chebar" (Ezek 1:1, 3; 3:15; 10:15, 20, 22) takes on geomythic significance if Seraiah's colophon-oracle unit indeed served as a foundation inscription claiming the Euphrates and the Babylonian land to the east of it as the new center of YHWH's attention. Since the Chebar was a tributary of the Euphrates, it would be a fitting place for Ezekiel to receive visions and form oracles, following the convention of priests and cult prophets receiving oracles in the loci anchoring communal devotion to the patron deity both in Israelite tradition (1 Sam 3; Isa 6) and following Mesopotamian convention as well.[43] For Ezekiel, the divine presence appearing to him was no longer

---

in Deut 27 and 31:9–13 and elsewhere, where the Levites are to read aloud the written torah in a ceremony declaring the terms of Israelite residency in the land YHWH has given them.

42. Rom-Shiloni, "Ezekiel as Voice," 16–18.

43. It may be worth noting, also, that the poet behind Ps 137 considers the

anywhere else but along the waters of Babylon that YHWH had designated the center of the cosmos,[44] and the ceremony involving Seraiah's colophon and the scroll to which it was attached was a ritual expression of this new reality.

But this is not the only way that Seraiah's colophon—and the act it details—could be understood. It is essential to note that Seraiah's colophon was part of the oracle-scroll deposited into the Euphrates.[45] As such, it too functioned as a genetic component of the foundation inscription. Indeed, this is indicated by the locution shared by both the oracle and the colophon, as Seraiah's colophon ends with the same catchword that concludes the Babylonian oracle:

> Thus says YHWH of hosts: the broad walls of Babylon shall be utterly overthrown, and her high gates shall be burned with fire; and the peoples shall labor for vanity, and the nations for the fire; and they shall be weary [ויעפו]. (Jer 51:58)

> And thou shalt say: Thus shall Babylon sink, and shall not rise again because of the evil that I will bring upon her; and they shall be weary [ויעפו]. (Jer 51:64a)[46]

The summative character of Jer 51:64 suggests that the oracle and colophon should be placed on par with each other, which carries major implications for the role of the scribe in the definition of YHWH's cosmic intentions. Like the scribes in Jer 36 who summarize the *Urrolle*'s contents in the presence of Jehoiakim (36:20), the scribal role in the colophon is to summarize and preserve the fundamental message of Jeremiah's oracles but also to facilitate and actualize them.[47] By submerging the colophon as *part* of the foundation inscription, a place for scribes is staked out within the new socioreligious order that the ceremony seems to have inaugurated,

---

Euphrates and its tributaries (על נהרי בבל in v. 1) a suitable place to compose and recite new liturgical material.

44. See William A. Tooman, "Ezekiel's Radical Challenge to Inviolability," *ZAW* 121 (2009): 510–11.

45. Lundbom, "Baruch, Seraiah," 103.

46. As Lundbom discusses, catchwords are standard colophonic features ("Baruch, Seraiah," 90).

47. David M. Carr, *Writing on the Tablet of the Heart: Origins of Scripture and Literature* (Oxford: Oxford University Press, 2005), 146–49.

and, within the book of Jeremiah, a substantial number of these scribes remained in the homeland between 597–587 BCE. There is no indication that Seraiah remained in Babylon after enacting the oracle-scroll ceremony, and it is clear that authoritative figures such as his brother Baruch and others such as Gedaliah ben Ahikam remained trusted executors of Jeremiah's word down to and even beyond the destruction of Jerusalem.[48]

Here we must consider that not only was Seraiah's oracle-colophon scroll embedded in the Euphrates, it was also embedded in the book of Jeremiah. I have argued elsewhere that an early version of Jer 1–25 plus the oracles against the nations was developed as a prophetic "charter collection" for the exiles of 597, with the anti-Babylon oracle and Seraiah's colophon serving as its finale.[49] The inclusion of Seraiah's oracle-colophon document into that literary collection rendered it as a sort of avatar of the submerged scroll, allowing the charter collection to function in numinous tandem with the foundation inscription submerged within the Euphrates. This approaches the convention of the "double document" in ancient Near Eastern scribal practice, where an official version remains sealed (or otherwise inaccessible) while a public copy could be consulted, examined, and studied.[50] In this case, the oracle-colophon scroll in the Euphrates served in the capacity of the former, while the Jeremianic charter collection served in the capacity of the latter. It served as a mythically vital, living liturgical work delineating the theology and social order of the 597 community preserving it.

The subsequent redactional addition of Jer 26–45 into this charter collection, however, changed the function of Seraiah's colophon. In this newer, more comprehensive corpus, Seraiah's colophon was the final example of *many* colophons throughout the work that demonstrated how scribes were the trustees of prophecy.[51] It is for this reason that immediately follow-

---

48. Leuchter, *Polemics of Exile*, 120–24.

49. Ibid., 69–70.

50. The duration of this practice extends down into the Hellenistic era and beyond. See Shaye J. D. Cohen, "The Judaean Legal Tradition and the Halakhah of the Mishnah," in *The Cambridge Companion to the Talmud and Rabbinic Literature*, ed. Charlotte Fonrobert and Martin S. Jaffee (Cambridge: Cambridge University Press, 2007), 126.

51. See Lundbom, "Baruch, Seraiah." See also the discussion further below. As per my discussion in *Polemics of Exile*, 146–47, I see the supplemental material currently in Jer 26–45 MT as purposefully interpolated into the Jeremianic charter collection to intervene between Jer 1–25 and the oracles against the nations. A function of this

ing Seraiah's colophon in the Masoretic Text sequence, we encounter the דברי ירמיהו notice; its presence at this literary juncture points back to the beginning of the work, extending the cosmic significance of Seraiah's oracle-colophon scroll back over the new material (and the colophons within this new material) it contained.[52] We may go further and view this new context for Seraiah's colophon as extending a deeper connection between scribes and Levites established in the book of Jeremiah,[53] with reference specifically to the role of Levites in the book of Deuteronomy. Like Moses, Jeremiah writes the oracle (51:60; cf. Deut 31:19, 22), and the oracle itself is characterized in the same terms as Moses' Deuteronomic address (Jer 51:60: את כל דברים האלה; cf. Deut 32:45). Seraiah is then directed to read the oracle (Jer 51:63) akin to the Levites' reading of the law (Deut 31:11–12) and is charged with depositing the document at a locus of mythic significance (51:63; Deut 31:26). In the context of the larger Jeremiah corpus, Seraiah's colophon contributes to the role of scribes as continuing the tradition of Levitical vigilance against social dissolution in the name of the YHWH, turning Jeremiah's written words into a new form of torah for them to teach and mediate to the entirety of the exilic population now bounded by the Euphrates River.[54] In this way, Seraiah's colophon is not only the closing strophe of the earlier prophetic charter collection for the exiles of 597, it is the final word on a broader account of scribes in exile—including those who were not part of Ezekiel's in-group—and their ability to sanctify space in the manner that Jer 9:11–12, 20 claim was abrogated in Jerusalem.

---

maneuver was to subsume this material within the דברי ירמיהו *inclusio* initially framing that earlier charter collection, thereby qualifying the new material as authentic and binding.

52. See the similar observation by Lundbom, *Jeremiah 37–52*, 504–5, though he views this as a secondary reworking by Seraiah of an extant corpus originally ending with Baruch's colophon akin to the LXX sequence.

53. Leuchter, *Polemics of Exile*, 168–76.

54. That these features are already part of Seraiah's colophon before the composition/addition of Jer 26–45 MT (since the LXX version of the colophon carries them as well) suggest that Seraiah's colophon was not redacted by the scribes who added Jer 26–45 to the earlier charter corpus. Rather, these features demonstrate the degree to which Deuteronomy affected the rhetorical modality of scribes in the last days of the monarchic era and should be credited to Seraiah himself if he is to be seen as the author of the original colophon.

CONCLUSION

The foregoing suggests a very different conceptual horizon than what obtains in Ezekiel. It is important to note that Jer 29 was redacted into its current form by scribes who arrived in Babylon after 587 and who advocated a more inclusive understanding of communal identity.[55] For them, life in exile could indeed be sanctified, just as Jeremiah's earlier letter to the exiles had claimed. However, this sanctity was not restricted only to the exiles of 597 as Ezekiel's oracles argued. Developing the implications of Seraiah's colophon both in the charter collection of Jer 1–25 plus the oracles against the nations and in the Euphrates submersion ceremony, YHWH's historical intention was facilitated through scribalism as much as through prophetic oracles. This was applied not simply to Jer 29 but to the totality of sources incorporated into Jer 26–45, expanded by exilic scribes into a discourse where scribal activity trumped geomythology as a definitive factor in communal legitimation. Put another way, sacred space in exile was not fixed to a ceremony at the Euphrates empowering the community settled there in 597, nor was it based in a fixed literary corpus such as the extant Jeremianic charter collection preserved by that group. Rather, sacred space and sacred communities were defined by the dynamic growth of a literary corpus.

In the end, it is ultimately the role of text during the period of the exile that delineated the boundaries of sacred space and communal identity. The first phase in this development revolved around the function of Serariah's colophon as perceived by Ezekiel's community and, one may argue, by Ezekiel himself. The submerged document and the Jeremianic charter collection set the spatial and ideological boundaries for the community; Ezekiel's activity both as a writer and performer of prophecy may be seen as a form of mediation between the two.[56] Ezekiel's own

---

55. Leuchter, "Personal Missives and National History: The Relationship between Jeremiah 29 and 36," in *Prophets, Prophecy, and Ancient Israelite Historiography*, ed. Mark J. Boda and Lissa M. Wray Beal (Winona Lake, IN: Eisenbrauns, 2013), 280–85.

56. Menahem Haran notes that Ezekiel's oracles function exclusively as literary texts rather than records of orally pronounced oracles ("Observations on Ezekiel as a Book Prophet," in *Seeking out the Wisdom of the Ancients: Essays Offered to Honor Michael V. Fox on the Occasion of His Sixty-Fifth Birthday*, ed. Ronald Troxel et al. (Winona Lake, IN: Eisenbrauns, 2005], 3–19). Given his priestly background, I would propose that these oracles originated at some point as oral discourses (the preferred mode of preexilic priestly instruction) but were textualized by Ezekiel and his sup-

education-enculturation with the Jeremianic charter collection stands behind some of the rhetorical commonalities often noted between both Ezekiel and Jeremiah's oracles.⁵⁷ Moreover, the elusive מקדש מעט of Ezek 11:16 might refer both to the temporal limitations of Mesopotamia as a sacred space *and* to the function of text as a surrogate sanctuary for a community in exile.⁵⁸ It is, after all, around texts (such as the Jeremianic charter collection) that communities were formed, and it was within such texts that the divine could be consulted;⁵⁹ this parallels the identical function of sanctuaries throughout Israel's landed preexilic history. And like the function of priests who mediated between the esoteric texts stored within such sanctuaries and the public (e.g., Lev 10:11), Ezekiel's prophetic activity constituted a bridge between such texts, the geo-mythology of the physical Mesopotamian space, and his in-group that resided there.

The introduction of Jer 26–45 into the earlier prophetic charter collection positioned various new examples of scribal colophons as parallels to that of Seraiah.⁶⁰ Narratives such as Jer 36 make clear that the text containing these new colophons, now added to the older charter corpus, were every bit as binding as the older material that Ezekiel and his community had venerated and were to be viewed as equal in potency to the earlier collection (Jer 36:32). At the same time, this newer text extended the sacred landscape beyond the Euphrates to the other locales represented by the

---

porters into documents that could function only within a textual universe—one that convention also restricted only to priests (van der Toorn, *Scribal Culture*, passim) and that is intimated by the textual-oral dynamic of Ezek 2:9–3:1. In that passage, the priest internalizes the written text, and its contents are therefore only accessible through the priests' oral proclamations.

57. On Ezekiel's use of Jeremiah's oracles, see Leuchter, *Polemics of Exile*, 158–59. On the effects of education-enculturation upon the rhetorical choices of the literati, see Carr, *Writing on the Tablet*, 148–49.

58. On מקדש מאט as a temporal designation, see Tooman, "Ezekiel's Radical Challenge," 507–8.

59. Jonathan Ben-Dov, "Writing as Oracle and Law: New Context for the Book-Find of King Josiah," *JBL* 127 (2008): 226–28, 232–36.

60. This, as I have argued elsewhere, resulted in the sequence of material that would become the MT version of the book. Contrary to the prevailing view, I see the construction of this sequence as predating the emergence of the LXX sequence, though I accept that the individual units preserved in the LXX sequence often reflect an older state of the sources common to both. See Leuchter, *Polemics of Exile*, 146–52.

colophons embedded therein. The book now containing Seraiah's colophon also established similar links to the village of Anatoth (32:6–15), the residential sectors in/around Jerusalem (36:1–8) and, indeed, everywhere that scribes carried on in their exegetical labors (45:5).

In the conceptual horizon of this expanded version of the book of Jeremiah, Ezekiel and his confederates were simply one group among many groups whose connections to YHWH remained intact. Despite the protest of Ezek 14:22–23, the post–587 BCE exiles were entitled to share in the covenantal identity of Ezekiel's in-group, at least insofar as the Jeremianic discourse was concerned. This explains why the later texts of Ezra-Nehemiah present the entire *golah* community as having adopted the separatist vision of Ezekiel on the one hand but also as relying upon Jeremiah's oracles of restoration on the other,[61] as well as how and why Babylon could remain a sanctified region even after the repatriates had returned to the homeland and rebuilt the temple.[62] Sacred space was no longer restricted or qualified by a geospecific mythology but was defined by the manner in which texts sanctified and defined communities along the Chebar, in Babylon proper, at Mizpah, and elsewhere.[63] In an ultimate irony, it was the destruction of Jerusalem as a sacred space that finally

---

61. On the connection between Ezra-Nehemiah and Ezekiel, see Rom-Shiloni, "Ezekiel as Voice," 44; Blenkinsopp, *Judaism*, 127–59. The importance of Jeremiah to Ezra-Nehemiah is evident not only from the overt reference to his prophecies in Ezra 1:1 but also from the various allusions to Jeremianic prophecy throughout the work. For recent studies that point to Jeremiah's influence on Ezra-Nehemiah, see Christiane Karrer-Grube, "Scrutinizing the Conceptual Unity of Ezra-Nehemiah," in *Unity and Disunity in Ezra-Nehemiah: Redaction, Rhetoric, and Reader*, ed. Mark J. Boda and Paul L. Redditt HBM 17 (Sheffield: Sheffield Phoenix, 2008), 150–59; Mark J. Boda, "In Order to Fulfill the Word of the Lord: The Impact of Haggai and Zechariah on Post-Exilic Historiography" (paper presented at the annual international meeting of the Society of Biblical Literature, St. Andrews, Scotland, July 8, 2013); Titus Reinmuth, *Der Bericht Nehemias: Zur literarischen Eigenart, traditionsgeschichtlichen Prägung und innerbiblischen Rezeption des Ich-Berichts Nehemias*, OBO 183 (Freiburg: Universitätsverlag, 2002), 290–96; David Shepherd, "Is the Governor Also among the Prophets? Parsing the Purpose of Jeremiah in the Memory of Nehemiah," in Boda and Beal, *Prophets, Prophecy*, 209–27.

62. Peter R. Bedford, "Diaspora: Homeland Relations in Ezra-Nehemiah," *VT* 52 (2002): 147–65.

63. The lone exception seems to be the community in Egypt, which receives strong condemnation in both Jeremiah (ch. 44) and Ezekiel (ch. 30). But even here there is room for interpretation, as both Jeremiah and Baruch are reported to be among the

brought to fruition YHWH's ancient promise to Jacob that his progeny would spread far and wide and be blessed wherever they settled (ופרצת ימה וקדמה צפנה ונגבה, Gen 28:14) through the texts transmitted and taught by the scribes among them.

Judahite remnant in Egypt, and it is inconceivable that either figure would be subject to the condemnation visited upon the prophet's adversaries in Jer 44.

EZEKIEL 15: A משל

John Ahn

1 And it happened that the word of Yahweh came to me saying:
2 Son of man, what is the vine stock in comparison to all the trees, the branch of the grapevine that is among the trees of the forest?
3 Isn't wood taken from it for service? Are they not used as a peg to hang each utensil?
4 Behold, it is put in the fire as fuel, both of its ends the fire has consumed, its middle is scorched. Can it be revived for service?
5 Behold, it has been rendered completely useless for service. Indeed, fire has consumed it, and it has been scorched and made utterly useless.
6 Therefore, thus says my Lord Yahweh, just as I set on fire to consume the branch of the vine among the tree of the forest, likewise I set the inhabitants of Jerusalem *on fire*.
7 I set my face against them like the fire that went out, the fire that consumed them so that you will know that I am Yahweh, the one who placed my face against them.
8 I set the land a waste because they acted in utter faithlessness, declares my Lord Yahweh.[1]

Forced migration studies on the exilic period have shed considerable new light on demarcating the threefold displacement of 597 BCE (Derivative Forced Migration and Development Induced Displaced Persons), 587 BCE (Purposive Forced Migration and Internally Displaced Persons), and 582 BCE events (Purposive Forced Migration and Internally Displaced Persons or Responsive Forced Migration and Refugees).[2] With the book

---

1. My translation of Ezek 15 MT.
2. John Ahn, *Exile as Forced Migrations: A Sociological, Literary, and Theological Study on the Displacement and Resettlement of the Southern Kingdom of Judah*, BZAW 417 (Berlin: de Gruyter, 2011); John J. Ahn and Jill Middlemas, eds., *By the Irrigation Canals of Babylon: Approaches to the Study of the Exile*, LHBOTS 526 (New York: T&T

of Ezekiel situated in exile or the forced migrations period, it is customary to begin the critical study of the book by acknowledging the two predominant schools of thought:[3] the historical-critical redactional approach of Walther Zimmerli and the holistic-canonical inner-biblical exegesis approach of Moshe Greenberg.[4] Scholars critically examining the book of Ezekiel fall somewhere between the Montagues and Capulets ("like warring camps")[5] or rigorously defend the poles. Those with sociocanonical interests, however, begin with the historical-critical (diachronic) and turn to the final form (synchronic) of the text. Interestingly, in more recent years, Ezekiel studies have been more about the Judahites left in Judah, the Babylonian captors, the exiled leaders, and the overall hegemony or postcolonial power or the lack thereof, among the forced migrants coupled with Ezekiel's influence on the Deuteronomist, the Holiness School, or the Priestly material.[6] Added to the debate is to what degree Ezekiel's call

---

Clark, 2012). Derivative Forced Migration (DFM) is a static migration that results from a new geopolitical and cartographical rearrangement (King Jehoiachin peacefully relinquishes Judah to the Babylonians establishing a newly expanded border for the Babylonians). Purposive Forced Migration (PFM) is usually profit driven, race related, religiously motivated, punishment, revenge, security for a dominating nation, among other purposes that instigate migration (Zekediah's rebellion or Gedaliah's murder or the need for additional Judean laborers in Babylon). In contrast to the first two, Responsive Forced Migration (RFM) is a voluntary migration due to tyranny, warfare, domestic, or even climate-related changes (Johanan, Jeremiah, and others who crossed a border and became refugees in Egypt and elsewhere).

Judeo-Babylonians: 597—DFM; 587—PFM; 582—PFM
Judeans (in the land): 597—DFM; 587—DFM; 582—DFM
Judeo-Egyptians (and possibly to the coastlands): 582—RFM

3. See Ralph W. Klein, "Ezekiel at the Dawn of the Twenty-First Century," in *The Book of Ezekiel: Theological and Anthropological Perspectives,* ed. Margaret S. Odell and John T. Strong, SymS 9 (Atlanta: Society of Biblical Literature, 2000), 1–14.

4. Walther Zimmerli, *Ezekiel: A Commentary on the Book of the Prophet Ezekiel,* vol. 1 trans. Ronald E. Clements, vol. 2 trans. James D. Martin, 2 vols., Hermeneia (Philadelphia: Fortress, 1979–1983); Moshe Greenberg, *Ezekiel 1–20,* AB 22 (Garden City, NY: Doubleday 1983); idem, *Ezekiel 21–37,* AB 22A (New York: Doubleday, 1997).

5. Steven Shawn Tuell, "Contemporary Studies of Ezekiel: A New Tide Rising," in *Ezekiel's Hierarchical World: Wrestling with a Tiered Reality,* ed. Stephen L. Cook and Corrine L. Patton, SymS 31 (Atlanta: Society of Biblical Literature, 2004), 241.

6. Risa Levitt Kohn, *A New Heart and a New Soul: Ezekiel, the Exile and Torah,* JSOTSup 358 (Sheffield: Sheffield Academic, 2002); Casey A. Strine, *Sworn Enemies: The Divine Oath, the Book of Ezekiel, and the Polemic of Exile,* BZAW 436 (Berlin: de Gruyter, 2013).

for a pure community is connected with Ezra-Nehemiah.⁷ The ideological bias or exclusivity found in Ezra-Nehemiah is suggested to be a continuation of Ezekiel's in-group against the out-group, that is, "us" against "them," in statements or phrases embedded in those "residing in Jerusalem" (ישבי ירושלים) or "on the soil of Israel" (על אדמת ישראל) against the "children [or sons] of your people" (בני עמך).⁸ The 597 displacement is at times called Jehoiachin's exile, but such a description is much too narrow because the first displacement involved not only the monarchy, but various social groups and classes that truly constituted the upper or elite and middle classes of skilled smiths, artisans, the priests, and the military. A more thorough discussion will follow in the end.

Before I address the issues in Ezek 15—that is, the literary genre of a משל, the placement of the text within the larger framework of Ezek 15–19, including the meaning of the vine imagery, and a brief reference on the dating of the chapter—a short self-reflexivity of Ezekiel may be a helpful starting point. Ezekiel is said to be a prophet,⁹ a priest and prophet,¹⁰ a writer or author,¹¹ a pastor (or rabbi) and lawgiver,¹² an angry yet yearning artistic poet,¹³ or simply a "displaced and resettled" person.

Ezekiel was likely a first or possibly a 1.5 generation¹⁴ Judeo-Babylonian who experienced Derivative Forced Migration (DFM)—a static form of migration after a nation's borders are redrawn due to war—and classified as a "Development Induced Displaced Person" (DIDP) resulting from Development Induced Displacement, that is, for the economic benefit of the host nation. It would not be improbable to assume that Ezekiel lived and worked as a corvée on the irrigation canals of Babylon with his fellow expatriates. Ezekiel seems to have been a member of an inner

---

7. Dalit Rom-Shiloni, *Exclusive Inclusivity: Identity Conflicts between the Exiles and the People Who Remained (6th–5th Centuries BCE)*, LHBOTS 543 (New York: Bloomsbury T&T Clark, 2013).

8. Ibid., 26, 140–50.

9. Gustave Hölscher, *Die Profeten: Untersuchungen zur Religionsgeschichte Israels* (Leipzig: Hinrichs, 1914), 298–315, esp. 307.

10. Walther Eichrodt, *Ezekiel: A Commentary*, trans. Cosslett Quin, OTL (Philadelphia: Westminster, 1970), e.g., 1, 22.

11. Johannes Herrmann, *Ezechielstudien*, BZAW 2 (Leipzig: Hinrichs, 1908), 7.

12. Rudolf Smend, *Der Prophet Ezechiel*, 2nd ed. (Leipzig: Hirzel, 1880).

13. Lawrence Boadt, "The Poetry of Prophetic Persuasion: Preserving the Prophet's Persona," *CBQ* 59 (1997): 1–21.

14. Ahn, *Exile as Forced Migrations*, 107–58.

circle of leaders who spoke about keeping Judah's national identity alive in Babylon. The Judeans with their collective experiences as the first wave of forced migrants—the privileged or elite classes of peoples, including the king, his royal family, the military, and the middle class of skilled metal and artisan workers that constituted the "think and action tank" in government, economic, education, and religious sectors—were displaced and resettled as an ethnic enclave in Babylon. Yet Ezekiel appears to have had a strong interest in events back at home in Judah, without compromising survival instincts and godly and spiritual direction for those in Babylon.

The literary imagery of the vine creates an imbroglio in the prophets (Ezek 15; 17:7; 18: 2; 19:10; cf. Isa 1:8; 3:14; 5:1, 3, 4, 5, 7, 10; 27:2; Jer 12:10; ch. 29). In the books of Isaiah and Jeremiah, the vine typically represents a positive image that turns into a wild branch (Isa 5) or a positive economic indicator "to plant" vineyards (Jer 29). In Ezek 15-19, however, the image of the vine lacks optimism or hope. A dramatic reversal by relegating the previous generation's view on sin and retribution being passed down from generation to generation (Jer 31:29; Ezek 18:2) is not at all a positive usage of the grape imagery. The passage is generally regarded as the sour or soured grape image. Although the view clearly reverses an outdated ideology that insinuates judgment passed down to the third or fourth generation[15]—an important social marker of exactly how many generations resided in Babylon—the imagery in Ezek 15 functions as a graphic poetic introduction to the unit found in Ezek 17-19.

Ezekiel 15 succinctly describes an image of a vine branch burned on both ends and the middle. This seemingly simple yet captivating depiction has held the imagination of many commentators. Many fundamentally begin by asking, Why specifically mention that the ends and the middle are all burned? Why go to lengths to state that because it is burned, it can never be made into anything useful (v. 5)? The apparent ending, "it is put into the fire for fuel," indicates an irreversible judgment of Judah (or Israel and Judah), but what is the implied message or lesson to be learned for the Judeo-Babylonians? Was this a definitive point that the thought of an immediate return to Judah, in advocating or advancing the words Shemaiah or Hananiah in Babylon was to be completely and fully uprooted, thereby indirectly endorsing Jeremiah's pro-*golah* posi-

---

15. Brevard Childs, *Biblical Theology of the Old and New Testaments* (Minneapolis: Fortress, 1992), 161–65.

tion? And although this charred image is more or less a first-generation image, by the time of the second or third generation, through inner-biblical exegesis or intertextuality, the motif rises to new heights as Second Isaiah recasts the motif in his preaching against the felling of a tree—a cypress, oak, or pine, to be used partly as fuel for preparing meals, or to warm oneself, and the mockery of fashioning it as a god and even outrageously worshiping it (Isa 44:14–17; cf. Ezek 15:2–5). Thus W. A. Irwin was insightful in identifying and considering Ezek 15 as the *Mitte* of the book of Ezekiel.[16]

The משל in Ezek 15 is traditionally divided into three parts. Verse 1 has been assigned as the messenger formula, verses 2–5 (original) as the message itself in a parable *Gattung*, and verses 6–8 (*formelhaft*) as the (later?) added explanation. In short, this succinct chapter has been seen as the microstructure of the entire book with an original core and its added interpolations by an ensuing generation's editor striving to preserve and maintain received traditions. But in order to fully appreciate and understand the imagery at large, Ezek 12 provides a helpful background.

In chapter 12, Ezekiel is commanded by God to literally enact going into exile or forced migration. So during the day Ezekiel prepares his "exilic pack" or "immigration bag" with the basic necessities of a skin (for holding flour or water), a mat (for sleeping on the cold desert ground), and a bowl (for eating and drinking)[17] before those who likely experienced the identical cultural trauma. Ezekiel prepares his own "migration bag" in the presence of the Judeo-Babylonians who lived that terrible moment a decade ago. Then in the evening he sets out to dig through the wall (12:3–6), enacting and actualizing the entire displacement and resettlement process from Judah to Babylon.

In the following section (vv. 8–9), there appears to have been much confusion regarding the meaning of the sign-act: For whom was the message intended and when was this going to transpire? Was this a reminder for the Judeo-Babylonians how they arrived in Babylon? Or was Ezekiel displaying another displacement from Babylon to another foreign nation or settlement? Or was this sign-act a preparation of some sort for the Judeo-Babylonians to return immediately, back to Judah or Jerusalem, as Hananiah and Shemaiah had been predicting (Jer 27–29)?

---

16. W. A. Irwin, *The Problem of Ezekiel: An Inductive Study* (Chicago: University of Chicago Press, 1943), 33–41.

17. Greenberg, *Ezekiel 1–20*, 209.

In Ezek 12:10 the sign-act is made clear. The principal "burden" still remains in Judah. Zedekiah will be captured while attempting to escape by burrowing through the wall at night. Ezekiel's sign-act precisely refers to the second displacement in 587. Again, in 12:14–16 Ezekiel says the prince, his auxiliaries, and his divisions will be scattered in all directions. However, a small number of the people will survive the sword, famine, and plague and be scattered to various countries (v. 15) so that they could recount and tell the story of shame, doom, and punishment of the 587 BCE aftermath. As for the remnant, they will be judged, living in fear and anxiety as the land becomes desolate and uninhabitable.

As the chapter stands, the second displacement of 587 is recounted before the first wave of the 597 audience. That there is still strong interest in the everyday routines and rituals that took place in Jerusalem was an important part of the first-generation Judeo-Babylonian way of life. As the community residing in Babylon is forewarned that Jerusalem will be completely destroyed and another wave of forced migrants will be displaced to Babylon, the interpolation in verse 12c makes very clear that Zedekiah's fate of being blinded after arriving in Babylon shows familiarity with displacement of the 587 community. Ezekiel 12 depicts a post-587 setting, but interestingly that which transpired in 582 is not evident. So it is with this background that we now turn to Ezek 15.

As mentioned above, Ezek 15 marks the beginning of a section of משל (see 2 Sam 12; 1 Kgs 4:33; Amos 5:19; Isa 28:26) or חידה (utterance with double meaning or "mocking words" in allegory; see Ezek 15–19).[18] Structurally, the text is parallel to Ezek 12, beginning with verse 1 as the introduction. The first half of the משל (vv. 2–5) relays the ill fate of the vine stock. The vine stock is burned, scorched, devoured by fire. The second half in verses 6–8, with the "conversation director" לכן (contrary to the indicator of consequence),[19] explains the image and its judgment. But before we proceed any further, let us briefly rehearse the vine vignettes depicted in the Hebrew Bible.

Recall in Num 13:23, when the Israelite spies went into the land of Canaan, the fruit from the vine was brought back by two persons. In Judg 9:12, the parable of the trees that went out to anoint a king over them,

---

18. William Brownlee, *Ezekiel 1–19*, WBC 28 (Waco, TX: Word, 1986), 212; Zimmerli, *Ezekiel 1*, 360.

19. Daniel Block, *The Book of Ezekiel: Chapters 1–24*, NICOT (Grand Rapids: Eerdmans, 1997), 458.

the vine said no because its fruit brought cheer to gods and mortals. In Gen 49 the vine represents Judah's endowment and lineage as royalty, with messianic representation. In Isa 5 the image of the vineyard is that of Judah and Jerusalem. The hope was for the cultivation of good grapes, but wild grapes were produced. Likewise, this metaphor is also employed by Jer 2:21—although Yahweh planted "a choice vine," it became wild—referring to the socioeconomic and religious infidelity of the southern kingdom of Judah.

The same point can be drawn out in both the major and minor prophetic literature, that the vine imagery usually depicts the kingdom of Judah that became wild, sour, or now burned. The same attestations is upheld by the traditions in the Book of the Twelve (Minor Prophets): Hosea (10:1; 14:7), Joel (1:11; 12; 2:22), Jonah (4:6), Micah (4:4), Haggai (2:19), and Zechariah (3:10; 8:12)—all powerfully reutilizing this imagery. Thus rightfully this motif even resurfaces in the intertestamental texts and the Dead Sea Scrolls into the New Testament Johannine literature, to depict Jesus' royalty or association with his messiahship—at the outset in the Gospel of John 2, where the water is turned into wine, one of the *egō eimi* passages, "I am the true vine" (John 15); and interestingly, in the end, on the cross, the "King of the Jews" is given soured wine (as the evangelist understood the soured royal imagery) or anesthetics for capital punishment.[20]

In general, vines are pruned biannually, in late winter and early summer.[21] And those pruned vine stocks that were cut down were thrown into the fire as daily fuel (something that was probably quite familiar to those living in Babylon). For us then, in the book of Ezekiel, this vine imagery (also in conjunction with other images) appears a total of three times, all clustered around chapters 15–19. This appears to be a quite deliberate and controlled means of limiting the usage of this metaphor to correspond to the three occurrences all set in the block of material in chapter 17, the fable of the eagle and vine: in chapter 18, the popular proverb; in chapter 19, Judah's mother—the entire Davidic dynasty is metaphorically depicted as the vineyard; and lastly, in chapter 15, the three scorched markings—judgment on Judah/Jerusalem[22] or Israel and Judah.

---

20. See the discussion of "vine" by Irene and Walter Jacob, "Flora," *ABD* 2:810.

21. Greenberg, *Ezekiel 1–20*, 266; Raymond Brown, *The Gospel according to John (XIII–XXI)*, AB 29A (Garden City, NY: Doubleday, 1970), 658–84.

22. For an overview on these imageries, see Block, *Ezekiel*, 522–54.

Referring to the vine stock burned on both ends and the middle, G. A. Cooke observed that the first burning referred to the exile of 597 BCE and the second burning to that of 587 BCE. However, he never completed his thought on what the third burning represented.[23] Walther Eichrodt says that the two ends point to Sargon's destruction of the Northern Kingdom and Nebuchadnezzar's carrying of Judah into Babylon. This then leaves the charred middle as the "still existing rump state with its capital, Jerusalem."[24] However, more recent scholarship has shown that this is most unlikely since there probably was a replacement temple in Mizpah with the center of economic commerce also having been moved to this area for export of balm, olive oil, and wine.[25]

Moshe Greenberg desperately tries to steer his readers away from the historicity embedded in the allegory, but ultimately the text prevents him from doing so. Greenberg associates the primary burning as Jehoiachin and Jerusalem with an impending and complete destruction of Jerusalem to follow.[26] But William Brownlee's explanation of this image is more narrowly framed around Zedekiah's reign (2 Kgs 15:1-4) in 587 BCE. The second or middle is then understood as that of the people falling in Jerusalem, and the third or the end represents all those who fled to foreign nations (Ezek 33:23-29) as God pursues them in judgment through the Chaldeans (Jer 43:8-44:30; Ezek 5:12; chs. 25-32). What is unclear, however, is where Gedaliah, who was in residence at Mizpah after the destruction of Jerusalem in 587 BCE (2 Kgs 25:22-26; Jer 40:7-43:7; Ezek 33:23-29), fits into this picture. But what is particularly obtuse in Brownlee's interpretation is that the third burning is a future event of those rebellious nations to whom Judean refugees flee (Jer 43:8-44:30; Ezek 25-30), "for those who escape by the sword at Jerusalem will be pursued by it in the diaspora" (Ezek 5:12).[27] This is quite unlikely and syntactically difficult to assert since the predicative element (נתן) in the phrase הנה לאש נתן לאכלה את שני קצותיו (12:4) is aspectually a completed action (perfect).

---

23. G. A. Cooke, *A Critical and Exegetical Commentary on the Book of Ezekiel*, ICC (New York: Scribner's Sons, 1937), 158.

24. Eichrodt, *Ezekiel*, 194.

25. J. N. Graham, "'Vinedressers and Plowmen': 2 Kings 25:12 and Jeremiah 52:16," *BA* 47 (1984): 55-58.

26. Greenberg, *Ezekiel 1-20*, 265-69.

27. Brownlee, *Ezekiel 1-19*, 213-14.

Zimmerli saw the first burning as the catastrophe under Jehoiachin (597 BCE). He completely dismissed and rejected the interpretation offered by Heinisch and Schumpp, who suggested that the first burning is that of Israel in 721 BCE and the other end being Judah in 587 BCE, leaving the charred group of the 597 in the middle (which became Eichrodt's position). In my view, Karin Schöpflin and others (R. E. Clements, Keith W. Carley) who continue to maintain this dual view of the Northern and Southern Kingdoms[28] being destroyed is an alternative view, though by and large the vine imageries in Ezekiel denote Judah and Jerusalem.[29]

Zimmerli's observations on this chapter are crisp and meticulous. He contends that the scorched vine stock imagery to Judah or, more specifically, to Jerusalem and its leaders. And although he saw the first burning as the catastrophe under Jehoiachin, the middle section being the displaced elites of Jerusalem (597 BCE), and the other end being the conflagration of 587 BCE,[30] Zimmerli's initial observation was more or less on the right path, going back to Cooke's original position—that the first burning is to be equated to that of the 597 BCE aftermath under Jehoiachin, who peacefully relinquished the throne for the sake of saving his people. The opposite end, then, is to be identified with the final destruction of Jerusalem during the idealistically Deuteronomic reign of Gedaliah until his assassination in 582 BCE, leaving the middle to 587 BCE. Indeed, from a priestly tradition, the *Mitte* is the temple, and even its destruction remains at the center.

What is significant about Ezek 15, along with 2 Kgs 24; Jer 43; 52; and Dan 6:10 is the presence of all three major conflagrations of Jerusalem. These chapters preserve a rare shadow of the third destruction and displacement of Jerusalem and its people. That Daniel prays three times a day toward Jerusalem suggests that he was remembering the threefold destruction of Jerusalem in 597, 587, and 582. However, Ps 137 attests to only the first and second displacements in 597 (vv. 1–6) and 587 (vv. 7–9), omitting the lament of the 582 BCE group, which suggests that the psalm was composed prior to the arrival of the third wave.[31] What is clear in

---

28. Karin Schöpflin, "The Composition of Metaphorical Oracles within the Book of Ezekiel," *VT* 55 (2005): 102.

29. For a detailed comprehensive treatment, see James A. Durlesser, *The Metaphorical Narratives in the Book of Ezekiel* (Lewiston, NY: Mellen, 2006), 39–81; Leslie Allen, *Ezekiel 1–19*, WBC 28 (Dallas: Word, 1994), 220; Greenberg, *Ezekiel 1–20*, 268.

30. Zimmerli, *Ezekiel 1*, 320.

31. John Ahn, "Psalm 137: Complex Communal Laments," *JBL* 127 (2008): 267–89.

Ezek 15 is that the *Sitz im Leben* encompasses the full range of the forced migrations of the sixth century BCE, leaving the 582 BCE event and displaced group as the final reference point. The editor of this unit in Ezekiel made sure that all three displacements were recorded and preserved in the national memory. Interestingly, the significance of this date according to Martin Noth's reconstruction based on Josephus's *Antiquities* 10.180–185 is that of Moab and Ammon (Edom unclear) losing their sovereignty (five years after the destruction of Jerusalem).[32]

At this juncture, what we need to keep in mind is the overall context and placement of Ezek 15, namely, within the short (graphic) cycle of Ezek 15–19. We read and see the vine imagery not only in Ezek 15, but also as previously mentioned in Ezek 17, 18, and 19. The allegory in Ezek 17 presupposes the relinquishing of the Davidic throne and kingdom by Jehoiachin in 597 BCE. Zedekiah's defection and wishful hope of dethroning the Babylonians (587) with assistance from Psammetichus II (594–588) is intended. The great eagles represent, respectively, Nebuchadnezzar and Psammetichus II, with the top cedar being the house of David (Jer 22:23). The vine branch depicts the entire kingdom of Judah. Zimmerli has noted, "Thus the literary placing of Ezek 17 between the dates of 8:1 and 20:1 would then be roughly the correct time, even if no compelling arguments can be brought in demonstration of it. Erbt's dating in the Persian era has rightly found no following."[33] The second half of Zimmerli's point may be substantiated, but not his dating between 8:1 (August/Sept 592) and 20:1 (July/August 591). These dates may be plausible, but they leave out Zedekiah's rebellion and the demise of 587. It is safer to keep the second date within the proximity of 29:1 or 29:17 (January 587 or March/April 571). But the point is that in Ezek 17 we have references to both the 597 and 587 destructions of Jerusalem in allegory.

Ezekiel 19 also references Zedekiah. But what is important in this chapter is verse 4, "the nations sounded an alarm against him ... they brought him with hooks to the land of Egypt." These words interestingly echo Jer 42–43, where the band that murdered Gedaliah flee to Egypt, Tahpanhes—"the men, the women, the children, the princesses, and everyone whom Nebuzaradan the captain of the guard had left with Gedaliah son of Ahikam son of Shaphan; also the prophet Jeremiah and

---

32. Martin Noth, *The History of Israel*, trans. Stanley Godman (New York: Harper & Row, 1960), 292.

33. Zimmerli, *Ezekiel 1*, 361.

Baruch son of Neriah. And they came into the land of Egypt" (43:6–7). This Jeremiah text speaks of the 582 BCE aftermath. And what we observe in Ezek 19, like Ezek 17, is an overlap of the two destructions, but this time around it is the latter two burnings in 587 and 582.

The placement and function of Ezek 15 at the outset of this historical and literary cycle not only depicts the threefold scorching of Jerusalem but also the foreshadowing and introductory *mashal* to the *meshalim*. Here lies a masterful composition. The three ensuing texts independently enumerate and symbolically add additional images to the destructions as represented by Ezek 17, 18, and 19. Read collectively, the section stands out as an artistic series.[34] And although we cannot precisely date Ezek 15, we can be reasonably certain that it must be post–582 BCE. Just like Ezek 12's post–587 conclusion, we also have a chapter with its final thoughts showing a literarily parallel ending. Ezekiel 15's scorched vine imagery (along with Ezek 17 and 19) depicts the 597 (DFM), 587 (PFM), and 582 (PFM) events.

Scholars working to recover the community or communities that shaped and helped edit the book of Ezekiel have indeed taken into account the temporal, spatial, and geographical markers found in this rich prophetic text.[35] As early as 1979, Brevard Childs observed that the final canonical shape of the book had complex preexilic, exilic, and postexilic oracles or oracular judgments calling for obedience. With issues of purity or holiness, idolatry or syncretistic worship in the land of Judah, the community with God in displacement, impending destruction of Jerusalem, restoration, and the temple, even a new vision of a new temple, these central themes have received thorough treatments in various scholarships. With more recent work focusing on issues of leadership oscillating between Judeo-Babylonians and those who remained in the land, the most promising direction for future investigation appears to be cultural or social trauma studies. "The interdisciplinary field of trauma and disaster studies has largely confirmed the profound effects of forced migration and captivity on individuals and communities."[36] Future work on Ezekiel

---

34. Ezek 15 as 597/587/582; Ezek 17 as 597/587; Ezek 18 as 587; Ezek 19 as 587/582.

35. Thomas Renz, *The Rhetorical Function of the Book of Ezekiel*, VTSup 76 (Boston: Brill, 1999), 1–26.

36. Louis Stulman and Hyun Chul Paul Kim, *You Are My People: An Introduction to Prophetic Literature* (Nashville: Abingdon, 2010), 149.

ought to focus on forced migrations, cultural or social trauma, and disaster and survival literature.[37] In support and agreement, an additional area of study is needed, that is, the power of generational demarcation and consciousness that foster acculturation and assimilation.

The importance of the first wave of forced migrants (597), the first generation of leaders that made life possible for all subsequent generations, needs to be recognized. An intriguing request by the first generation of elders in Ezek 14 and 20 presents a unique depiction of everyday life. It is difficult to assess fully if this particular group of elders is the same group that visited Ezekiel's house in chapter 8. Nevertheless, the elders in Ezek 14 and 20 are important in-group of first-generation leaders from 597. They may have set the social and theopolitical agenda for subsequent forced migrants who would arrive ten and fifteen years later, inasmuch as for the second-, third-, and even fourth-generation Judeo-Babylonians confronting issues of assimilation or acculturation, socioeconomic upward movement through their professional guild-related skills clashed with received traditions that Ezekiel represents. It appears as if these elders represent a forward-thinking group that sought more than just survival.

Ezekiel 14 begins with Ezekiel's response that there is idolatry in the hearts of the elders, questioning their rational for consulting the Lord (14:1–5). Commentators employing Ezek 20 to complement Ezek 14, and vice versa, have offered several possible interpretations of the phrase "let us be like the nations, as the families of the lands, worshiping wood and stone" (20:32), as the volition of these elders. Ezekiel's rejection of the elders' request is broadly construed with the overall rejection of idolatry, which was still prevalent in the homeland, stressing the presence of foreigners and their idolatry in Judah (14:7) with a full rehearsal of the exodus or wilderness traditions that initially brought about God's injunction against idols in Egypt and elsewhere (Ezek 20).

Ezekiel 14:6–10 particularly speaks against a significant group causing abomination in the land. A group of foreigners were practicing idolatry with prophetic endorsement (14:8). The identity of this group has been generally understood as the 587 community, but in my view it may also

---

37. Margaret S. Odell, *Ezekiel*, SHBC (Macon, GA: Symth & Helwys, 2005), 10; David G. Garber Jr., "Traumatizing Ezekiel, the Exilic Prophet," in *From Genesis to Apocalyptic Vision*, vol. 2 of *Psychology and the Bible: A New Way to Read the Scriptures*, ed. J. Harold Ellens and Wayne G. Rollins, Praeger Perspectives: Psychology, Religion, and Spirituality (Westport, CT: Praeger, 2004), 215–35.

represent the 582 group, since foreigners who have joined the Lord were present. And because Ezek 12 and 13 speak to the destruction of Jerusalem in 587, with false prophets condemned in Ezek 13, the likelihood of Ezek 14 being a reference to both 587 and 582 remains high. The 582 group bears the iniquity for the total destruction of the land. Even if Noah, Daniel, and Job petitioned for the land, only they would be saved—not even their children or the remnant and clearly not the land (14:16). At this point, the elders are told that a wave of forced migrants will arrive with their sons and daughters. They are told not to feel compelled to assist them because of their evil deeds. When they fully realize why God brought forth such judgment on the people, ironically, the elders will discover comfort (14:22) and learn to side with God.

When examining Ezek 14 and 20, scholars generally reference Ezekiel passages that speak against idolatry (Ezek 6), in addition to Deut 4:27–28; 28:36, 64; 29:16; 2 Kgs 19:18; Isa 37:19; and Jer 2:27; 39:1–18,[38] to magnify the danger and opposition to any form of syncretistic worship. The sign-act and oracle in Ezek 20:45–49 (21:1–5 MT), which begins by asking Ezekiel to turn to the Negev or the south, to proclaim fire on every green tree that will be consumed and continue to burn into the north—possibly routes or sources of wood needed for idol makers—closes with the elders' response to Ezekiel. They mock and reduce Ezekiel's prophecy to a ממשל משלים (20:45–49 [21:1–5 MT]). An important context for unpacking Ezek 14 and 20 is Isa 44.

Isaiah 44:9–20 appears to be a blueprint for fashioning gods out of metal and wood. The pericope seems to reflect the everyday work of the second- or third-generation Judeo-Babylonian community's engagement as iron- or silversmiths who hammer and forge (Ezek 22:20–22) or carpenters or carvers who start by drafting with a stylus and then proceed to cut down a cedar, holm, or oak to carve an image. After the idols are fashioned, the prophet especially criticizes the idol makers for prostrating or bowing down and offering prayers for deliverance to them (Isa 44:15, 17). In short, these idol makers cannot be foreigners or even Babylonians but second- and subsequent generation Judeo-Babylonians in the idol-making business. The injunction is set against this particular segment of the Judeo-Babylonian community. The rhetoric is that there is only one true God.

---

38. Dalit Rom-Shiloni, "Facing Destruction and Exile: Inner-biblical Exegesis in Jeremiah and Ezekiel," *ZAW* 117 (2005): 189–205.

Those in the skilled profession are thoughtless and should be put to shame. Although less striking in tone in comparison to Ezekiel's damnation-by-fire speech, Second Isaiah's point appears to be that even if he cannot force this group to stop from such profitable line of work, the message seeks to bring awareness or consciousness of work that is in opposition to Yahwistic faith.[39]

The engraver or carpenter is especially singled out. He who begins by planting the cedar and waiting for the rain to nourish it uses the same felled tree as fuel for kindling a fire to stay warm, to fashion a god, and to cook (44:16). As a satire or sarcasm, the polemic is that there is no discernment on the part of the second- and subsequent generation Judeo-Babylonian idol makers. That this particular segment of the community do not seemed to be concerned or even bothered by such judgment is precisely the point. Having eyes and refusing to see and ears and refusing to hear may have been the ideology to survive against internal religious threats. Ezekiel 22, 37, and 44 describe Levites who have backslid by worshiping idols. The community seems to be split on whether to restore them to their former post or to completely reject them and prevent them from serving again.

Isaiah 44:9–20 may be a continued series or cycle that started in the first generation of elders in Ezek 14 and 20. The local predicament before the elders and future generations may have been that they were simply a skilled group of Judeo-Babylonian smiths and carvers fashioning idols in Babylon for profit—conspicuous consumption. The ritual to bow down to the idols to manifest that the divinity has entered or the deity has been freed to take shape in the ironwork, stone, or tree is precisely the uncompromising point and polemic for Ezekiel and Second Isaiah. A contrasting narrative not to bow down to an idol or image even in spite of innuendos of a consuming fire is reflected in the court narratives of Daniel. From a social class–related reading, the elders in Ezek 14 and 20 are the voices of an important in-group, possibly representing the entire guild of Judeo-Babylonian artisans who may have been collectively saying that although they are idol makers and even bow down and to worship the idols fashioned by their own hands, in order to fully integrate and especially advance, in their

---

39. In Diaspora settings, socioreligious challenges tend to repeat. For example, notice the parallel account of Demetrius and the guild of idol makers in Ephesus being confronted by Paul that erupted into a riot that eventually forced Paul to leave Ephesus (Acts 19).

hearts, they were nevertheless centrally Yahwistic—even when the rest of the community perceives otherwise. And so their words, "Let us be like the nations, like the tribes of the countries, and worship wood and stone" (20:32), are simply asking for some provisional acceptance or approval that they are simply doing their job. And to this request, Ezekiel says no. There is no room for such acculturation or assimilation in Ezekiel's orthodox system. Indeed, Ezekiel's extended rehearsal of salvation history closes with a reference that even if Noah, Daniel, and Job petitioned, the Lord God would not be inclined to accept (Ezek 14:20). The sign-act to speak to the south—whose route would eventually traverse to the north, a possible source of delivery for raw material (forest land), where every green tree grows—would be set ablaze (20:47).

Beyond the basic observation that Ezek 15 shares lexemes, themes, and illustrative depictions with Ezek 14, 20, and Isa 44:16–20, what makes Ezek 15 unique is the inclusion of the 582 community. From a priestly point of view, that is, religious orthodoxy, social status, and ethnic purity, the arrival of the 587 group would be a signal for some caution. With the arrival of the 582 group, even those who may have held a neutral view on the 587 group would have turned against the 582 group. In other words, if there were any mixed feelings about accepting the 587 group, the silence on the 582 group appears to be sign of rejection. Without going into details (I have attempted to reconstruct the 582 community elsewhere),[40] those who were in power may have refused to acknowledge this final group because of their ethnicity. In short, if Gedaliah was indeed pro-Deuteronomic, between 587 and 582, he would have had a pro-immigration or integration of foreigners in his policies to help sustain and even revive a fractured and scattered remnant community (Jer 40:9–11). With the information that there was some economic recovery in Mizpah by harvesting an abundance of summer fruit (possibly for export to Babylon; Jer 40:13), one cannot rule out the possibility of an integration policy of Judeans mixing with people from Ammon, Edom, Moab, and other satellite nations—the people of the land—with the very poor remnant of Judeans. It is this integrated and inclusive Judean and non-Judean work-force that constituted the 582 community. Intermarriage would not have been prohibited, though not fully endorsed or promoted. What we have in Ezek 15 may be an attempt to show that in spite of the rejection of the 582 group, through a משל, this particular segment of the

---

40. Ahn, *Exile as Forced Migrations*, 98–101.

community of mixed Judeans with foreigners are remembered by the purists of 597 or possibly by the urging of the 587 group. Interestingly, the children or the community descending from this 582 group resurface in Third Isaiah, as third- or fourth-generation inclusive Judeo-Babylonians. They say: "Do not let the foreigner joined to the Lord say, 'The Lord will surely separate me from his people'" (Isa 56:3). A parallel caricature of the 582 group may be seen in Jer 40–44.[41]

Ezekiel 15:1–4 depicts collectively the 597, 587, and 582 communities as the royal vine or simply and exclusively the 597 community that has been reduced to almost nothing, like a peg on which hangs a vessel. Verses 5–6 then may represent the voices of the 587 community, and verses 7–8 reflect the 582 community. In verses 1–4, drawing attention to the entire charred image, the middle is accented, highlighting the destruction of the temple, the conflagration, the holocaust, and loss of children (Ps 137:7–9). The syntax in Ezek 15:4 is somewhat rough: הנה לאש נתן לאכלה את שני קצותיו אכלה האש ותוכו נחר היצלח למלאכה. The text actually reads smoother if we simply read הנה לאש נתן לאכלה את שני קצותיו ותוכו, omitting אכלה האש. The intrusion of אכלה האש draws the reader's attention to a known fact that in 587 fire burned the house of the Lord, the king's house, and all the houses of Jerusalem, every residence or home (Jer 52:13). Home, nation, and all the markers of identity for the 597 community, those who had hoped that they could one day return, was now gone, destroyed by fire.

The Septuagint's rendering of verse 4 offers a different perspective. Foremost, the fire is set as a catharsis (κάθαρσιν), which is coupled with a reference to a year (ἐνιαυτὸν) or a full seasonal cycle for pruning. In addition, there is a deliberate omission of the accusative phrase, the "two ends and its middle." The verse moves quickly to the "end" (τέλος), stressing that the end is burned. The eclipse of both the 597 and 587 groups, quickly advancing to impress on the 582 group, is surprising. This then turns the rhetorical question at the end of verse 4 into something completely different than originally intended in the Masoretic Text. Since the end is completely burned, it cannot possibly be serviceable or made economically profitable (ἐργασίαν) again. The 582 community cannot and will not be restored. There is no hope in verse 4 of the Septuagint's rendering,

---

41. Mark Leuchter, *Polemics of Exile in Jeremiah 26–45* (Cambridge: Cambridge University Press, 2008).

whereas in the Masoretic Text the phrase למלאכה היצלח attempts to offer a small glimmer of restoration.

Verse 5 of the Masoretic Text and Septuagint are worth comparing in full:

הִנֵּה בִּהְיוֹתוֹ תָמִים לֹא יֵעָשֶׂה לִמְלָאכָה אַף כִּי־אֵשׁ אֲכָלַתְהוּ וַיֵּחָר וְנַעֲשָׂה עוֹד לִמְלָאכָה:

οὐδὲ ἔτι αὐτοῦ ὄντος ὁλοκλήρου οὐκ ἔσται εἰς ἐργασίαν. μὴ ὅτι ἐὰν καὶ πῦρ αὐτὸ ἀναλώσῃ εἰς τέλος, εἰ ἔσται ἔτι εἰς ἐργασίαν.

In the Masoretic Text, the generic remark on the unprofitability of the whole vine branch becomes intensified, since Judah's center is scorched, that is, the temple in 587. Judah is now truly useless and unfit for any kind of service since its only remaining iconic symbol for those in the Diaspora was the temple. With the temple reduced to nothing by flames, it is truly charred. The passive-reflexive *niphal* verbs—the fire has devoured it (Jerusalem), has scorched it, and made it utterly useless—answer the rhetorical question posed in verse 4 as affirming that, indeed, it can never be used for anything. The Septuagint's rendering has eliminated all traces of any hope for restoration and continues to hammer down the end, the 582 group, calling them completely useless and unprofitable, ironically placing the blame of Jerusalem's burning on them.

In verse 6 of the Masoretic Text, לכן draws the משל to an explanation that the fire and the destruction, including all the inhabitants of Jerusalem, took place by Yahweh's authority. The destroyer of Zion is not Nebuchadnezzar, Nebuzaradan, or the Babylonians but the Lord God. The Septuagint (aorist imperative) also follows the Masoretic Text in having Ezekiel frame the Lord's speech in the first person. Rightfully, in both the Masoretic Text and Septuagint, verse 6 echoes the opening image established in verse 1. The explanations are contextually driven, against the leadership and inhabitants of Jerusalem in 587 in the Masoretic Text and Gedaliah and the inhabitants of Jerusalem of 582 in the Septuagint.

Verses 7 and 8 are clearly additions in the Masoretic Text. The faint voice of the 582 community is heard. But the inclusion of this final group does not have a favorable ending. The strongest language of Yahweh's judgment, that the Lord's face or presence is set against "them," takes destruction and consumption by fire to a whole new level. The finale is the complete abandonment of the land, which resulted because of the transgressions of the 582 group. Perhaps it may have been best if the 582 community was not represented in the text. I think this is the point that the Ezekiel school of thought is making. The volition of wanting to be included results in the overall responsibility and judgment. This is the only group that receives the words, "they acted faithlessly."

The translators of the Septuagint recognized that verses 7–8 were additions. Perhaps the reason for blaming the 582 community for the defilement of the land, as seen in verses 4 and 5, allows for a creative ending in verses 7 and 8. To mark a new explanation or point, the tradents of the Septuagint began by emending the aspectual or completed action of the Hebrew verbs. The tense in Greek becomes an indicative future, perhaps reading a prophetic present, but more likely indicative of their own contextual settings, suggesting that the community in fact returned from that fire to rebuild a return migrations community; or through inner-biblical exegesis, the tradents are casting the shadows of Daniel's three friends in the fiery furnace, a true trial by fire during the time of Antiochus the IV, suggesting that the fire is used as a means of purification—as any priest would see in a sacrifice— with the genitival use of ἐπ' αὐτούς that the Lord will place the Lord's face over them (not against): καὶ δώσω τὸ πρόσωπόν μου ἐπ' αὐτούς ἐκ τοῦ πυρὸς ἐξελεύσονται καὶ πῦρ αὐτοὺς καταφάγεται καὶ ἐπιγνώσονται ὅτι ἐγὼ κύριος ἐν τῷ στηρίσαι με τὸ πρόσωπόν μου ἐπ' αὐτούς (Ezek 15:7 LXX), truly depicting that the believer, as an individual or community, will come out of the fire sanctified. This is a radical theological shift from a first generation's fire of judgment to a subsequent generation's view on a fire of holiness. The editor adds an important message because it was God who burned the community and God is holy; and should such an event happen again, they will come out of the fire knowing that the Lord was with them in the holocaust.

In the final verse of the Septuagint, like the Masoretic Text, a statement on the condition of the land being desolate is unfortunately pronounced. Indeed, the land is truly overrun and ruled by foreigners or those who are nonpurists, causing the land to be defiled. Both the Septuagint and the Masoretic Text agree on this closing point.

> 1 And a word of the Lord came to me saying:
> 2 And you, son of man, what has become of the wood of the grapevine, among all wood of the vine branches that is among the wood of the forest?

3 Will they take wood out of it in order to make it profitable? Will they receive from it a peg to hang any vessel?
4 It is given to the fire to be consumed, according to the annual purification; the fire destroyed and leaves off the end; will it be profitable again?
5 Even if it is restored, will it not be profitable? Not the least so because the fire has consumed the end, it will not be profitable.
6 On account of this, say the following: The Lord says the wood of the vine in the forest, which I have given up to the fire to be consumed, thus I have given *up on* the inhabitants of Jerusalem.
7 Now, I will set my face over them; out of the fire they will come, even though fire will devour them; they will come to know that I am the Lord, the one to establish my face over them.
8 And I will set the land to destruction for the trespasses committed, says the Lord.[42]

In conclusion, Ezek 15 is a carefully thought out and construed משל. In forced migrations, the communities of 597, 587, and 582 are all represented and attested. In the Masoretic Text, the burning of the temple is highlighted without ever verbally mentioning this painful experience in 587. The 582 group is blamed for the desolation of the land in the Masoretic Text. Likewise in the Septuagint, the sole culprit for all of Judah's destruction is the 582 group. From the perspective of a priestly Judeo-Babylonian, Persians of Judean descent, or hellenized Jews, the land remains desolate because it is occupied by foreigners. Perhaps this משל may explain how the Ezekiel school accommodated changes in the exilic community, producing an oracle that somehow allowed for the 597 group to modestly accept the 587 group as viable by producing an oracle addressing judgment against the 582 group. This perhaps parallels what is going on in the book of Jeremiah, as it developed in exile, which also made a case for the 587 exiles through the construction of Jer 26–45 and the harsh depiction of the 582 group in Jer 40–44.

---

42. My translation of Ezek 15 LXX.

The Cultic Dimension of Prophecy in the Book of Ezekiel

Corinna Körting

The choice of Ezekiel as the subject of questions of cult seems, at first glance, to not be surprising at all. Already the first chapter introduces Ezekiel naturally as the one who saw visions, who heard the word of the Lord, and who has a priestly pedigree (vv. 1–3). Nevertheless, research has looked at this differently. The prophet, who speaks his word out of his own religious experience, like a glowing stream of lava, and the word, formed by the prophetical experience to its accomplished poetic form—as Walther Zimmerli describes it[1]— stood in the center of interest, not the priest.

Zimmerli intended to correct this picture by taking questions of form and life setting into account. For him, it was necessary to look at the possibility of whether there had been an office for prophets in the service of Israel that explains the connection. This was in 1954. Bernard Lang could in 1981 still conclude that the question of why a Judean priest acts as a prophet is hardly touched on in research literature.[2] This situation has changed completely since then. A lot of scholarly work has been done in this field.[3] One of the results is that the question itself has also changed. An example of this change is offered by the title of an article by Corrine L. Patton: "Priest, Prophet, and Exile: Ezekiel as a Literary Construct."[4] Most

---

1. Cf. Walther Zimmerli, "Die Eigenart der prophetischen Rede des Ezechiel: Ein Beitrag zum Problem an Hand von Ez. 14 1–11," *ZAW* 66 (1954): 1.

2. Bernhard Lang, *Ezechiel: Der Prophet und das Buch,* EdF 153 (Darmstadt: Wissenschaftliche Buchgesellschaft, 1981), 77.

3. For recent literature, see Karl-Friedrich Pohlmann, *Ezechiel: Der Stand der theologischen Diskussion* (Darmstadt: Wissenschaftliche Buchgesellschaft, 2008).

4. Corrine L. Patton, "Priest, Prophet, and Exile: Ezekiel as a Literary Construct," in *Ezekiel's Hierarchical World: Wrestling with a Tiered Reality,* ed. Stephen L. Cook and

scholars no longer expect to find a real person behind Ezekiel, no priest and prophet in one person, but a literary construct that combines important elements of both.

While the discussion on the "person" seems to be answered, and the search for an office that combines the abilities of both a priest and a prophet with the help of form-critical tools seems to be unnecessary, the obvious combination of both traditions in the book of Ezekiel remains a challenge. At this point I shall enter the debate in order to contribute some thoughts on the relationship between prophetical message and cultic legislation, based on Ezek 14:1–11. This search for the function of a combination of different traditions in a prophetical book is accompanied by the question of how they supplement each other in the specific historical or constructed historical situation, a time without a temple—the exile.[5]

TERMINOLOGICAL AND CONTEXTUAL CONNECTIONS
BETWEEN THE SACRAL LAW AND EZEK 14

Already in 1954, Zimmerli made observations regarding the connections between sacral law, especially Lev 17, and Ezek 14.[6] Here the discussion

---

Corrine L. Patton, SymS 31 (Atlanta: Society of Biblical Literature, 2004), 73–89; cf. as well Matthijs J. de Jong, "Ezekiel as a Literary Figure and the Quest for the Historical Prophet," in *The Book of Ezekiel and Its Influence*, ed. Henk Jan de Jonge and Johannes Tromp (Aldershot: Ashgate, 2007).

5. The discussion in research on the historical background of the book as well as its literary history is overwhelmingly broad. A good overview is given by Thomas Renz, *The Rhetorical Function of the Book of Ezekiel*, VTSup 76 (Leiden: Brill, 1999), 27–38. For the literary history, see Pohlmann, *Ezechiel*, 29–73. While not being able to enter the discussion sufficiently in this place, I understand the book of Ezekiel as a literary construct with a longer history of *Fortschreibungen*. On this question see esp. Karin Schöpflin, *Theologie als Biographie im Ezechielbuch: Ein Beitrag zur Konzeption alttestamentlicher Prophetie*, FAT 36 (Tübingen: Mohr, 2002), 352–53. She discusses the book of Jeremiah, the Holiness Code (or the *Umkehrtheologie*), and the Deuteronomists' theology of repentance. Her book marks a change of the image of the prophet in research, a fact that makes it interesting and probably necessary to take also the postexilic references on prophets and priests into account; the major part of the book might stem from late exilic and early postexilic times.

6. Zimmerli, "Eigenart der prophetischen Rede," 12–13; Lang, *Ezechiel*, 97–99. Moshe Greenberg collects the parallels he finds between Ezek 14 and Lev 17 in *Ezekiel 1–20*, AB 22 (New York: Doubleday, 1983), 248–55. The connection has been disputed as well under the question of dependency. This is answered mainly in three ways:

should be started with a brief comment on specific terms, נָשָׂא עָוֹן and כָּרַת מִן, that connect the passage with sacral law, before continuing with some major differences between Ezek 14 and sacral law to point to the prophetical surplus. In order to be brief, I have chosen only those examples that are most relevant. They do not cover the whole range of connotations to sacral law.

Regarding נָשָׂא עָוֹן, Zimmerli suggested two main interpretations. Outside the Priestly writings he translated it as "to forgive sins" (Exod 34:7; Num 14:18);[7] for the Priestly writings and Ezekiel he chose the translation "to carry guilt"—with three different connotations.[8] Relevant for Ezek 14 is the third variant, which connects Ezek 14 with sacral law, used in connection with specific cases of prohibition against eating the sacrifice and in cases of incest or violating a vow.[9] Looking at these passages, Zimmerli concluded that in all these cases "to carry guilt" seems to be comparable to a priestly diagnosis for a severe illness. The impact of this illness will definitely follow but varies from case to case.[10]

Despite Zimmerli's interpretations, a discussion on the meaning of נָשָׂא עָוֹן was nevertheless unavoidable and can be followed currently. For

---

either Ezekiel is taking up material from sacral law (see Avi Hurvitz, *A Linguistic Study of the Relationship between the Priestly Source and the Book of Ezekiel: A New Approach to an Old Problem*, CahRB 20 [Paris: Gabalda, 1982]; Jan Joosten, *People and Land in the Holiness Code: An Exegetical Study of the Ideational Framework of the Law in Leviticus 17–26*, VTSup 67 [Leiden: Brill, 1996], 12–15), or Ezekiel and the redactors of the Holiness Code are drawing on the same traditions with a mutual influence upon each other (see Ronald E. Clements, "The Ezekiel Tradition: Prophecy in a Time of Crisis," in *Israel's Prophetic Tradition: Essays in Honour of Peter R. Ackroyd*, ed. R. J. Coggins et al. [Cambridge: Cambridge University Press, 1982], 128–30), or sacral law is dependent on Ezekiel (see Klaus Grünwaldt, *Das Heiligkeitsgesetz Leviticus 17–26: Ursprüngliche Gestalt, Tradition und Theologie*, BZAW 271 [Berlin: de Gruyter, 1999], 147–50, 376).

7. "Der die Schuld vergibt" (Zimmerli, "Eigenart der prophetischen Rede," 9).

8. First, "to carry guilt" as the task for the scapegoat on the Day of Atonement (Lev 16:22); Aaron, carrying the guilt of the people (Exod 28:38; Lev 10:17); and, in this perspective, also Ezek 4:4–17 and Isa 53:11. Second, "to carry guilt" for the purpose of "being responsible" (Num 18:1). Third, "to carry guilt" in the context of sacral law, used in cases of violating the sacred realm, touching a taboo. See Zimmerli, "Eigenart der prophetischen Rede," 9–10.

9. Cf. Exod 28:43; Lev 5:1, 17; 7:18; 17:16; 19:8; 20:17, 19; 22:16; Num 5:31; 30:16; Ezek 44:10, 12.

10. Zimmerli, "Eigenart der prophetischen Rede," 12.

example, Baruch Schwartz votes for a consistent reading of נָשָׂא עָוֹן as "to carry/bear sin," or "carry/remove sin," but it is never indicative of punishment per se.[11] Nevertheless, he needs to state that consequences do follow. Jacob Milgrom says in contrast: "In sum, *nāśāʾ ʿāwôn* is a nonexpiable, irremediable divine sentence. In all cases where the punishment is not stated, it is forthcoming—irrevocably. ... [P]erhaps one might say that the punishment ... expiates for the sin (explicitly, m. Yoma 8:8), but the punishment itself is unavoidable."[12]

In the direct context of the נָשָׂא עָוֹן formula, consequences for eating a carcass (Lev 17:16), for incest (20:17, 19), or for cursing God (24:15) are announced as "they shall be cut off [כרת *niphal*] in the sight of their people" (20:17) or "they shall die childless" (20:20). In Ezek 14 the consequences are expressed in two closely related ways, in verse 8 with כָּרַת and in verse 9 with שָׁמַד (to destroy). Both occurrences have YHWH as subject: וְהִכְרַתִּיו מִתּוֹךְ עַמִּי ("and I will cut you off from the midst of my people"; Ezek 14:8).[13] This formula is used in the Priestly legislation and the Holiness Code as a punishment inflicted for crimes that involve a breach of the covenant.[14] The meaning of כָּרַת is not completely clear, however. The question is whether one is dealing with the death penalty when speaking about "cutting off from the midst of the people." The least we can state is that in sacral law the dissociation from the people, which means from the cultic community, results in losing the life-providing contact with the community, with the cultic ritual, with God.[15]

---

11. Baruch J. Schwartz, "The Bearing of Sin in the Priestly Literature," in *Pomegranates and Golden Bells: Studies in Biblical, Jewish, and Near Eastern Ritual, Law, and Literature in Honor of Jacob Milgrom*, ed. David P. Wright et al. (Winona Lake, IN: Eisenbrauns, 1995), 9–10. The discussion has been taken up by Gary A. Anderson, *Sin: A History* (New Haven: Yale University Press, 2009), 18–21.

12. Jacob Milgrom, *Leviticus 17–22*, AB 3A (New York: Doubleday, 2000), 1490; see also idem, *Leviticus 1–16*, AB 3 (New York: Doubleday, 1991), 295.

13. For the parallel use of these two terms, see Gerhard F. Hasel, "כָּרַת *kārat*," TDOT 7:344. Cf. Andrew Mein, *Ezekiel and the Ethics of Exile*, OTM (Oxford: Oxford University Press, 2001), 181: "more often the responsibility for punishment is YHWH's." On YHWH's responsibility, see also Hasel, TDOT 7:348.

14. Cf. Mein, *Ezekiel and Ethics*, 181.

15. Offense against the Sabbath law in Exod 31:14 or the case of child sacrifice (Lev 20:2) requires the death penalty. That the formula does not necessarily stand for the death penalty and that the consequences are somewhat open are also found in Ezek 4:4–6, where Ezekiel has to carry guilt but definitely does not die. According to

Besides the two terminological examples that point to the priestly background,[16] there are two that seem to clearly point to a prophetical or at least a nonpriestly and nonsacral background. The first is שׁוּב (Ezek 14:6), "(call) to return"; the second is לֵב, "heart" (14:3, 4, 7).

In the context of prophecy, שׁוּב has often been understood as a key term of prophetic speech (cf. 2 Kgs 17:13). Despite the fact that there is an ongoing discussion as to how much room there is left for a true turn to God in the message of most of the prophets and how early the call to turn has been used in the history of prophecy,[17] the terminology itself is connected with the prophetical task. The function of the call to turn can be described as twofold: (1) a call to make those who listen change their minds and turn back to God, a basic reorientation;[18] or (2) a proof of the guilt of the people because they did not leave their false gods and the wicked ways in order to turn back to God.[19]

Finally, taking up לֵב (heart), we come to a term even more broadly represented in the Old Testament than שׁוּב, but nevertheless carrying throughout the prophetic literature connotations decisive for Ezek 14. Inside the human heart are both blindness against God and trust in God. The heart can be stubborn and evil (cf. Jer 7:24; 17:5), and it tends toward

---

Joosten, the meaning of "cutting off" as punishment for certain transgressions gets three main interpretations in research: "a) death penalty imposed by human agency, b) excommunication, and c) some type of divine punishment" (*People and Land*, 80). Cf. Grünwaldt, *Heiligkeitsgesetz Leviticus 17–26*, 149, who stresses the meaning of excommunication. "Das 'Ausrotten' will das unheilvolle Wirken von Menschen oder Dingen auf Israel bzw. auf die Welt unterbinden" (150).

16. Another relevant connection is given by אִישׁ אִישׁ, "any single person." Nearly all of the twenty-seven verses of the OT where the expression is used are of priestly origin. In prophetic literature we find Isa 53:3; Mic 7:6; and Ezek 14:4, 7. For this context it is interesting that the expression is used four times in Lev 17 (vv. 3, 8, 10, 13).

17. See Konrad Schmid, *Literaturgeschichte des Alten Testaments* (Darmstadt: Wissenschaftliche Buchgesellschaft, 2008), 170–71.

18. See Joseph Blenkinsopp, *Ezekiel*, IBC (Louisville: Westminster John Knox, 1990), 72.

19. With the function of a demonstration of guilt, a *Schuldaufweis*. See M. Graupner and H.-J. Fabry, "שׁוּב *šûb*," *TDOT* 14:496–97. Paul M. Joyce explains the function as follows: "The call to repentance here offers just a hint of the possibility of a new future. Yet no new beginning can be envisaged until after the judgement is complete—and then it will depend not upon Israel's own response but upon the obedience that YHWH himself will grant as a gift (cf. 11:19; 36:26–27)." See *Ezekiel: A Commentary*, LHBOTS 482 (New York: T&T Clark, 2007), 124, also 20–23.

idolatry (Hos 10:2). The stubborn heart stands in opposition to the heart that turns, שׁוּב, to God (cf. Jer 9:13; 13:10).[20]

While the terminology of Ezek 14 already points to the interwovenness of prophetical and priestly language, the same is true of the situation the text describes. Ezekiel 14 starts with a rather unusual scene. The elders of Israel come to Ezekiel and sit down before him. Their wish is not explicitly expressed, but it is clear that they expect something of the prophet/priest.[21] Forms of בּוֹא and the phrase וַיֵּשְׁבוּ לְפָנָי ("to come" and "sit before") are used together in three situations in the book of Ezekiel (Ezek 14:1; 20:1; 33:31).[22] Three times the elders or the people come to listen to the word of God, but, in the end, they are not willing to follow. "To come and to sit before" is often connected with coming before God to question him and to get advice. It is said about David as an individual and about the Israelites or their elders as a group. Interestingly, the only textual example outside Ezekiel where a prophet is surrounded by the elders *sitting before him* does not point definitely to a situation questioning God. The elders do sit before Elisha to be witnesses for God's word coming true, not seeking it for themselves (see 2 Kgs 6:32–7:2). David, on the other hand, comes before the Lord and sits down praying (2 Sam 7:18; 1 Chr 17:16). "To sit down before" is to be found as well in Judg 20:26 and 21:2. This time, it is again the people: they come, sit down before the Lord, and cry, fast, and sacrifice—a cultic situation.[23] The references we can consult do not clearly point to a prophetic situation. Therefore a cultic or priestly situation must also be taken into account, strengthened by the fact that the passage in Ezek 14:1–11 closes with a priestly admonition. Israel may not defile itself any longer with all its transgressions (v. 11).[24] The whole situation also fits with what we read in Lev 10:10–11 or

---

20. Cf. H.-J. Fabry, "לֵב *lēb*," *TDOT* 7:429, 433.

21. Rudolf Mosis describes the יָשַׁב of the elders as an official assembly with a legal act. See "Ez 14:1–11—ein Ruf zur Umkehr," *BZ* 19 (1975): 190–91.

22. Also, Ezek 8:1 has to be mentioned. The elders are sitting in front of Ezekiel. Only the third term, בּוֹא, is missing.

23. We can read Ezra 10 along the same lines: Ezra is directly called *priest* while standing up talking to the sitting people—sitting before the house of God (Ezra 10:9). Moreover, being directly connected to the real high priest Aaron, his actions, particularly with regard to the law, have to be regarded as fully legitimate (cf. Ezra 7:1, 11; H. G. M. Williamson, *Ezra, Nehemiah*, WBC 16 [Waco, TX: Word, 1985], 91; Zech 3:8).

24. Coming from a different point of view, namely the task of preexilic priesthood and the problem of an exilic priesthood, Schwartz collects a wide range of argu-

Ezek 44:23 and 22:26 about the task of the priests. They shall teach the people to distinguish between clean and unclean.²⁵ In later prophecy, we find the same phenomenon of a mixture of genres or offices. In Hag 2:11 the Lord speaks to the prophet Haggai and tells him to ask the priests for a ruling on consecrated meat. In Mal 2:7 the text speaks about the task of the priest to guard knowledge, and the people shall seek instruction from his mouth, for he is the messenger of the Lord of Hosts.

If we call the situation in the beginning and the closure a priestly one or one of expectation of priestly advice, the whole scene seems to change to a prophetic one between verses 2–10, though they are not completely distinguishable here as well.²⁶ The situation is a prophetic one first and foremost in the way God speaks to Ezekiel. From verse 3 to verse 11 is a long direct saying by God that questions the possibility of consulting him (דָּרַשׁ, v. 3). The elders have sinned (v. 3) with idolatry, and everybody among them who seeks prophetic advice shall be cut off from the midst of the people. The text goes even further. Prophetical words that are spoken anyway are to deceive the prophet and the inquirer.²⁷ Finally, *both* shall be cut off. The passage has often been called a prophetic admonition,²⁸ but it seems to be both prophetic and priestly.

Is it now possible to say something about the function of a combination of priestly and of prophetic terminology in Ezek 14:1–11? It seems that שׁוּב and נָשָׂא עָוֹן complement one another. While the prophetic call

---

ments concerning why Ezekiel's role cannot be understood as one of a priest and why there was no exilic priesthood. Some should be mentioned here: Ezekiel has never performed priestly duties; cultic service was utterly unthinkable without a temple, and "the priest's task of תורה in the sense of instruction was not an independent undertaking, separate from his cultic duties." See "A Priest out of Place: Reconsidering Ezekiel's Role in the History of the Israelite Priesthood," in Cook and Patton, *Ezekiel's Hierarchical World*, 63–64, 68. In contrast to his approach, I have read Ezek 14:1–11 in the context of postexilic prophecy and Ezra, where we find the combination of offices. On Ezekiel as an idealized figure and an idealized priest, see Patton, "Priest, Prophet, and Exile," 73–74, 84–89.

25. See Mein, *Ezekiel and Ethics*, 147.

26. Regarding form and genre, see Ronald M. Hals, *Ezekiel*, FOTL 19 (Grand Rapids: Eerdmans, 1989), 91–93.

27. In contrast, William H. Brownlee says that the Lord has a word ready for them. See *Ezekiel 1–19*, WBC 28 (Waco, TX: Word, 1986), 202.

28. See K. Arvid Tångberg, *Die prophetische Mahnrede: Form- und traditionsgeschichtliche Studien zum prophetischen Umkehrruf*, FRLANT 143 (Göttingen: Vandenhoeck & Ruprecht, 1987), 103–6.

to repentance is directed to the whole house of Israel, the threat to carry one's own sin points to the individual. There is a slight hope for the group but punishment for the individual. The use of terminology stemming from varying backgrounds sharpens the difference in perspective for the individual and the community.

With לֵב (heart), a category is added that complements the sacral law with a prophetic perspective. Those who have their idols in their hearts are unclean at the innermost level. Idolatry and uncleanness are synonymous (cf. Ezek 36:25 or Jer 2:23). The uncleanness that is often gained by touching—for example, a carcass of an unclean beast or corpse (cf. Lev 5:2–3)—reaches the innermost part of a person and makes the relationship with God impossible.[29] Some scholars read verses 3, 4, and 7 as thoughts coming up. They are thinking about acquiring idols and are therefore in "grave danger of … falling into sin and guilt." This way of reading, sometimes also linked to dating the text clearly before the exile,[30] as a warning seems somehow to weaken the assertion. But apart from the dating, even if it is just the thought or, as suggested here, the innermost part of a person that is reached, anyway the person is defiled. Idolatry is on his or her heart and mind, and God knows. It cannot be hidden.

If we look at the passage from the background of sacral law, a light is also shed on the strong reaction of the idolater questioning God. It is not possible for God to simply remain silent. In a way, our passage is an enhancement of what we can read in Ezek 7:26. There the prophet, the priest, and the elders keep silence. Sin silences the oracle.[31] In Ezek 14, however, the idolater, the unclean, tries to come closer to the holy God. This behavior needs punishment.[32]

Consequences for the Discussion on Individual and Collective Guilt

The use of נָשָׂא עָוֹן links our passage in Ezek 14 with Ezek 18 and the discussion around individual and collective guilt. Much has been said about

---

29. This is different in priestly literature: "Only when a *deed* has been done is a sin 'borne' in the priestly system" (Schwartz, "Bearing of Sin," 13).
30. See Brownlee, *Ezekiel 1–19*, 201.
31. See Greenberg, *Ezekiel 1–20*, 252.
32. See 1 Kgs 22:19–23, where the lying spirit in the mouth of the false prophets brings divine retribution upon Ahab and Jehoshaphat.

this. In general one can outline the results of speaking about Ezekiel's prophecy as the turning point in perspective from collective to individual guilt and responsibility.[33] Konrad Schmid argued convincingly against such a simple view on the problem. Although I am aware that his point is presented far too briefly, one of his major arguments is that law has always had the individual in focus.[34] Some aspects should be added to his argument. In nonsacral law the consequences for order inside a community provide the background for the definition of deeds that need punishment. Nonconfirmation of punishment means ignoring the God-given order, allowing chaos.[35] In biblical sacral law, the consequences of individual misbehavior for the community are fundamental as well but probably even more in focus when it comes to the various regulations as found in nonsacral law.

Another key term should also get attention, however. The reason for "carrying guilt" is given in verse 11. Everybody, in this case the inquirer and the prophet, has to carry his or her own guilt because the house of Israel may not defile (וְלֹא־יִטַמְאוּ) themselves anymore with all their transgressions. This problem is pointed to already in 4:9–17, in a prophetic sign-action. Ezekiel has to bake bread on dung, which is unclean.[36] Guilt leads to defilement, not just of the guilty person but of the whole community. The problem of uncleanness is its prolongation. "Like contagious disease, it spreads and becomes more virulent unless it is cured and purified."[37] This means that the relationship of the whole community with YHWH is at issue.[38]

---

33. Joyce describes the passage as "overwhelmingly collective" (*Ezekiel*, 124; cf. 23–26).

34. Konrad Schmid, "Kollektivschuld? Der Gedanke übergreifender Schuldzusammenhänge im Alten Testament und im Alten Orient," *ZABR* 5 (1999): 193–222; cf. Barnabas Lindars, "Ezekiel and Individual Responsibility," *VT* 15 (1965): 454; Gordon H. Matties, *Ezekiel 18 and the Rhetoric of Moral Discourse*, SBLDS 126 (Atlanta: Scholars Press, 1990), 191–93; Joel S. Kaminsky, *Corporate Responsibility in the Hebrew Bible*, JSOTSup 196 (Sheffield: Sheffield Academic, 1995), 166, on Ezek 18.

35. One example out of narrative texts is 1 Sam 15:1–23. Saul violates God's order to punish the Amalekites. His excuse to offer God the best of the loot does not count.

36. In the context of this passage, also, the sign-action of laying down and *carrying the guilt* of the people is mentioned.

37. Milgrom, *Leviticus 1–16*, 310.

38. See Matties, *Ezekiel 18*, 134.

I want to add one more thought, as an aside. In the beginning I mentioned that carrying guilt has, according to Zimmerli, three different connotations in priestly literature. I have discussed the relevant one for Ezek 14. Some other passages in the priestly literature are interesting as well under the perspective of individual responsibility. For example, Exod 28:38 (cf. Lev 10:17) states that Aaron shall take on himself any guilt incurred in the holy offering that the Israelites consecrate. Aaron carries guilt. In Lev 16:22 it is the scapegoat carrying the guilt of the people of Israel. In Ezek 4:4–6 it is Ezekiel himself who carries in a sign-act the guilt (NRSV "punishment") of the people. These possibilities (not even speaking about Isa 52–53) are excluded for the guilty individual Ezek 14 speaks sharply about.

If we use priestly categories in the context of a discussion on individual and collective guilt, the results are twofold: the individual has to carry his or her own guilt, which means also to take over the God-given consequences. Being guilty, however, is never simply a case between God and the individual; the whole community is involved.[39] Consequences have to be taken over for the sake of the house of Israel.

Ezekiel 14—A Text for the Templeless Age?

Thomas Renz writes: "The text discusses the relevance of God's word for the exilic community."[40] Andrew Mein argues: "We must ask why these ritual concepts, drawn originally from the regulations of the temple in Jerusalem, appear to have struck such a chord with an audience of exiles, and thereby to have helped maintain a distinctively Jewish community."[41] Both would agree that the text stems from exilic times and has an exiled audience in focus. Renz lays stress on the problem of inquiring of God, the prophetic perspective, while Mein takes the templeless situation with its loss of ritual into account, the priestly situation. What both perspectives have in common is the danger of losing the relationship with God. No word could be heard, no atonement would be reachable.

The guilt lies with the people. They have the idols in their hearts; they have set their guilt as a stumbling block before them. The text does not

---

39. On the combination of corporate and individualistic concerns in Ezek 18, see Kaminsky, *Corporate Responsibility*, 168–78.

40. The guiding question, according to Renz, is how the community can survive (*Rhetorical Function*, 73, 232).

41. Mein, *Ezekiel and Ethics*, 137.

point directly to the fact that there is no temple and no active cult. But making the elders sit together before Ezekiel, prophet and priest, shows that they are still regarded as a cultic community awaiting the teaching of the priestly torah. Taking up priestly terminology and concepts makes clear that also in new surroundings it is true and relevant that God is holy and therefore his people shall be holy. It is not by chance that the parallels between Ezek 14 and the sacral law, specifically Lev 17, are to be found. Israel remains a cultic community, expecting expiation or judgment according to the sacral law.

For a community in exile, the text makes clear that there is still a future perspective, based on individual responsibility. Hope for the future finds its expression also in the formula וְהָיוּ לִי לְעָם וַאֲנִי אֶהְיֶה לָהֶם לֵאלֹהִים "they shall be my people and I will be their God" (Ezek 14:11). It is taken up in 37:23, where salvation becomes explicit. God himself cleanses the Israelites from the defilement of idolatry. The ideal bond shall be restored. The formula connects Ezek 14 as well with two other passages, 11:20–21 (in this passage a punishment is still included) and 36:26–29, that name the conditions for the hope for the new beginning: God gives a new heart and a new spirit, and they shall be his people and he will be their God.

While the priestly aspects of the text received much attention in this paper, the prophetical side stood somehow in the background. I have said already that it is the prophet who announces the sacred law in the specific scene of Ezek 14. The prophetic task is enlarged.[42] Yet Ezekiel's prophecy is more. The historical background of "exile" has been questioned over and over again, at least for parts of the book. On Ezek 14 scholars say that the text discusses theoretical questions, indistinct and timeless.[43] Indeed, the situation described in the text seems to be constructed like the situation Ps 137 paints. Both texts show paradigmatic situations of gathering the people, getting teaching, or expressing grief. If one takes Ezek 14 as such an "ideal" situation, as a literary, constructed scene, one has to go further by asking about the task of prophecy. In contrast to what has been said in the beginning, prophecy as the expression of the prophet's religious experience, now we have to speak about prophecy as *Schriftauslegung*. With

---

42. Differently, Patton says that the portrait of Ezekiel asserts the priesthood over prophecy ("Priest, Prophet, and Exile," 88–89).

43. Pohlmann, *Das Buch des Propheten Hesekiel*, ATD 22.1 (Göttingen: Vandenhoeck & Ruprecht 1996), 197; cf. Mosis, "Ez 14:1–11," 188; Schöpflin, *Theologie als Biographie*, 310–11.

the sacred law material at hand,[44] the exile provides the background for (1) an enlarged understanding of prophecy that adds priestly tasks to the prophetic office—in surroundings where there is no temple and no cult—done by *Schriftauslegung*; and (2) the establishing of a new, clean cultic community against a hostile outside.[45] This is to be experienced also in postexilic times. So I can conclude by repeating: the establishment of a new, clean cultic community against a hostile outside is the goal of the text—in exile and beyond.

---

44. On the literary character of enlarging Ezekiel's prophecies, see Ronald E. Clements, "Chronology of Redaction in Ezekiel 1-24," in *Ezekiel and His Book: Textual and Literary Criticism and Their Interrelation,* ed. Johan Lust, BETL 74 (Leuven: Leuven University Press, 1986), 288-89. Cf. Clements, "Ezekiel Tradition," 129-34; in evaluating the relation of Ezek 40-48 and the Holiness Code, he stresses the mutual influence of these compositions. The purpose is a charter for the rebuilding of the Jerusalem temple.

45. Lindars, "Ezekiel and Individual Responsibility," 460.

EZEKIEL AS DISASTER/SURVIVAL LITERATURE: SPEAKING ON BEHALF OF THE LOSERS*

Louis Stulman

War ravages and debilitates; it numbs the senses and renders ordinary language useless. It shatters dreams and constructions of self and community. War devastates everyone, but it annihilates the losers; bodies are desecrated and families are splintered, faith is destroyed, and voices are shamed into silence. Albert Hourani aptly observes:

> Defeat goes deeper into the human soul than victory. To be in someone else's power is a conscious experience which induces doubts about the ordering of the universe, while those who have power can forget it, or can assume that it is part of the natural order of things and invent or adopt ideas which justify their possession of it.[1]

No wonder we rarely read the stories of the defeated or see a human face on the displaced; rarely do we tally the number of dead, maimed, and bereaved, except as war trophies. Instead, the inflated narratives of the victors monopolize memory.

The prophetic corpus in the Hebrew Bible is a striking exception to the rule. This "war literature" speaks on behalf of the losers, the dispossessed, the disappeared. It bears witness to their pain. It lines out their abyss in a wide range of expressions. And perhaps most remarkably, it imagines their survival.

---

* A form of this essay appeared originally in Louis Stulman and Hyun Chul Paul Kim, *You Are My People: An Introduction to Prophetic Literature* (Nashville: Abingdon, 2010), 145–60. Used by permission.

1. Albert Hourani, *A History of the Arab Peoples* (New York: Warner, 1991), 300–301.

The book of Ezekiel, more than most, conforms to these contours. It opens a dark shadowy window into the pain of displaced people. This stunning literary artifact refuses to cover up and banish memory. At the same time, it dares to map out a path of hope through the massive debris of loss. Ezekiel is a "manifesto for exiles,"[2] a survival trajectory for the crushed and conquered; or put more modestly, this diasporic text is literature of resistance in the struggle for community survival.

While acknowledging its towering contributions, twentieth-century scholarship has by and large relegated Ezekiel to secondary status.[3] This tendency may be due to its idiosyncratic character; more likely, it is the result of the book's surplus of violence and unrelenting blame. Donald E. Gowan suggests that the brutal nature of Ezekiel's message and his insistence "on the completeness of the death of the people of God"[4] contribute to the "unenthusiastic, if not negative judgment ... by some interpreters."[5] The text's harsh portrayal of God has done little to foster interest. The book portrays the God of Israel as exacting and punitive. Its judgment oracles are beset by brutal, even horrific, imagery. Its rigid internal community boundaries are designed to separate insiders from outsiders and good insiders from bad insiders. Even the tradition's hopeful utterances are rather detached and calculated. Unlike Isaiah's lyrical hope or Jeremiah's combative hope, Ezekiel's constructions of hope grow out of a piety that honors ritual and purity over morality and intimacy.

---

2. Margaret S. Odell, *Ezekiel*, SHBC (Macon, GA: Smyth & Helwys, 2005), 10.

3. This is not to say that Ezekiel has been ignored by recent scholarship. On the contrary, one can even speak of a resurgence of interest during the past decade; see Risa Levitt Kohn, "Ezekiel at the Turn of the Century," *CurBR* 2 (2003): 23; see also Andrew Mein, *Ezekiel and the Ethics of Exile*, OTM (Oxford: Oxford University Press, 2001); Margaret S. Odell and John T. Strong, eds., *The Book of Ezekiel: Theological and Anthropological Perspectives*, SymS 9 (Atlanta: Society of Biblical Literature, 2000); John F. Kutsko, *Between Heaven and Earth: Divine Presence and Absence in the Book of Ezekiel* (Winona Lake, IN: Eisenbrauns, 2000); Paul M. Joyce, *Ezekiel: A Commentary*, LHBOTS 482 (New York: T&T Clark, 2007); Daniel Smith-Christopher, *A Biblical Theology of Exile*, OBT (Minneapolis: Fortress, 2002); also note the outstanding commentaries by Leslie Allen, Joseph Blenkinsopp, William Brownlee, Ronald Clements, Moshe Greenberg, and of course Walther Zimmerli. To some degree, an intense interest in the social realities of exile has fueled recent interpretation.

4. Donald E. Gowan, *Theology of the Prophetic Books: The Death and Resurrection of Israel* (Louisville: Westminster John Knox, 1998), 122.

5. Ibid.

Akin to Isaiah and Jeremiah, though, Ezekiel is beset by an empire's designs toward world domination. It deals with the harsh realities of hegemony and the resultant collapse of long-standing national arrangements. In particular, Ezekiel's implied readers cannot elude the menacing maneuvers of Babylon; and so it bears witness to the horror of war and the trauma of displacement. Yet rather than faltering under the weight of the superpower's social systems and its symbolic universe, Ezekiel constructs a nonviolent script of resistance. This alternative rendering of the universe in the first place imagines the overpowering reality of YHWH over and against rival forces—mythic and geopolitical. Indeed, Ezekiel refers the whole matrix of geopolitical contingencies to this reality, in terms of judgment and sustaining hope for the future. In this manner, Ezekiel joins the prophetic chorus as disaster literature *and* survival literature. It addresses the atrocities of war while seeking to uncover a passage through the horror.

The Anatomy of Trauma

From beginning to end, the book of Ezekiel pulsates with the pain of war and occupation, exile and captivity. It dares to ponder the unthinkable: the loss of land, temple, capital city, and dynastic claims, indeed even the collapse of Israel's royal theology. It is not difficult to understand why Ezekiel's contemporaries would have interpreted such tragic circumstances as the nullification of God's promises. Land occupation, the Jerusalem temple, and a strong dynastic government long symbolized divine blessing and favor. Their dismantling threw the entire world into disarray. And Ezekiel speaks to the barrage of broken promises and shattered dreams.

While Ezekiel is only one of several prophetic traditions that addresses these focal concerns, its preoccupation with exile and captivity is clearly distinctive; the lingering social and symbolic damage of war completely dominates its literary and symbolic horizons. Perhaps no other prophetic writing enters the liminal world of exile more fully and more directly than Ezekiel. Exile frames the text. It defines the text. It engulfs the text in pain and leaves an indelible mark on it. Ezekiel can hardly be read apart from the realities of military conquest and displacement.

Ezekiel envisions exile (and the fall of Jerusalem) as the principal social crisis of community life. It not only represents the reality on the ground but also a metaphor for the end of all that is valued. Exile catapults an indigenous people into a community of strangers; it limits access to established social structures and power arrangements. Exile hurls Israel into an unclean land. It casts grave doubts on Israel's election tradition. It rocks the very foundations of Israel's identity, especially in its priestly forms. Forced migration, moreover, poses a serious threat of accommodation and loss of "self." It creates an enormous hole in Israel's symbolic universe. It jeopardizes the belief in a meaningful world and ruptures coherent networks of meaning. It imperils trust in God. It creates a disturbing *absence* from formative symbols and institutions, cultural givens, and beloved structures. And this devastating absence threatens to nullify Israel's long and cherished metanarrative. Forced relocation results in the apparent absence of a God who is by self-decree ever present (according to Buber) and at the same time ever elusive (according to Terrien).[6] It calls into question the very character of the covenant God, who is capable of creating newness and hope for captive people.

No wonder exile serves as such a resonant metaphor for many today. And no wonder recent scholarship has employed trauma and disaster studies as a window into this world.[7]

The interdisciplinary field of trauma and disaster studies has paid considerable attention to the effects of forced migration and captivity on individuals and communities. In the second half of the twentieth century in particular, researchers began to study war neuroses and captivity with scientific scrutiny. And anatomies of trauma began to crystallize, often vacillating between mimetic and antimimetic theories.[8] Although we need not universalize the experience of deported people or reduce the impact

---

6. Martin Buber, *I and Thou*, 2nd ed. (Edinburgh: T&T Clark, 1958); cf. Phil Huston, *Martin Buber's Journey to Presence* (New York: Fordham University Press, 2007); Samuel L. Terrien, *The Elusive Presence: Toward a New Biblical Theology*, Religious Perspectives (San Francisco: Harper & Row, 1978).

7. See, e.g., David G. Garber Jr., "Traumatizing Ezekiel, the Exilic Prophet," in *From Genesis to Apocalyptic Vision*, vol. 2 of *Psychology and the Bible: A New Way to Read the Scriptures*, ed. J. Harold Ellens and Wayne G. Rollins, Praeger Perspectives: Psychology, Religion, and Spirituality (Westport, CT: Praeger, 2004), 215–35; Daniel L. Smith-Christopher, "Reassessing the Historical and Sociological Impact of the Babylonian Exile (597/587–539 B.C.E.)," in *Exile: Old Testament, Jewish, and Christian Conceptions*, ed. James M. Scott, JSJSup 56 (Leiden: Brill, 1997), 7–36; idem, "Ezekiel on Fanon's Couch: A Postcolonialist Dialogue with David Halperin's *Seeking Ezekiel*," in *Peace and Justice Shall Embrace: Power and Theopolitics in the Bible: Essays in Honor of Millard Lind*, ed. Ted Grimsrud and Loren L. Johns (Telford, PA: Pandora, 1999), 108–44.

8. Ruth Leys, *Trauma: A Genealogy* (Chicago: University of Chicago Press, 2000).

of victimization to rigid formal structures, the trauma of exile, like that of grief itself, is manifestly "formful." Focusing on individuals rather than communities, Judith Herman argues that captivity or coercive control "seeks to destroy the victim's sense of autonomy."[9] It creates feelings of distrust, fear, and alienation. It degrades, creates the loss of will to live, as well as "the intrusive symptoms of post-trauma stress disorder,"[10] including "the hopelessness of depression,"[11] hyperarousal, the loss of connectivity, rage, and self-hatred. Under extreme circumstances, captives shut down "feelings, thoughts, initiative, and judgment."[12] The loss of memory and the capacity to feel is observable in the tragic creation of children soldiers.

Irahim Aref Kira states that survival-threatening experiences such as exile or forced migration can "shatter … assumptions and beliefs about self and objects," undermine "behavioral and emotional independence," and are potent enough to dismantle "the schema, the beliefs, the assumptions, and judgments about the self and the world."[13] Put differently, the trauma of exile can destroy faith, coherent networks of meaning, and constructions of communal and individual identity. Interestingly, when describing those responsible for producing the book of Ezekiel—namely, Jewish refugees in Babylon—Henry McKeating notes that "their survival is at stake because their identity is at stake. They have lost most of what defined them."[14]

A Traumatized Prophet

Life and death, survival and trauma, are always before us on the pages of Ezekiel. While one can discern these signs throughout the book, its two major characters, Ezekiel and YHWH, exhibit the most profound signs of victimization. As a result of war, exile, and captivity, both show striking symptoms of traumatic violence and dislocation. First the prophetic figure.

The tradition presents its hero as a survivor whose life is inundated in pain. The portrait of the prophet as captive or refugee is so embedded

---

9. Judith Herman, *Trauma and Recovery* (New York: Basic Books, 1992), 77.
10. Ibid., 87.
11. Ibid., 94.
12. Ibid., 84.
13. Ibrahim Aref Kira, "Taxonomy of Trauma and Trauma Assessment," *Traumatology* 7, no. 2 (2001): 73–86.
14. Henry McKeating, *Ezekiel*, OTG (Sheffield: Sheffield Academic, 1993), 75.

in the texture of the book that it is hardly possible to imagine the prophet apart from this social location. Ezekiel introduces himself in solidarity with his displaced community. With his fellow Judeans, Ezekiel is a casualty of war, a victim of coercive control and political captivity. He speaks as a displaced person and as a wounded healer whose world has been fractured beyond recognition. Like his compatriots, Ezekiel is caught between and betwixt worlds. He resides in the country of his incarceration and yet lives with a marked sense of nostalgia for his beloved city that lies in ruins. This profound sense of displacement creates a palpable hybridity.

No less than Jeremiah, Ezekiel is a person of deep suffering. And like his contemporary, Ezekiel's pain can be encoded in his body as well as in his oracles, symbolic actions, and visionary reports. At the outset of the prophetic drama the reader learns that Ezekiel must ingest a scroll with "words of lamentation and mourning and woe" to fulfill his vocation (Ezek 2:10). This act prepares him to bear witness to death and destruction in word, symbolic action, and in his *bios*.

The depiction of the impending destruction of Jerusalem in chapters 4–24 is a case in point. Here the prophet's language is scathing; his visionary reports and symbolic acts are shocking. Violence dominates the symbolic topography. Gowan notes that when Ezekiel employs this language "he is not *imagining* a wrathful, vengeful God, nor expressing his own anger. He speaks of things he and his audience have already seen."[15] Perhaps Gowan says more than he should in this regard. Nonetheless, the prophet's rhetoric of disaster, often used in the name of divine judgment, is seemingly refracted through the lenses of war and the trauma of captivity. In other words, Ezekiel's language of terror, although sometimes formulaic, reflects the horror of war itself. Ironically, Ezekiel does not primarily deploy this language against dangerous outsiders, the perpetrators of violence, but rather against insiders who supposedly pose the most profound danger to the survival of the community. Although the prophet's derisive rhetoric serves in part to rein in those who resist community order, it also reveals signs of trauma and encroachment; that is, Ezekiel's harsh and punitive language is indicative of a society that feels itself at risk and in grave danger—a community that has been overexposed to the destructive forces of war.

---

15. Gowan, *Theology of the Prophetic Books*, 122.

In addition to proclaiming a message of terror, Ezekiel carries the pain of war within his own body. The prophet's life serves as a "sign" for the community at large (e.g., 12:6; 24:24). The prospect of captivity leaves the prophet "in bitterness in the heat of [his] spirit" (3:14). Like a prisoner of war, he lives in isolation, restrained and silent (3:22–26). Ezekiel lies on his left and then right side to represent a prolonged period of siege (4:4–8). Also indicative of siege and deportation, he suffers scarcity and defilement (4:9–17) as well as shame and humiliation (5:1–4). To symbolize Judah's captivity, Ezekiel packs his bag for a period of exile (12:1–6). To convey the terrible violence inflicted upon Jerusalem, he eats his "bread with quaking" and drinks his water "with trembling and with fearfulness" (12:17–20); when Ezekiel's wife dies, he is forbidden to find solace through customary forms of mourning (24:15–27). Yet even this most personal form of grief holds communal import: like the prophet's bereavement, the people of Israel will suffer the loss of their beloved temple, "the delight of [their] eyes," as well as the death of "[their] sons and daughters." Despite these crushing blows, the nation, like the prophet, is banned from conventional mourning rituals. Such symbolic performances convey the end of Judean culture as it was long known (cf. Jer 16:1–9).

The text's portrayal of the prophetic psyche also reflects symptoms of traumatic violence. Early- and mid-twentieth-century studies often subjected Ezekiel's personality to psychological analysis. Drawing on the work of E. C. Broome, for instance, Abraham Heschel notes that Ezekiel exhibits "behavioristic abnormalities consistent with paranoid schizophrenia," including "delusions of persecution and grandeur."[16] More recent interpretive perspectives tend to view Ezekiel's behavior—or rather the literary portrayal of the "disordered" personality—as more indicative of trauma and posttraumatic stress than psychosis or paranoid schizophrenia.[17]

For instance, like those who suffer unspeakable violence, Ezekiel appears detached and disconnected, often vacillating between worlds. He manifests a fixation with violence and death, even when imagining the future (37:1–14). And he undergoes dissociative episodes, constriction, or paralysis, hyperarousal, helplessness, and the loss of control (as

---

16. Abraham Joshua Heschel, *The Prophets* (New York: Harper & Row, 1963), 505–6.

17. For an insightful study of the traumatic impact of exile on Ezekiel, see David G. Garber Jr., "Trauma, History and Survival in Ezekiel 1–24" (Ph.D. diss., Emory University, 2005).

perhaps suggested by the phrase "the hand of the LORD"). Even the formulaic expression בן אדם, "son of man" or "Mere mortal" or "O mortal" (NRSV), conveys vulnerability and disempowerment. This address is a constant reminder of Ezekiel's frailty and mortality. Ezekiel is an earthling whose existence, like that of Adam, is drawn from the earth (אדמה) and sustained by the breath or spirit of God. And God's spirit almost always overpowers and silences the diminutive prophet.

Strangely similar to the exercise of repressive control, YHWH's interaction with Ezekiel is intense and overpowering. The commanding voice of YHWH dominates the landscape; it dwarfs both prophet and people. It is authoritative and assertive. It monopolizes symbolic and discursive space, relegating dissent to the margins. As a result, Ezekiel does not readily challenge the divine perspective, even when it suggests the unthinkable (e.g., 20:25). The prophet does not oppose the divine point of view, even when it appears excessively punitive. The force of YHWH's directives is too powerful, and, ultimately, Ezekiel is overwhelmed into submission. Because YHWH is exacting, dangerous, and, above all, holy, neither Ezekiel nor his readers defy this God or attempt to circumvent God's holy resolve. Such a piety honors conformity over engagement and submission over dissent; it is more positional than personal.

This is not to imply that countervoices are absent from the book. Although Ezekiel's landscape is governed by an all-consuming voice, the text still provides dark windows into the complex and fractured interiority of the prophet and the refugee people. Ezekiel must be told three times, for instance, to eat the scroll, before he obeys (2:8–3:3). And he leaves his initial encounter with YHWH "in bitterness in the heat of … spirit" (3:14). When confronted with the wholesale destruction of Jerusalem, the prophet intercedes: "Ah Lord GOD! will you destroy all who remain of Israel as you pour out your wrath upon Jerusalem?" (9:8). In another case, Ezekiel falls to the ground and pleads with YHWH for the remnant of Israel (11:13).

While the voices of Judean refugees are usually subdued, occasional expressions of resistance and despair emerge. The Jerusalem elders insist, "The LORD does not see us, the LORD has forsaken the land" (8:12); prophet and people recite the conventional saying, "The parents have eaten sour grapes, and the children's teeth are set on edge" (18:2); some contend, "The way of the LORD is unfair" (18:25), "The way of the LORD is not just" (33:17; see also 37:11). As a rule, however, these dissenting/lamenting voices are few in number and limited in scope. And they are placed in the mouths of others—most often YHWH and Ezekiel—as disputation speeches are used against those who supposedly uttered them (see also 9:9; 11:3; 12:21–25; cf., however, 33:10).

Thus the text locates the prophet in a symbolic universe that is largely free of moral incoherence and ambiguity. Not only is there little tolerance for dissent, resistance, and vexation in this world, there is also little acknowledgment of gratuitous suffering and divine injustice. Meaning-making is by and large coherent, symmetrical, and monologic. If there is *any* moral slippage, it is found in the promissory language where YHWH's unilateral and sovereign speech destabilizes a rigid act-consequence schema. Constructions of newness are not for Israel's sake or because Israel is deserving but for God's sake and for the preservation of God's reputation. Otherwise, the book's governing categories are stable, well-defined, and in effect seamless.[18]

A Traumatized God

Notwithstanding this symbolic symmetry, something strange and unexpected takes place: YHWH eventually becomes fully immersed in Israel's pain and alienation. This metamorphosis is most clearly evident in the second of three vision reports that organize the book of Ezekiel. In this particular vision report (esp. 8:1–11:25), we discover that the sovereign and holy God is susceptible to the anguish of war and displacement. No longer detached and unscathed, as in chapters 1–3, YHWH is drawn into Israel's fractured world as a wounded participant. In solidarity with traumatized Israel, YHWH astonishingly becomes a displaced God and in so doing identifies with the endangered refugee community, even to the point of humiliation. Ultimately this radical displacement becomes a source of healing and newness for suffering Israel. But before hope can blossom, YHWH must feel the full brunt of Israel's pain and alienation.

In the inaugural vision, the prophet encounters YHWH arrayed in splendor in the heavenly throne room. This glimpse into the divine world, of course, draws on traditional forms, such as fire, light, glory, cloud, spirit, and the bow, several of which are reminiscent of the wilderness tradition—the

---

18. One could think of the world created by Ian McEwan in his much acclaimed *Atonement* (New York: Anchor, 2003). Briony, Robbie, and Cecilia experience the devastation of a morally exacting world in which one offense has lingering and haunting consequences.

formative period *before* YHWH takes up residence in the temple. Indeed, the wheels on the divine chariot drive home the point that God's heavenly throne is not tied to the monarchy or the state—whether Judean or Babylonian; and, as importantly, it demonstrates that God's abode is constructed for transit. YHWH will go wherever YHWH desires!

Besides traditional symbols, the vision is also influenced by Mesopotamian traditions, demonstrating, among other things, that the servants/spirits of the Babylonian gods are harnessed to the chariot throne of YHWH and so are subservient to YHWH. Margaret Odell notes that the use of Mesopotamian iconography not only reinforces claims of YHWH's universal rule, but it also subverts hegemonic claims, stressing that YHWH, not Mesopotamian rulers, controls the destiny of Israel.[19] The God of the losers—not unlike the God of Hebrew slaves—is sovereign and impervious to self-aggrandizing human leaders and military machines. This God stands over and against mighty Babylon *and* captive Israel. As divine ruler, YHWH commands *all* forces in the created order—until something unexpectedly occurs; divine vulnerability eclipses divine sovereignty.

In the second major vision in the book, YHWH is driven out of the temple by idolatry, violence, and injustice (8:1–10:22 and 11:1–25). The Holy One cannot dwell in such a setting. So the כְּבוֹד אֱלֹהֵי יִשְׂרָאֵל moves "from the cherub to the threshold of the house" (9:3; 10:3–4), leaves the threshold of the house, and hovers over the cherubim at the entrance of the east gate of the house of the Lord (see 10:18–22). Then the divine glory rises above the city, passes by the Kidron Valley, and eventually "heads east, stopping at the Mount of Olives."[20]

This move is replete with danger. Treks eastward can be perilous. Humanity is banished east of Eden to a life of conflict, danger, and death (Gen 3:24). At risk and in grave danger, Cain is evicted from the divine presence to live out his life as vulnerable refugee, east of Eden (Gen 4:16). Angry and despondent, Jonah leaves Nineveh and sits "down east of the city" (Jonah 4:5; see also Isa 2:6; Ezek 25:4, 10). The east represents a faraway place of vulnerability, banishment, and exile—in large measure because menacing superpowers (Babylon in particular), Israel's tormenters, reside east of Jerusalem.

---

19. Odell, *Ezekiel*, 13–38.
20. Ibid., 125.

When YHWH departs from the Jerusalem temple for the eastern regions, YHWH becomes an outcast in solidarity with the diasporic community. YHWH not only takes up residence in the borderlands; YHWH becomes a "displaced person" there. God becomes an exile! Like the community with which the God of Israel identifies, YHWH suffers massive disjunction. It would seem that this God has little choice than to participate in this dangerous setting. Even though YHWH is sovereign and free, YHWH is not insulated from Israel's wreckage. Like the Judean exiles, YHWH is forced to leave the safety of land, city, and temple—driven out by corruption and gratuitous violence. And like any other refugee, YHWH is shattered and traumatized beyond words. Terrorized at home and humiliated in exile, YHWH suffers the debilitating loss of reputation (similar to the so-called Jerusalem elite living in exile) as well as the disorienting chaos of a world gone amok in moral insanity. YHWH is shamed by the battery of events and by Israel's misdeeds. And, in response, YHWH lashes out (1) to restore a damaged reputation, (2) to rectify the wrongs done against him, and (3) to clean up the symbolic mess. These actions are evident in part in the oft-used statement of recognition, "Then you/they will know that I am the LORD" (e.g., 13:23).

The violence that erupts from YHWH's mouth mirrors the rage of a war-torn people. It also represents a "measured" response to a crumbling world on the brink of destruction; that is, YHWH is angry for good reason! The world is on the verge of collapse. The enemy is at Jerusalem's gates. Judah's leaders have lost their way. Families are splintered; hostages have been taken. And the temple has been desecrated. However, rather than lashing out at Babylon, the geopolitical agent of disaster, YHWH targets Israel. Perhaps the converse would be too dangerous in diaspora, even for YHWH (cf., however, the language against the empire in Jeremiah). Regardless, Israel, not Babylon, is the focus of YHWH's attention.

Ultimately YHWH's exile from the temple leads to an alliance with the traumatized community—in location, in rage, in suffering, and eventually in hope (11:22–24). As John Kutsko notes, "the divine *kābôd* would be available to Israel in exile, as it was available to Israel in the wilderness."[21] Again landless and in the wilderness, YHWH returns to this liminal place, now as a refugee among dispirited refugees. "Therefore tell the exiles: This is what the sovereign LORD says: Though I exiled them

---

21. Kutsko, *Between Heaven and Earth*, 97.

among the nations and scattered them among the countries, yet I will be a sanctuary to them for a little while [לְמִקְדָּשׁ מְעַט] in the countries where they have gone" (11:16).

In the third and final vision (Ezek 40–48), the exiled God returns to the temple. God's "banishment" is over. The "glory of the God of Israel" enters the temple by the east gate and fills the sanctuary (43:5; 44:4), not unlike earlier descents of the divine presence into the holy place (e.g., 1 Kgs 8:11; cf. 2 Chr 5:14; 7:2). The prophetic drama ends with a consecrated, thoroughly purged, and coherent symbolic universe where YHWH feels at home (43:6–9). The array of religious improprieties, including "vile abominations" (8:9) and temple wall portraits of "all kinds of creeping things, and loathsome animals, and all the idols of the house of Israel" (8:10), are altogether gone. Now the divine residence in the restored temple becomes a source of blessing for the world, although it is still predominantly in the service of a beleaguered Judean community. The location of this vision, however, should not be overlooked: the prophet sees the new temple and the return of YHWH while residing in exile. Thus it is stillborn in the maelstrom of war, upheaval, and estrangement.

It is no accident that Ezekiel concludes with a triumphant note that YHWH is present in the new city of God (48:35). Indeed, the name of the city "from that time on shall be, The Lord is There." These last two words of Ezekiel—יהוה שמה, "YHWH is there"—respond to the danger lurking in the text.

But what exactly is that danger? What threatens faith and jeopardizes the coherent constructions of the universe? What places trust in God at risk? Most concretely, it is the harsh reality of war and captivity. And Ezekiel dares to speak to these destructive realities. This courageous text participates fully in Israel's fractured world and gives this world of loss its own name. Deploying priestly categories, Ezekiel names the abyss *absence*.[22] From opening vision to concluding doxology, the book of Ezekiel throbs with the pain of absence—the absence of land, temple, king, city, and most painfully God. And this tangible absence creates a dreadful sense of disconnection and shattered reality, which converge as a raging assault against hope.

---

22. The theme of divine absence and presence in the book of Ezekiel has been treated most thoroughly by Kutsko, ibid., 26.

Yet amid all the wreckage comes YHWH—Judah's displaced God, the God of the losers—to fill the absence and repair a ruptured world. In the vortex of loss, Ezekiel claims, the traumatized community can discover the mystery that "God is hidden in the pain and suffering of the world."[23] To be sure, YHWH is there! Such an utterance affirms that nothing can separate God's people from God's presence. It asserts that this God is accessible in the most unlikely places, even in the faraway country of Babylon. Or as Peter Craigie so eloquently notes, Ezekiel "reminds us forcibly that there is no place and no circumstances in which the experience of God may be denied. Perhaps it is even true that God's presence is known at the place and in the circumstances in which it is least expected."[24]

---

23. Ibid., 135.
24. Peter C. Craigie, *Ezekiel*, Daily Study Bible (Philadelphia: Westminster, 1983), 13.

Forced Migration and the Visions of Zechariah 1–8*

Frank Ritchel Ames

Introduction

Forced migration, the relocation of members of a community due to armed conflict, infrastructure project, or natural disaster, is a persistent social phenomenon. In our day, organized violence and threats of violence "have generated tides of refugees."[1] At the end of 2009, the number of "persons of concern" (refugees, asylum seekers, internally displaced persons, returnees, stateless persons, and similar) counted by the United Nations High Commissioner for Refugees (UNHCR) exceeded 36 million.[2] The dynamics of conflict-, project-, and disaster-induced displacement differ from one instance to the next, but the outcome is the same: members of a community are made to leave their homeland to establish themselves elsewhere, welcomed or unwelcomed, either as refugees in a foreign land or as internally displaced persons within their own country. The trauma does not reach the same level in every case, but forced

---

* An earlier version of this paper was originally presented in the Exile (Forced Migrations) in Biblical Literature program unit at the SBL Annual Meeting, New Orleans, 23 November 2009.

1. Norman Etherington, "War, Demographic Consequences of," *Encyclopedia of Population*, ed. Paul Demeny and Geoffrey McNicoll, 2 vols. (New York: Macmillan, 2003), 2:965.

2. United Nations High Commissioner for Refugees (UNHCR), "Total Population of Concern to UNHCR: Refugees, Asylum-Seekers, IDPs, Returnees, Stateless Persons, and Others of Concern to UNHCR by Country/Territory of Asylum, End-2009," table 1. Online: http://www.unhcr.org/globaltrends/2009-Global-Tends-annex.zip.

migration is traumatic. Displaced persons experience disorienting psychosocial effects and destabilizing socioeconomic losses; it is tragic, for the resultant harm can be devastating and intractable.

This paper explores the cascading outcomes of forced migration and evidence of those outcomes in a late sixth-century community of Judean exiles, the community addressed in the visions of Zech 1–8. My approach is comparative, offers a sociological model, and applies the model in understanding both text and community. I argue that the impacts of forced migration—namely, diminished resources and security and increased morbidity and mortality—foster extension and inclusion in exiled households and communities.

Forced migration has been a constant throughout human history and is a crucible that shaped ancient Israel and early Judaism. One could argue that forced migration is a defining element in the national consciousness of ancient Israel and the religion of early Judaism, and some consider it to be *the* defining event. Daniel L. Smith asserts that "the most sociologically significant event is precisely the military defeat and mass deportation of Judeans to a foreign environment composed of a dominant Babylonian population and other conquered peoples."[3] *Exile*, a traditional term for conflict-induced displacement, is a prominent biblical motif. The Primary History[4] tells how prototypical ancestors were banished from idyllic gardens, driven from cultivated lands, swept from the earth, and scattered abroad; how matriarchs and patriarchs sojourned in foreign countries to survive famines; how liberated but obstinate descendants wandered in wilderness regions and claimed new territories; how chiefdoms and kingdoms flourished and failed, and their citizens were captured. The poets of ancient Israel and early Judaism lament displacement and celebrate restoration, and the prophets repeatedly threaten deportation and promise return. Woe and weal are bound up in exile and restoration, and, east of Eden, all are exiles and can say with Moses, "I have been a stranger in a strange land" (Exod 2:22 KJV).

---

3. Daniel L. Smith, "The Politics of Ezra: Sociological Indicators of Postexilic Judaean Society," in *Persian Period*, vol. 1 of *Second Temple Studies*, ed. Philip R. Davies, JSOTSup 117 (Sheffield: JSOT Press, 1991), 75.

4. On the use of the term *Primary History* in reference to the complex epic that extends from Genesis through 2 Kings, see David Noel Freedman, *The Unity of the Bible*, Distinguished Senior Faculty Lecture Series (Ann Arbor: University of Michigan Press, 1993), 6.

Embedded in story, song, and prophecy are glimpses of the social realities of ancient Israel and early Judaism, and these realities can be teased out of texts that always complicate and often confound historical, social, and literary inquiry. As scholars know all too well, there is nothing simple about biblical texts, which tend to represent nationalistic views of elite urban males, portray exceptional—not ordinary—experiences, and commingle the understandings of earlier authors and later editors. Genre and provenance remain problematic, but it is nonetheless possible to reconstruct aspects of ancient culture from biblical texts explored in conjunction with archaeological and comparative data. There is need for caution and restraint but also reason enough for pursuing a text-based comparative ethnography with a degree of confidence. First—drawing insight from Carol Meyers—one can argue that "the division between preindustrial and contemporary smallholders is not so great as some would suppose."[5] It is the ubiquity of communities, the universality of human needs, and the constraining influence of environments that make cross-cultural comparisons credible and useful.[6] Social patterns are survival patterns, and communities, for conscious and unconscious reasons, adopt patterns that help them survive in environments that offer limited choices. Individuals within communities do not and cannot always make optimal decisions—they may not have options, but social groups in similar circumstances will react in similar ways and over time will develop similar strategies to survive and to thrive. For this reason, comparative data is useful for understanding ancient societies and inscribed experiences. Even highly ideological textual data is useful, though for a different reason: texts address social concerns and in doing so expose social realities. Verisimilitude, a literary concept applied to fiction, is useful in exploring biblical genres as disparate as historical narrative and apocalyptic vision. A text's semblances of reality, present in the relational behaviors of characters and the social dynamics portrayed, tend to replicate social dynamics whether the characters and events are historical, merely realistic, or utterly fantastic. It matters little for social analysis. The representation may be factual or fictional, historical or imaginative, accurate or approximate, but the social dynamics that are portrayed will mimic the social dynamics of the author's world.

---

5. Carol L. Meyers, "The Family in Early Israel," in *Families in Ancient Israel*, ed. Leo G. Perdue et al.; Family, Religion, and Culture (Louisville: Westminster John Knox, 1997), 4.
6. Ibid.

Readers cannot make good sense of the text unless the dynamics that are portrayed are recognizable and realistic. If the interactions are not, the story will not capture the imagination, will seem contrived and inauthentic, and will be disregarded. Authors may create imaginative worlds, but the social patterns within these worlds tend to be quite unimaginative. For these reasons, texts from exiled communities expose the social dynamics of forced migration, and the observed dynamics of forced migration can illuminate texts from exiled communities.

Baseline Outcomes of Forced Migration

Forced migration has three baseline outcomes, and the first is a diminishing of resources and security. Losses may include (1) domicile, which provides shelter, safety, privacy, and storage; (2) land, which provides sustenance and income and is itself a form of wealth; (3) property such as food and water, furnishings, clothing, tools, instruments, supplies, books and artwork, and personal items; and (4) domestic animals, which are a form of wealth and a source of food and income. But the losses are not solely material. Refugees and internally displaced persons also lose, through death or separation, family members, friends and neighbors, and unknown but important community members. Social networks and community infrastructures are fractured. The loss of material and human resources is compounded by the loss of what these provide: adequate food and water; protection from the natural elements, predatory animals, and human aggression; and care for the helpless and aging. The effects are cascading.

Modern Iraq provides an instance of the trauma and cascading outcomes of forced displacement. More than 725,000 people were displaced by sectarian violence between February 2006 and March 2007.[7] By the end of 2007, "approximately 75,000 children were living in camps or temporary shelters."[8] Sectarian violence accounts for only a portion of the displacements. There are about 1.9 million displaced persons within

---

7. Norwegian Refugee Council, *Iraq: A Displacement Crisis* (Geneva: Internal Displacement Monitoring Centre, 2007), 7.

8. Karim Khalil, "Political Stalemates and Deepening Humanitarian Crises: Internal Displacement in the Middle East," in *Internal Displacement: Global Overview of Trends and Developments in 2007*, ed. Edmund Jennings (Geneva: Internal Displacement Monitoring Centre, 2008), 58.

Iraq, with an equal or greater number living as refugees in neighboring countries. The UNHCR refers to the Iraqi situation as the "largest population movement since 1948 in the Middle East."[9] Based on field interviews reported by the Norwegian Refugee Council, unmet needs among the displaced included shelter, food and water, healthcare, employment, and education, with long-term housing being a priority for displaced persons, for "temporary housing ... makes them extremely vulnerable to homelessness and secondary displacement."[10] There are many unmet needs. Displaced persons take only what can be packed or carried, and those who often have little to begin with suddenly have less. Many have nothing. Forced migration diminishes individual, family, and community resources with rippling effects.

Displacement is evidence of inadequate security and further decreases security. The road, encampment, and relocation are less safe than prior household and village, especially for women, who, together with children, make up 80 percent of those displaced in war.[11] In a 2002 report commissioned by the United Nations Development Fund for Women, Elisabeth Rehn and Ellen Johnson-Sirleaf write:

> Violence against women in conflict is one of history's great silences. We were completely unprepared for the searing magnitude of what we saw and heard in the conflict and post-conflict areas we visited. We knew the data. We knew that 94 percent of displaced households surveyed in Sierra Leone had experienced sexual assaults, including rape, torture and sexual slavery. That at least 250,000—perhaps as many as 500,000—women were raped during the 1994 genocide in Rwanda. We read reports of sexual violence in the ongoing hostilities in Algeria, Myanmar, Southern Sudan and Uganda. We learned of the dramatic increase in domestic violence in war zones, and of the growing numbers of women trafficked out of war zones to become forced labourers and forced sex workers.[12]

---

9. Norwegian Refugee Council, *Iraq: A Displacement Crisis*, 12.
10. Ibid.
11. Elisabeth Rehn and Ellen Johnson-Sirleaf, *Women, War, Peace: The Independent Experts' Assessment on the Impact of Armed Conflict on Women and Women's Role in Peace-Building*, Progress of the World's Women 1 (New York: United Nations Development Fund for Women, 2002), 19.
12. Ibid., 9.

They add, "But knowing all this did not prepare us for the horrors women described."[13] Coauthor of the report, Johnson-Sirleaf, the president of Liberia, leads a nation recovering from a fourteen-year-long civil war "in which more than half the country's women suffered some form of sexual or gender-based violence."[14] I will not and need not describe the atrocities but will point to the "collapse of women's protection" during conflict and displacement.[15] Thoraya Ahmed Obaid, executive director of the United Nations Population Fund (UNFPA), says, "Far from being a specific niche issue, sexual violence is an indicator of the most severe breach of human security."[16] In short, conflict-induced migration decreases the security of women, though the safety of every member of the community diminishes. Ironically, conflict-induced migration also increases the responsibilities of women, for in the absence of men killed in combat more women will serve as the de facto heads of households or without the assistance of a spouse.

Forced migration has a second consequence: increased morbidity and mortality. The 1960s expression, "War is not healthy for children and other living things,"[17] is true, and as Richard M. Garfield and Alfred I. Neugut point out, "The phrase is so understated that one hesitates to ask how unhealthy war might be."[18] Displacement weakens and kills, and in the long run may be more harmful than the conflict or disaster that caused the displacement.[19] Bluntly, the aftermath is more deadly than the attack. The Centers for Disease Control and Prevention (CDC) characterizes the mortality rates that attend forced displacement as "extremely high," and during acute emergency phases as high as "60 times the crude mortality rate …

---

13. Ibid.

14. United Nations Population Fund, *Report on the International Symposium on Sexual Violence in Conflict and Beyond, 21–23 June 2006* (Brussels: UNFPA, 2006), 9.

15. Khalil, "Political Stalemates," 58.

16. T. A. Obaid, "Introduction," *Forced Migration* 27 (2007): 6. For additional information about the UNFPA, see http://www.unfpa.org/public/.

17. On the origin of the poster saying, see Steven Heller, "War Is Not Healthy: The True Story," *AIGA Design Archives*, n.p. Online: http://www.aiga.org/content.cfm/war-is-not-healthy-the-true-story.

18. Richard M. Garfield and Alfred I. Neugut, "The Human Consequences of War," in *War and Public Health*, ed. Barry S. Levy and Victor W. Sidel (Washington, DC: American Public Health Association, 2000), 27.

19. Ibid.

among non-refugee populations in the country of origin."[20] In nonemergency situations in developing countries, one expects the mortality rate to be less than 0.5 deaths per day among 10,000 persons; for children under the age of five, the rate is one death per day.[21] The rate increases markedly under forced migration. A three-year drought in Ethiopia placed ten million persons at risk of starvation in 2000, and a large number from the Gode district in Somali were displaced.[22] The crude mortality rate peaked at 6.3 deaths among 10,000 per day; for children under five, it reached 12.5.[23] The UNHCR emergency threshold for a humanitarian crisis is double the baseline mortality rate or approximately the deaths of two children under the age of five among 10,000 persons per day.[24] Baseline rates vary by region from 0.19 in Latin America to 1.14 in Sub-Saharan Africa.[25] West Darfur provides a disturbing instance. In Murnei, crude mortality rates reached 9.5 persons among 10,000 per day during the acute phase of the displacement and dropped to 1.2 persons per day after settlement in the camp. Surveys were taken of 215,000 people by Médecins sans Frontières from April to June 2004. Abstractions mask the gravity of the situation: about 204 people died each day during flight and about 26 people died each day in the camps.[26] According to the CDC:

> Children, particularly those aged <5 years, usually account for most deaths in such situations. Malnutrition, diarrheal diseases, acute respiratory infection, malaria, and measles account for 60%–95% of reported deaths in famines and complex emergencies. For children aged <5 years, measles is a leading cause of mortality during these emergencies.[27]

---

20. Centers for Disease Control and Prevention, "Famine-Affected, Refugee, and Displaced Populations: Recommendations for Public Health Issues," *MMWR* 41, no. 13 (July 24, 1992): n.p. Online: http://www.cdc.gov/mmwr/preview/mmwrhtml/00019261.htm.

21. Centers for Disease Control and Prevention, "Mortality during a Famine—Gode District, Ethiopia, July 2000," *MMWR* 50 (2001): 286. Online: http://www.cdc.gov/mmwr/PDF/wk/mm5015.pdf.

22. Ibid., 285.

23. Ibid., 286.

24. Robert Lidstone, "Health and Mortality of Internally Displaced Persons: Reviewing the Data and Defining Directions for Research" (Washington, DC: Brookings-Bern Project on Internal Displacement, 2007), 4.

25. Ibid., 5.

26. Ibid., 6.

27. Centers for Disease Control and Prevention, "Mortality during a Famine," 287.

In horrific ways, displacement increases morbidity and mortality.

A third effect is a pragmatic response to diminished resources and security and increased morbidity and mortality. Forced migration alters social relationships and identities. For pragmatic reasons, households and eventually communities tend to become more extensive and inclusive. By extensive and inclusive, I mean that displaced families and communities, having lost members through death or separation, add members who were previously excluded. Displaced people in Iraq, for example, are routinely taken in by an "extended family."[28] To meet basic needs, families that have lost members reestablish households that include increasingly distant relatives, nonrelatives, and foreigners. Ruth Katz and Yoav Lavee, who studied families in modern Israel, report that "to ease material and economic difficulties, many immigrants choose to live in multi-generational households."[29] Families, in time and of necessity, become increasingly inclusive. Adoptions, intergenerational and nonfamilial coresidencies, and interracial and cross-cultural marriages tend to increase.

Amy E. Wagner summarizes a range of relevant findings for urban settings: Families extend when young adults are unemployed, older adults are ill, relatives immigrate, and financial resources diminish.[30] Not unexpectedly, extended families are more common in medium-sized agricultural societies because larger families offer economic advantages.[31] Flannery explains:

---

28. Norwegian Refugee Council, *Iraq: A Displacement Crisis*, 11.

29. Ruth Katz and Yoav Lavee, "Families in Israel," in *Handbook of World Families*, ed. Bert N. Adams and Jan Trost (London: Sage, 2005), 497.

30. Amy E. Wagner, "Extended Families," *International Encyclopedia of Marriage and Family* 2:539–40. Wagner references, among others, J. E. Benson, "Households, Migration, and Community Context," *Urban Anthropology* 19 (1990): 9–29; D. Y. Ford, and J. J. Harris, "The Extended African-American Family," *Urban League Review* 14 (1991): 71–83; J. E. Glick, "Nativity, Duration of Residence and the Life Course Pattern of Extended Family Living in the USA," *Population Research and Policy Review* 19 (2000): 179–98; J. E. Glick, F. D. Bean, and J. V. W. Van Hook, "Immigration and Changing Patterns of Extended Household Structure in the United States: 1970-1990," *Journal of Marriage and Family* 59 (1997): 177–91; J. L. Pearson et al., "Black Grandmothers in Multigenerational Households: Diversity in Family Structure and Parenting Involvement in the Woodlawn Community," *Child Development* 61 (1990): 434–42.

31. Patricia B. Christian, "Family, Extended," *Encyclopedia of Anthropology*, ed. H. James Birx, 5 vols. (Thousand Oaks, CA: Sage, 2006), 3:944.

in subsistence systems, the nuclear family is simply not a viable economic unit. In many parts of the [ancient] Near East, married sons remain attached to the household of their father because the combination of two tasks—cereal agriculture and the grazing of herd animals—requires a division of labor beyond the capacity of a nuclear family. By 5500 B.C. many Near Eastern villages not only grew wheat, barley, lentils, and peas for food, but also raised flax for linen and had added cattle and pigs to the herding of sheep and goats. A family of 15–20 simply had more manpower to perform all the disparate tasks in such an economy.[32]

Pragmatic interests dominate, and necessity and proximity result in extended and blended families across cultural boundaries. Necessity and proximity have a similar and compounding effect on larger social groups, where, over time, pragmatic interests foster assimilation and mitigate antagonism.

As a result, reconfigured families and communities slowly develop amended identities. This outcome relates to changes in the recomposition of families, juxtaposition of communities, and realignments of larger social frameworks. Identity is socially constructed and relates to roles and relationships in cultural contexts,[33] and identity changes for the displaced family, which is now a foreign or refugee family. Members within the family, of necessity, will assume new responsibilities and cross cultures, and language acquisition plays a part. The ability to master the elements of a second language diminishes with age,[34] and the younger members of households may acquire abilities and cultural understandings that deauthorize parents and grandparents. There may be a subtle shift of authority toward younger members of the social group.[35] Displacement alters the identities of individuals and, over time, the corporate identities of communities.

---

32. K. V. Flannery, "The Origins of the Village Revisited: From Nuclear to Extended Households," *American Antiquity* 67 (2002): 424.

33. V. Colic-Peisker, and I. Walker, "Human Capital, Acculturation and Social Identity: Bosnian Refugees in Australia," *Journal of Community and Applied Social Psychology* 13 (2003): 338.

34. Michael H. Long, "Maturational Constraints on Language Development," *Studies in Second Language Acquisition* 12 (1990): 251–85.

35. Ruth Katz and Yochanan Peres, "The Sociology of the Family in Israel: An Outline of Its Development from the 1950s to the 1980s," *European Sociological Review* 2 (1986): 150.

The consequences discussed are not the only effects, nor are they isolated or static. This description of cascading outcomes is a simplification, but the model provides useful categories for understanding forced displacement in ancient Israel and early Judaism and for reading texts such as Zech 1–8.

Outcomes of Forced Migration in Zechariah 1–8

Diminished resources and security, increased mortality and morbidity, and altered social relationships and identities are experiences that inform Zech 1–8, an early postexilic document that preserves visions and oracles dated from 520 to 518 BCE (cf. 1:1; 7:1). Zechariah envisions the creation of a new Zion in an apocalyptic composition that advances from a brief introduction (1:1–6), to eight night visions (1:7–6:15), to a series of concluding oracles (7:1–8:23), which also serve as a transition from the "realized" visions of chapters 1–6 to the "frustrated" visions of chapters 9–14.[36] The future that is envisioned and promoted by the prophet may be characterized as an undoing of exile in which the consequences of Judah's forced migration are reversed. Though complex in redaction, Zechariah, in its canonized form, preserves a vision that would "encourage obedience and engender hope for a generation living in circumstances falling short of the prophetic ideal."[37] The outcomes of forced migration identified in comparative studies are, to greater and lesser degrees, observed in Zechariah.

First, resources and security, which were diminished in exile, are restored in abundance in Zechariah's vision of the future. Zechariah's first vision (1:7–17) is that of a conversation between Yahweh and four riders who have returned from patrolling the earth and are standing in a glen of myrtle trees, a lush Edenic setting. In the vision, the angel of the Lord laments that Yahweh, who commands a supernatural army, has withheld mercy for seventy years. In the vision, however, Yahweh responds "with gracious and comforting words," which Zechariah is to convey to others:

> Thus says the LORD of hosts: I am very jealous for Jerusalem and for Zion. And I am extremely angry with the nations that are at ease; for

---

36. Mark J. Boda, "From Fasts to Feasts: The Literary Function of Zechariah 7–8," *CBQ* 65 (2003): 407.

37. Ibid. See also Louis Stulman, "Reading the Prophets as Meaning-Making Literature for Communities under Siege," *HBT* 29 (2007): 153–75.

while I was only a little angry, they made the disaster worse. Therefore, thus says the LORD, I have returned to Jerusalem with compassion; my house shall be built in it, says the LORD of hosts, and the measuring line shall be stretched out over Jerusalem. Proclaim further: Thus says the LORD of hosts: My cities shall again overflow with prosperity; the LORD will again comfort Zion and again choose Jerusalem. (1:14–17)[38]

The prophet envisions a time in which "cities shall again overflow with prosperity" (1:17), a reference implying the loss of resources in past displacement.

In Zechariah's second vision, 1:18–21, a vision of four horns and four blacksmiths, the prophet learns that the horns of the nations that scattered Judah will themselves be scattered. Although the imagery is somewhat ambiguous, the prophetic message is not. The nations that scattered Judah will themselves be scattered; security will be restored. The third vision also sees a secure future: the reinhabited city will not need walls for protection, for Yahweh will protect the city (2:1–5). The prospects of restored safety and prosperity are reiterated in the concluding oracles. When representatives from Bethel ask the priests and prophets about fasting rituals, they recall the words that the prophets used to proclaim "when Jerusalem was inhabited and in prosperity" (7:7), something lost that they hope will be regained. In 8:10–12 the message of the prophet is a message of prosperity:

> For before those days there were no wages for people or for animals, nor was there any safety from the foe for those who went out or came in, and I set them all against one other. But now I will not deal with the remnant of this people as in the former days, says the LORD of hosts. For there shall be a sowing of peace; the vine shall yield its fruit, the ground shall give its produce, and the skies shall give their dew; and I will cause the remnant of this people to possess all these things. (8:10–12)

Forced displacement brought "disaster," a loss of security and essential resources, but Zechariah proclaims that Yahweh will "do good to Jerusalem and to the house of Judah" (8:15).

Second, mortality and morbidity, which conflict-induced displacement increases, decrease in the world envisioned in Zech 1–8. In his third vision, 2:1–5, Zechariah observes a man surveying the dimensions of Jerusalem and learns from his angelic guide that "Jerusalem shall be inhabited

---

38. Scripture quotations are from the NRSV unless otherwise noted.

like villages without walls" (2:4a). Two reasons are given for the unusual design: its human and animal population will permit no boundaries, and Yahweh will protect the city (2:4b). In the renovation of Judah that Zechariah envisions, life and health surpass death and disease. This motif also reappears in the concluding oracles. In 8:4 the prophet declares, "Old men and old women shall again sit in the streets of Jerusalem, each with staff in hand because of their great age. And the streets of the city shall be full of boys and girls playing in its streets."

Third, social relationships and identities change in Zechariah's postexilic world, and the transformation that the prophet envisions for the immediate and distant future have personal and communal aspects. The introduction to Zech 1–8 emphasizes moral transformation: the Lord of Hosts says, "Do not be like your ancestors, to whom the former prophets proclaimed, '… Return from your evil ways and from your evil deeds'" (1:4). Preexilic identity and identification with the ancestors change to a postexilic identity in which evil and ancestral identities are traded for righteousness. In the new order, communal relationships also evolve. Comparative studies suggest that one would find in the visions and oracles evidence of movement toward extension and inclusion, and this is the case. Yahweh's command, "Render true judgments, show kindness and mercy to one another; do not oppress the widow, the orphan, the alien, or the poor; and do not devise evil in your hearts against one another" (7:9–10), which was neglected by Judah's ancestors, is expected in new Zion, where "Jerusalem will be called the faithful city" (8:3; cf. 8:17). Moreover, the community becomes inclusive. Zechariah's final oracle for the postexilic community and for the new Jerusalem—which will be a city without walls—is this:

> Peoples shall yet come, the inhabitants of many cities; the inhabitants of one city shall go to another, saying, "Come, let us go to entreat the favor of the LORD, and to seek the LORD of hosts; I myself am going." Many peoples and strong nations shall come to seek the LORD of hosts in Jerusalem, and to entreat the favor of the LORD. Thus says the LORD of hosts: In those days ten men from nations of every language shall take hold of a Jew, grasping his garment and saying, "Let us go with you, for we have heard that God is with you." (8:20–23)

The permeability of the community is captured in its reference to "men from nations of every language" seeking to accompany the Jews to Jerusalem (v. 23). The prophet sees "many peoples and strong nations" seeking the Lord in Jerusalem.[39] There is, however, no reference in the visions to family extension or inclusion.

Conclusions

Comparative studies suggest that the effects of forced migration include diminished resources and security, increased mortality and morbidity, and altered social relationships and identities, including pragmatic, survival-oriented acceptance of the extension of families and the inclusion of outsiders. These patterns may be observed in contemporary displacement situations and in Zech 1–8, though social patterns are not especially prominent within the book.

That forced migration promotes extension and inclusion at the family and community level invites additional explanation and raises questions about inclusive and exclusive rhetoric in the Hebrew Bible. My conclusion is that forced displacement creates a need for extended families and inclusive communities that transcends ideologies of separation; in short, ideology bends to the pragmatics of survival. Jeremiah's instructions to exiles are altogether pragmatic:

> Build houses and live in them; plant gardens and eat what they produce. Take wives and have sons and daughters; take wives for your sons, and give your daughters in marriage, that they may bear sons and daughters; multiply there, and do not decrease. But seek the welfare of the city where I have sent you into exile, and pray to the Lord on its behalf, for in its welfare you will find your welfare. (Jer 29:5–7)

When the welfare of outsider and insider are linked, and each has a stake in the security and prosperity of the other, ideology shifts toward extension and inclusion.

---

39. Baseline outcomes of forced displacement are also evident in Zech 9–14. The arrival in Jerusalem of Zion's humble king ushers in a return to security (9:9–15) and an abundance of resources: "grain shall make the young men flourish, and new wine the young women" (9:17), and there will be adequate produce for everyone (10:1). Moreover, an envisioned exile of half the population of Jerusalem involved the looting of houses and raping of women (14:2).

SCAT! EXILIC MOTIFS IN THE BOOK OF ZECHARIAH

Mark J. Boda

There is little question that the book of Zechariah is concerned with the restoration of the community of God in the wake of the Babylonian period,[1] a period that saw the destruction of the city of Jerusalem, the death or exile of the elite of the kingdom of Judah, and the incorporation of the state of Judah into the Babylonian Empire. In this book, where restoration plays such a key role, one should be able to discover what is often considered its contrast, that is, exile, and so this paper will provide insight into the perspective on exile found in the book of Zechariah.[2] The perspective found throughout this book is that of the Jewish community living in Yehud in the early Persian period, even though at times those addressed include communities living in the Diaspora, especially in the Mesopotamian context (see Zech 2:10–13 [Eng. 6–9]).[3]

In the present work I will focus on explicit references to exile as forced migration, that is, the movement of a person or population from

---

1. See David L. Petersen, "Zechariah's Visions: A Theological Perspective," *VT* 34 (1984): 195–206.
2. Although older critical scholarship has often treated this book as two separate literary entities, Proto- and Deutero-Zechariah (and some even add Trito-), in the present work I join a recent trend in scholarship in focusing on the book as a whole. See Mark J. Boda, *Haggai-Zechariah Research: A Bibliographic Survey,* Tools for Biblical Studies 5 (Leiden: Deo, 2003). I will not ignore evidence of compositional development, as I give attention to various parts of the corpora that share elements in common. On my theory of compositional development see Boda, *Zechariah,* NICOT (Grand Rapids: Eerdmans, forthcoming).
3. On this Yehudite perspective see John Kessler, "Diaspora and Homeland in the Early Achaemenid Period: Community, Geography and Demography in Zech 1–8," in *Approaching Yehud: New Approaches to the Persian Period,* ed. Jon L. Berquist, SemeiaSt 50 (Atlanta: Society of Biblical Literature, 2007), 138–39, 143.

one location to another, the first location typically being that associated with the ancestral home of the person or people group. I am well aware that "exile/forced migration" is part of a much broader motif or imagistic complex related to the cataclysmic destruction of a city or nation, both physically and sociologically, by a greater power. Exile appears to me to be a subsidiary image/motif within this broader complex, and this broader complex seems to dominate Zechariah. This means that in the present work I will not have in view all motifs within the book of Zechariah that are related to restoration or to the dystopia that precedes it. Here I will progress through the corpus and consider various pericopae in which exile is a major motif.

Human Exile

Foundational Vision-Oracles (Zech 1:7–2:9 [Eng. 5]; 4:1–6a; 4:10b–6:15): Zechariah 2:1–4 (Eng. 1:18–21)

At the core of the book of Zechariah lies an original sequence of seven night visions with accompanying short oracles in chapters 1–2 and 4–6. Within this sequence, visions 1–3 (1:7–17; 2:1–4 [Eng. 1:18–21]; 2:5–9 [Eng. 1–5]) and 8 (6:1–8) are focused on restoration issues, and one might expect that there would be some reference to the exilic experience. One might be tempted to draw in the first vision report with its reference to the "seventy years," but the use of this motif here in the night vision reports as well as in the broader ancient Near Eastern and biblical witness shows that this motif is related to the period of the desolation of a city, possibly due to ensuring the passing of a generation or more specifically of a king.[4] So also the reference to the exhaustion of Yahweh's wrath in "the land of the north" in the final vision report (6:1–8) may suggest to some the exilic motif, but there the focus is on the punishment of the aggressor nation, not the exile of the people.

---

4. The focus of the first night vision is on an unspecified experience of the discipline of Yahweh by Jerusalem and the cities of Judah that involved unspecified nations who enhanced this discipline beyond the intention of Yahweh. The reversal of this situation involves the return of Yahweh to Jerusalem with compassion, comfort, and election, the rebuilding of the temple and city, and the restoration of material prosperity to the region. There is no explicit reference to forced migration or exile. See further Boda, *Zechariah*.

It is really only in the second night vision in 2:1–4 (Eng. 1:18–21) that the motif of exile clearly comes to the fore.[5] The first night vision prompted an oracular pronouncement that promised two divine measures that would rectify deplorable conditions in Jerusalem and Judah, the first being the anger of Yahweh toward the nations who exceeded his disciplinary intention, and the second the compassion of Yahweh to return to and restore Jerusalem and the cities of Judah. The second night vision fills out the first of these measures.

The vocabulary used in this section includes *horns, plowers* (farmers), *scattering, terrifying,* and *throwing.* The mention of four horns suggests two oxen, something expected for the act of plowing or threshing (notice the use of pairs of animals in 1 Kgs 19:19; Deut 22:10).[6] In this agricultural context the term *scattering* (זרה *piel*) refers either to the scattering of a flock (Ps 44:12; Jer 31:10) or to the scattering of chaff in the act of threshing (Prov 20:26).[7] The regular link between זרה *piel* and winds (Ezek 5:10, 12; 12:14–15; Jer 49:32, 36) may suggest the latter image, but it must be noted that wind is not mentioned in this particular pericope.[8] *Terrifying* (להחריד) is used for the act of driving off a group of animals in Isa 17:2, Deut 28:26, and Jer 7:33, and *throwing* (*piel* of ידה) is used only twice elsewhere in the Hebrew Bible, to refer to throwing stones (Lam 3:53) and to shooting arrows (Jer 50:14) at an enemy. The overall picture here appears to be that of a team of oxen used for an agricultural enterprise (either plowing the land or threshing grain) who have either become loose and

---

5. See further Boda, "Terrifying the Horns: Persia and Babylon in Zechariah 1:7–6:15," *CBQ* 67 (2005): 22–41.

6. Isaiah 28:24–28 shows that חרשים do more than just plow, they also plant and thresh. Animals used in farming include עֶגְלָה (heifer/young cow, Judg 14:18; Hos 10:11, which thresh and possibly also plow/harrow), בָּקָר (ox, 1 Kgs 19:19–20; Job 1:14; Amos 6:12, which plow; Elijah in 1 Kgs 19 uses twelve pairs of oxen), and שׁוֹר and חֲמוֹר (ox and donkey, Deut 33:17, the former possessing horns; cf. Ps 69:32).

7. Carol L. Meyers and Eric M. Meyers (*Haggai, Zechariah 1–8: A New Translation with Introduction and Commentary,* AB 25B [Garden City, NY: Doubleday, 1987], 137) note here only the image of winnowing, assuming this for all references to זרה; so also Marvin A. Sweeney, *The Twelve Prophets,* 2 vols., Berit Olam (Collegeville, MN: Liturgical Press, 2000), 582.

8. The image of winnowing can also be discerned in the use of זרה *qal* in Isa 30:24; 41:16; Jer 4:11; 15:7; Ruth 3:2. For the regular association of the root זרה with the exile, see Kessler, "Diaspora and Homeland," 144: Lev 26:33; 1 Kgs 14:15; Jer 31:10; 49:32; Ezek 5:2, 10, 12; 6:8; 12:14, 15; 20:23; 22:15; 36:19; Ps 106:27.

scattered a flock of sheep or have been involved in threshing grain, which scattered the chaff among the nations. Four farmers then appear on the scene to bring an end to the present fiasco by throwing stones at the team of oxen in order to drive them off.

This night vision describes at first the exile of Judah, Jerusalem, and Israel (2:2 [Eng. 1:19]), before secondly focusing on Judah alone (2:4 [Eng. 1:21]),[9] using the language of scattering (either chaff or sheep), and identifies the cause of this exile as two powerful nations (the horns of the nations). Although the focus of the vision soon shifts to Judah, matching the trend seen in the first night vision (esp. note 1:12–17), the initial reference to both Judah and Israel suggests that the two nations represented by the horns are probably Assyria and Babylon, those nations that successively scattered Israel and Judah.[10] This suggests that Mesopotamia is the region to which Israel and Judah were scattered. No reference is made to when Judah, Israel, and Jerusalem were scattered nor why the exile took place.

Secondary Levels in the Vision-Oracles (Zech 2:10 [Eng. 6]–3:10; 4:6b–10a; 6:9–15): Zechariah 2:10–17 (Eng. 6–13)

While the remainder of the core night vision material does not contain an explicit reference to the exile of Judah, Israel, or Jerusalem, the secondary materials that make up 2:10–17 (Eng. 6–13), chapter 3, 4:6b–10a, and 6:9–15 do.[11] Some have seen the reference to Joshua as a brand plucked from the fire and the depiction of him with unclean clothing as evidence of the exilic motif.[12] However, this can only be sustained if "the fire" is a reference to the exile, and this is not made explicit in this context. Throughout the book of Zechariah Jeshua is never clearly identified as a member of the exilic community, even though in 6:9–15 he receives a crown made from

---

9. See ibid., 145, for the legitimacy of the presence of all three in 2:2 (Eng. 1:19) and only Judah in 2:4 (Eng. 1:21).

10. See Boda, "Terrifying the Horns," 26 n. 17, for the interlinking of Assyria and Babylonia in Hebrew tradition, esp. Jer 50:17–18; Gen 10:8–12.

11. See Boda, *Zechariah*.

12. E.g., Meyers and Meyers, *Haggai, Zechariah 1–8*, 188, 221; also Byron G. Curtis, *Up the Steep and Stony Road: The Book of Zechariah in Social Location Trajectory Analysis*, Academia Biblica 25 (Atlanta: Scholars Press, 2006), 134, who speaks of the "fires of evil and the unclean land of exile."

materials brought by members of this community.¹³ If this reference to "a brand plucked from the fire" is drawing on Amos 4:11,¹⁴ where a similar phrase follows an allusion to the destruction of Sodom and Gomorrah, then the focus is on the destruction of Jerusalem rather than on the exile of the people.¹⁵ This conclusion is strengthened by Yahweh's reference to the election of Jerusalem immediately prior to the description of Jeshua as a firebrand. An exilic connection is evident in the passing reference to the arrival of members of the exilic community (הַגּוֹלָה) from Babylon (אֲשֶׁר־בָּאוּ מִבָּבֶל) in 6:10. The term הַגּוֹלָה probably serves only as a technical term for "exile" and so offers little insight into the Zecharian perspective on exile, besides the fact that this group is composed, at least at the outset, of those who come from Babylon.¹⁶ Near the end of 6:9–15 reference is made to those who will come from רְחוֹקִים (far off) to build the temple (6:15). This more generic term broadens the potential exilic community while emphasizing the aspect of distance from Jerusalem in the exilic experience and is one often used in prophetic material to describe the diasporic communities.¹⁷ Far more revealing, however, is the treatment of the exile in the oracular section that brings closure to the first panel of night vision reports and comprises 2:10–17 (Eng. 6–13).

In the first part of this oracular section (2:10–13 [Eng. 6–9]), the exilic community is exhorted to flee from Babylon. The one addressed is "Zion," suggesting that the exilic community is related to the preexilic inhabitants of Jerusalem. A variety of images is used to describe the motif of exile. The first is seen in the phrase כְּאַרְבַּע רוּחוֹת הַשָּׁמַיִם פֵּרַשְׂתִּי אֶתְכֶם (as/according to the four winds of the heavens I have scattered you). There are two key challenges to understanding the image in play in this phrase, first the meaning of the verb פרש piel,¹⁸ and second the

---

13. Contra Kessler, "Diaspora and Homeland," 150, who cites Hag 1:1.
14. See Sweeney, *Twelve Prophets*, 596.
15. As Michael H. Floyd, *Minor Prophets, Part 2*, FOTL 22 (Grand Rapids: Eerdmans, 2000), 374: "Joshua is comparable to a burned stick from that fire in the sense that he, as a legitimate descendant of the Jerusalem priesthood, is one of the few remaining traces of the cult that was destroyed." The focus is on Joshua's survival from the destruction, not on the exile.
16. Cf. Kessler, "Diaspora and Homeland," 152–53.
17. Ibid., 153, who notes Isa 33:13; 43:6; 49:12; 60:4, 9; Jer 30:10; 51:50; Dan 9:7.
18. Peter R. Ackroyd (*Exile and Restoration: A Study of Hebrew Thought of the Sixth Century B.C.*, OTL [Philadelphia: Westminster, 1968], 179) translates this phrase here as "for like the four winds of heaven I have caused you to take wing," citing G. R.

meaning of the preposition כ. The verb פרש *piel* is typically employed with words for hands (either כפים or ידים) to indicate a human extending the palms/hands to pray (Isa 1:15; Jer 4:31; Ps 143:6) or even to swim (Isa 25:11), or to Yahweh entreating the people (Isa 65:2). Only here and in Ps 68:15 (Eng. 14) does the verb appear without a noun for hand, and in the latter it appears to refer to the scattering of an army in defeat, especially in light of references to scattering in 68:2 (Eng. 1) ("Let God arise, let his enemies be scattered [פוץ], and let those who hate him flee [נוס]") and 68:31 (Eng. 30) ("He has scattered [בזר *piel*] the peoples who delight in war"). Support for this image may also come from the *niphal* stem of this root, which occurs only one time in the Hebrew Bible.[19] Ezekiel 17:21 describes the survivors of a defeated army being scattered to every wind.[20]

This reference to "wind" in Ezek 17:21, that the scattering is "to every wind," may offer some help for the second key challenge to understanding this image, that is, the function of the preposition כ. The dominant sense of this preposition is "general agreement," and it is often used to introduce a simile or comparison. If that is the sense here, the scattering of the people is being compared to the scattering of the four winds, that is, in the same way that the four winds are scattered, so also Zion was scattered.[21] But this preposition is also used to introduce the manner or norm

---

Driver, "Studies in the Vocabulary of the Old Testament: II," *JTS* 33 (1931): 252. While פרש does appear with כנף to signify a bird (or birdlike creature) spreading out the wing or taking wing in the Hebrew Bible (Deut 32:11; Job 39:26; Jer 48:40; 49:22; cf. Exod 25:20; 37:9; 1 Kgs 6:27; 1 Kgs 8:7//2 Chr 5:8; 2 Chr 3:13), even with כנף omitted in 1 Chr 28:18, it is important to note that these cases involve the *qal* of פרש while in the present case the *piel* of פרש is used. Odd here is the witness of the OG, which has συνάξω, suggesting an original Hebrew *Vorlage* of כנס (to gather; see Ps 33:7; Qoh 2:8, 26; 3:5; Neh 12:44; Esth 4:16; 1 Chr 22:2), which provides a completely different reading unrelated to the motif of exile.

19. Some (e.g., *BHS*) have suggested that פרש *niphal* in Ezek 34:12 should read פרש *niphal*. There it refers to the scattering of a flock of sheep.

20. While one would usually associate the *niphal* with the *qal*, a *piel*::*niphal* relation is attested at times in Hebrew Bible (*IBHS* §23.6.2), besides the fact that the semantic range of the *qal* of פרש is strikingly similar to that of the *piel*. The *qal* is used for spreading out/stretching over a cloth, covering, garment, tent, net, letter, scroll, and sail, as well as (akin to *piel*) stretching out the hand (Lam 1:10; Prov 31:20) and stretching out the palm in prayer (Exod 9:29, 33; 1 Kgs 8:22, 38, 54; 2 Chr 6:12, 13, 29; Ezra 9:5; Job 11:13; Ps 44:21). See also Lam 4:4, where it refers to breaking bread, and Mic 3:3, chopping up meat.

21. E.g., Floyd, *Minor Prophets*, 368.

of an action, as in Ps 51:3 (Eng. 1): "Have mercy on me, O God, according to your steadfast love."²² If that is the sense, the scattering could be accomplished based on the principle of the four winds (as four directions) or by manner of the four winds. This sense is closer to the use of the preposition לְ with the *niphal* in Ezek 17:21, that is, the scattering is "to" the four winds. The four winds here are used to indicate the four basic directions as found in Ezek 42:20 and 1 Chr 9:24 (cf. Jer 49:36; Dan 11:4).

Other vocabulary that appears in Zech 2:10–13 (Eng. 6–9) includes שָׁלַל/שָׁלָל (plunder/plundering), terms regularly used for the despoiling of a nation by an opposing army (Isa 10:6; Jer 50:10; Ezek 26:12; 29:19; 38:12; 39:10; Hab 2:8). When the verb is followed by an accusative it can designate the person from whom plunder is taken or it can refer to the plunder itself. In light of the use of שָׁלָל in Zech 2:13 (Eng. 9), where in the reversal the nations who plundered now become plunder for their slaves, it is more likely that it is the people who are the plunder of the foreign army. Such plunder is taken back to the home country, revealing its relevance to the exilic motif in this passage. The use of the verb נגע (to touch) fits within this broader imagistic world as well, either as reference to the sexual abuse²³ or to the violence²⁴ associated with ancient war.²⁵ Thus the vocabulary used in 2:10–13 (Eng. 6–9) suggests the image of a defeat of an army or nation in war that leads to a scattering of the army/nation, as well as pillaging, violence, and possibly rape. The reference to the community as a female inhabitant living within the domicile of another female (יוֹשֶׁבֶת בַּת־בָּבֶל) and as slaves (עֲבָדִים) suggests the final condition of a nation defeated in war and taken away into exile.²⁶

---

22. *BHRG* §39.10.1.(ii).

23. For נגע with the preposition בְּ for a sexual act see Prov 6:29 (possibly also Gen 26:11); cf. Gen 20:6 (where the preposition אֶל is used) and Ruth 2:9 (where accusative).

24. נגע with the preposition בְּ can refer to someone violently striking (Gen 26:11; 32:26, 33; Josh 9:19; 2 Sam 14:10; Jer 12:14), to a wind blowing violently (Ezek 17:10; Job 1:19), or to God's physical touch of creation (Amos 9:5; Pss 104:32; 144:5).

25. The image of touching the pupil of the eye is also employed here to strengthen the sense of connection between the people and Yahweh and to highlight the preciousness of the people to Yahweh. Various phrases are used to refer to the pupil of the eye in the Hebrew Bible: in Ps 17:8 it is אִישׁוֹן בַּת־עָיִן (pupil of the daughter of the eye), in Lam 2:18 it is בַּת עַיִן (daughter of the eye), in Deut 32:10 and Prov 7:2 it is אִישׁוֹן עֵינוֹ (pupil of his eye).

26. On such servitude see Meyers and Meyers, *Haggai, Zechariah 1–8*, 137:

Zechariah 2:10–17 (Eng. 6–13) identifies those who are exiled as Zion. At first the one who exiled Zion is identified as Yahweh himself (2:10 [Eng. 6]), but later it is made clear that "the nations" played a role. The location of the exile is identified as the "land of the north" (2:10 [Eng. 6]), a location identified in the prophetic tradition with the Mesopotamian region in general (e.g., Jer 46:10; 59:9) and due to connections to the destruction of Judah and exile of the people (e.g., Jer 6:22; 10:22) and the return and restoration of Judah (e.g., Jer 3:18; 16:15; 23:8; 31:8), with Babylon in particular.[27] That Babylon is in view here in Zech 2 is made explicit in the reference to "daughter Babylon" in 2:11 (Eng. 7).[28] Nevertheless, the reference to "the four winds of the heavens," may represent a broader geographical destination.[29] There is no reference to the time when exile took place and no reason is given for the exile.

Prose Sermonic Material (Zech 1:1–6; 7:1–14; 8:14–23):
Zechariah 7:1–14

Surrounding the expanded inner core of vision-oracles lie the prose sermons of 1:1–6 and chapters 7–8 (minus 8:1–13). While 1:1–6 is silent on human exile as forced migration, one does find evidence in chapters 7–8, just prior to the key rhetorical turning point in this second prose sermon. Zechariah 7:14 employs the verb סער *piel*, a form that appears only here in the Hebrew Bible. A *pual* form, however, appears in Isa 54:11, and *poel* or

---

"Exiled groups served a variety of other purposes, by providing skilled and unskilled labor both for urban needs and for the development of unsettled regions." However, for some reason, the Meyers (p. 167) see the servitude in this context as referring to Yehud, rather than as the context demands to those still exiled in Babylon.

27. See David L. Petersen, *Haggai and Zechariah 1–8: A Commentary*, OTL (Philadelphia: Westminster, 1984), 174–75; Sweeney, *Twelve Prophets*, 587.

28. "Land of the north" also appears in the final night vision report in 6:1–8, which is immediately followed by the arrival of exiles from Babylon, suggesting that the fulfillment of the divine decrees against the land of the north in the final night vision has resulted in the release of the exiles in 6:9–10, something foreshadowed in 2:10–17 [Eng. 6–13].

29. See Kessler, "Diaspora and Homeland," 146, who sees here a recognition of both "a past, widespread dispersion and a more focused one (Babylon)," reminding us not "to collapse all the expatriate communities into the one in Babylon." Contra Meyers and Meyers, *Haggai, Zechariah 1–8*, 163, who see in this reference to the four winds "cosmic overtones," which "make it transcend historical realities."

pual form in Hos 13:3. The nuance of Isa 54:11 is uncertain, but Hos 13:3 clearly refers to chaff being blown away from the threshing floor by a great wind.[30] One cannot be certain that the threshing image is in play here, but it is certainly plausible. A key feature in this depiction of the exile, however, is that the land is left desolate (שמם *niphal*) and desolated,[31] that is, the wind here was so powerful it removed everyone from the land.

In Zech 7:14 those who are exiled are not clearly identified, although it is assumed it is those who previously had inhabited Jerusalem, the Negev, and the Shephelah (7:7). Yahweh claims to have personally exiled the people by not listening to their cries and instead sending them away. The destination of their exile is identified generally as "all the nations" (כָּל־הַגּוֹיִם). The reason for their exile is explicitly stated in 7:7–13 as the refusal of the people to respond to the prophetic word. The broader context as well suggests that the exile took place seventy years prior to this prophetic sermon, that is, around 588 BCE.

Secondary Oracles among the Prose Sermons (Zech 8:1–13): Zechariah 8:6–8, 11–13

Inserted into the second prose sermon in chapters 7–8 are two key pieces in 8:1–13. The first in 8:1–8 is an oracular collection, while the second in 8:9–13 a cohesive prose sermon. Although diverse in origin, the two sections are connected by common vocabulary in their closing verses, 8:6–8

---

30. Some have suggested repointing יִסְעָרוּ (*qal*) in Hab 3:14 to יְסֹעֲרוּ (*pual*; see BHS; HALOT 2:762). See also the nominal forms סְעָרָה (high wind, Ezek 1:4; 13:11, 13; Jer 23:19; 30:23, etc.) and סַעַר (tempest, Jer 23:19; 25:32; 30:23; Ps 83:17; Amos 1:14; Jonah 1:4, 12), both of which are used in connection with Yahweh and his judgment. Notice especially Isa 41:15–16, where the image of threshing is used to refer to the reversal in the exilic period and how winnowing (זרה *qal*) precedes a wind (רוּחַ) that carries away the chaff (see 41:15, מֹץ), a storm (סְעָרָה) that scatters (פוץ, *hiphil*) it. Also Isa 40:24 where reference is made to the storm wind (סְעָרָה) carrying away stubble; cf. Petersen, *Haggai and Zechariah 1–8*, 294.

31. There is some confusion on the noun שַׁמָּה in the lexicons. This noun can refer to an object of horror or to a wasteland but also to a place without inhabitant; see Isa 13:9; Jer 2:15; 4:7; 46:19; 48:9; 50:3; 51:29, 53. In Zech 7:14 the verb נָשַׁמָּה and noun שַׁמָּה refer to a deserted land, a conclusion supported by the phrase מֵעֹבֵר וּמִשָּׁב, which points to the cessation of human activity (see Ezek 35:7).

and 8:11–13: שְׁאֵרִית הָעָם הַזֶּה (the remnant of this people) and the *hiphil* of ישע (to save).[32]

Here the image used is that of a remnant, a remainder, that which is left over after a catastrophe from a previously existing larger entity (see esp. Isa 44:17).[33] This is a common motif in the Hebrew Bible, used often but not exclusively for those who survived the destruction and exile of Israel and Judah.[34] There are both negative and positive dimensions to this motif.[35] Negatively it assumes severe judgment/discipline of a group, but positively it assumes that a group has not been eliminated. While this term does appear in the book of Haggai (1:12, 14; 2:2), besides the meaning of Zerubbabel's name (seed of Babylon), there is no indication there that this remnant is one that had survived an exilic experience. However, in Zech 8:1–13 it is clear in verses 6–8 that this remnant is a community that is removed from the land since they are in need of salvation: מֵאֶרֶץ מִזְרָח וּמֵאֶרֶץ מְבוֹא הַשָּׁמֶשׁ (from the land of the rising and from the land of the setting of the sun, 8:7). In verses 11–13 this exilic dimension is not as explicit. According to verse 13, they are "a curse among the nations," but this could mean that those living in the land are an example of curse within the international community. However, in light of the preceding reference to an international setting in verses 6–8 and the close affinities between the two passages, it is likely that "among the nations" here refers to an exilic context.

Alongside the remnant motif is that of "curse" (קְלָלָה) in 8:13. While this term is used for the curse that will befall those who are disobedient to the covenant, especially in the book of Deuteronomy (11:26; 28:15, 45; 30:1), its appearance here in relation to the nations reflects the use of this term in Jeremiah, where it refers to the resultant state of that curse having falling upon a people or land (Jer 24:9; 25:18; 42:18; 44:8, 12, 22;

---

32. See Boda, *Zechariah*, for further links between these two pericopae and evidence that these two oracles reflect processes that brought together not only Zech 1–8 in its present form, but also Haggai-Zechariah 1–8.

33. See Meyers and Meyers, *Haggai, Zechariah 1–8*, 417; Kessler, "Diaspora and Homeland," 149, both of whom argue the term שְׁאֵרִית here taps into the larger theological motif of remnant found elsewhere in the Hebrew Bible.

34. See Gerhard F. Hasel, *The Remnant: The History and Theology of the Remnant Idea from Genesis to Isaiah*, 3rd ed., AUMSR 5 (Berrien Springs, MI: Andrews University Press, 1980).

35. See Lester V. Meyer, "Remnant," *ABD* 5:670.

49:13; cf. 18:16; 19:8; 50:13), appearing alongside the terms אָלָה (curse), שַׁמָּה (object of horror), חֶרְפָּה (reproach), חֹרֶב (ruin), and שְׁרֵקָה/שְׁרִיקָה (object of hissing).

In Zech 8:1–13 those who are exiled are described as "my people" (8:7) and the "house of Judah/house of Israel" (8:13). The latter reflects "an understanding of its addressees as members of a broader unity."[36] The location of the group called "my people" ranges from the distant east (the land of the rising ... of the sun; אֶרֶץ מִזְרָח ... הַשֶּׁמֶשׁ) to the distant west (the land of the setting of the sun, אֶרֶץ מְבוֹא הַשָּׁמֶשׁ, 8:7).[37] The location of the groups called "house of Judah/house of Israel" is "among the nations" (בַּגּוֹיִם). There is no indication as to who exiled the community, although Yahweh's statement in 8:11, "But now I will not treat the remnant of this people as in the former days," suggests that Yahweh is the one responsible, even though "the former days" in this context are not the days of "exile" but rather the hardship experienced by the early Persian period community before the foundation of the temple was laid (see Hag 2:15–19). In Zech 8:1–13 no indication is given why the exile was necessary, nor when it took place.

Oracles of Zechariah 9–10

The first major section of Zech 9–14 is composed of the oracular material in chapters 9–10, introduced by the literary marker מַשָּׂא in 9:1. Within this literary complex there are two references to human exile: 9:11–13 and 10:6–11.

Zechariah 9:11–13

In Zech 9:11–13 Yahweh addresses first Daughter Zion and then her sons Judah and Ephraim. Here the exilic community is identified as "prisoners" (אָסִיר), who have been incarcerated in a waterless pit. In the Hebrew Bible,

---

36. Kessler, "Diaspora and Homeland," 148.

37. Because Meyers and Meyers (*Haggai, Zechariah 1–8*, 418, 430) do not see evidence for a return from the Egyptian diaspora, they consider this reference to the east/west as "eschatological." However, see Kessler, "Diaspora and Homeland," 151, who notes how this may be "a simple merism, thus designating the exiles wherever they may be" or "may be an explicit inclusion of the Egyptian diaspora," as per Ackroyd, *Exile and Restoration*, 213.

אָסִיר often refers to someone who performs forced labor (Judg 16:21, 25; Job 3:18; cf. Gen 39:20; Pss 68:7 [Eng. 6]; 69:34 [Eng. 33]; 79:11; 102:21 [Eng. 20]; 107:10). The use of a בּוֹר to refer to a prison is common in the Hebrew Bible (Gen 37:20, 22, 24, 28–29; 40:15; 41:14; Isa 24:22; Jer 38:6–7, 9–11, 13; Lam 3:53). The use of the terms אָסִיר and בּוֹר is reminiscent of Joseph (cf. Gen 37:20, 22, 24, 28–28; 40:15; 41:14 with 39:20), while the phrase מִבּוֹר אֵין מַיִם בּוֹ (a waterless pit) is reminiscent of Jeremiah (see Jer 38:6).[38] The invitation to these prisoners is to return to בִּצָּרוֹן, a *hapax legomenon* in the Hebrew Bible. Although insecure, the root בצר may offer some insight into its meaning. The *qal* passive participle of that root is used multiple times in the Hebrew Bible to describe a city or wall as "fortified," that is, inaccessible to opposing forces.[39] Here then those who were imprisoned within an inaccessible stronghold are invited to freedom in another inaccessible stronghold.

In Zech 9:11–13 the exilic community is identified as Judah and Ephraim, who are considered the sons of Zion. However, no indications are given as to where, why, or when the exile took place, nor who was responsible for the exile.

Zechariah 10:6–11

Zechariah 10 begins with a focus on Judah as Yahweh makes many promises to his flock, the house of Judah. This reaches a climax in the opening line of 10:6 with the promise that he will strengthen the house of Judah, a summary statement of the promises in 10:3a–5. It is at that point that the house of Joseph is introduced into the discourse, with the declaration that Yahweh will save the house of Joseph and bring them back. The overall

---

38. See Meyers and Meyers, *Zechariah 9–14: A New Translation with Introduction and Commentary*, AB 25C (New York: Doubleday, 1993), 140–42. Such connections to "prisoners" and a "pit with no water in it" "involves language referring to the condition of exile," especially in light of the fact that Joseph is often treated as "diaspora hero" story.

39. In reference to an עִיר: Num 13:28 Deut 1:28; 3:5; 9:1; Josh 14:12; 2 Sam 20:6; 2 Kgs 18:13//Isa 36:1; 2 Kgs 19:25//Isa 37:26; 2 Chr 17:2; 19:5; 32:1; 33:14; Neh 9:25; Isa 25:2; 27:10; Ezek 36:35; Hos 8:14; Zeph 1:16. In reference to a חוֹמָה: Deut 28:52; Isa 2:15; Jer 15:20. See ibid., 142, for their connection to the mid-fifth-century fortresses in the western portion of the Persian Empire in order to guard against the Greeks; see Kenneth G. Hoglund, *Achaemenid Imperial Administration in Syria-Palestine and the Mission of Ezra and Nehemiah*, SBLDS 125 (Atlanta: Scholars Press, 1992).

flow suggests that Judah's return has been accomplished, and now Judah will play some kind of role in the restoration of Joseph from exile. Exile is described in 10:9 using the verb זרע, a word used countless times in the Hebrew Bible to refer to sowing seed (e.g., Gen 26:12) and another time figuratively to sowing Israel (Hos 2:25). While this image does imply the scattering of seed, this kind of scattering is far more dynamic than that encountered earlier in the book.[40] The seed has potential for new life, and that is precisely what happens in the latter half of the verse as they along with their children come to life (חיה) and return to the land. The image of sown seed is also appropriate in reference to the dispersion of the northern tribes, one that had taken place at a much earlier point in history and that entailed a deeper embeddedness in foreign soil.[41] While the term *gather* (קבץ *piel*) is one of the most common verbs used for the return to the land after exile,[42] it is used in Mic 4:12 to refer to the gathering in of sheaves, which would fit the present context with seed that has sprouted and reached maturation.[43]

In Zech 10 the exilic community is identified as the house of Joseph (10:6) and Ephraim (10:7). The declaration in 10:6 that the future salvation will be "as though I had not rejected them" suggests that Yahweh is the one who exiled them. The location of exile is identified as "the peoples" (עַמִּים) and "distant places" (מֶרְחַקִּים) in verse 9, and more specifically in verse 10 as the land of Egypt and Assyria. No indications are given as to why or when the exile took place in this chapter.

Zechariah 12–14

The oracular material now found in 12:1–13:6 and chapter 14 contrasts radically with that found in chapters 9–10, a shift that can be attributed

---

40. See Meyers and Meyers, *Zechariah 9–14*, 216, who contrast the image here with that of winnowing earlier in Zechariah.

41. Cf. ibid., who note that while winnowing was appropriate as an image for the southern kingdom, planting was better for the northern kingdom due to "the long duration—the rootedness—of Ephraim's exile."

42. Deut 30:3–4; Isa 11:12; 43:5; 54:7; 56:8; Jer 23:3; 29:14; 31:8, 10; 32:37; Ezek 11:17; 20:41; 28:25; 34:13; 36:24; 37:21; 39:27; Mic 2:12; 4:6; Zeph 3:20; Zech 10:8, 10; Pss 106:47; 107:3; Neh 1:89; 1 Chr 16:35; cf. Ezek 29:13.

43. So also Floyd, *Minor Prophets*, 478: "The scattering of Israel ... thus becomes comparable to a great 'sowing' (*zrʿ*, 10:9aα; *RSV* 'scatter'), from which the resulting harvest is now being reaped in the process of restoration."

to elements introduced in the prophetic sign-act of 11:4–16.⁴⁴ The material looks to a future day when the nations will attack Jerusalem and be defeated. While the first depiction in chapter 12 emphasizes Jerusalem's complete success against the nations, the second depiction in chapter 14 describes an initial defeat of Jerusalem that is followed by success due to Yahweh's intervention. This initial defeat involves the taking of spoil (שָׁלָל), the capturing of the city, the plundering of houses, the raping of women, and the exile (גּוֹלָה) of half of the city. This future vision is strikingly reminiscent of the depiction of the exile in 2:10–13 (Eng. 6–9).

Those exiled in 14:2 are the inhabitants of the city of Jerusalem, but the destination of their exile is not provided. The nations prompted by Yahweh are responsible for this exile. No reason is given for the exile. Its timing is clearly in the future ("a day is coming," 14:1). Interestingly, the focus remains on those left behind in the city rather than on those who are exiled.

Shepherd Units (10:1–3a; 11:1–3; 11:4–16; 11:17; 13:7–9)

The last major literary unit in Zech 9–14 is that of the shepherd units, which pepper the account in 10:1–3a; 11:1–3; 11:4–16; 11:17; 13:7–9. Among these units only 13:7–9 contains vocabulary that may be connected to exile. There the verb פוץ (scatter) is used to describe the action of the sheep after their shepherd is violently struck by the sword.⁴⁵ On its surface it appears that this text does not refer to a group that goes into exile, since after the sheep are scattered, two parts in the land are cut off and perish, while a third is left in it to be refined. However, if this depiction is relying on Ezek 5 (vv. 2–4, 12),⁴⁶ then it is possible that the two parts include those who are cut off from the community and sent into exile

---

44. See Boda, "Reading between the Lines: Zechariah 11:4–16 in Its Literary Contexts," in *Bringing out the Treasure: Inner Biblical Allusion and Zechariah 9–14*, ed. Mark J. Boda and Michael H. Floyd, JSOTSup 304 (Sheffield: Sheffield Academic, 2003), 277–91.

45. The root פוץ in the *hiphil* often is used for the scattering of Israel in exile (Deut 4:27; 28:64; Ezek 11:16, 17; Jer 9:15 [Eng. 16]; 13:24; Neh 1:8). The *hiphil* is used for the scattering of a flock in Jer 23:1, 2, the *niphal* in 1 Kgs 22:17; Ezek 34:6, 12; Jer 10:21, and the *qal* (as here) in Ezek 34:5. See further Meyers and Meyers, *Zechariah 9–14*, 388.

46. Petersen, *Zechariah 9–14 and Malachi: A Commentary* (OTL; Louisville: Westminster John Knox, 1995), 131.

(כרת *niphal*; cf. Exod 12:15; Num 19:20), as opposed to those who perish. Furthermore, the reference to portions of the community alongside reference to scattering is strikingly similar to the reference to portions of the city alongside reference to exile in 14:2. If exile is in view, the image of exile here draws again on the agricultural context of sheepherding as well as the priestly context of ritual law. It is not the exilic community, however, that is refined through the fire but rather that group which is left in the land.

The identity of those exiled in Zech 13:7–9 is not made clear nor is their destination, and it may not be outside the land at all. Their fate is uncertain, although there are indications that a significant number would not survive. The timing of this exile appears to be in the future.

Divine Exile

To this point we have tracked the presentation of the exilic motif/image in relation to humans on the earthly plane within the book of Zechariah. However, there is another dimension to the exilic motif/image in the book that is rarely considered, that is, the exile that occurs within the heavenly realm.

Exile of a Babylonian Deity

Such a forced migration appears in the penultimate night vision of Zech 5:5–11. There a female figure called either "their eye" or "their iniquity" in verse 6[47] and later identified as "wickedness" in verse 8 is transported by stork-winged women to the land of Shinar (Babylon), where she is placed on a pedestal within a shrine. That this migration is forced is made clear by the need for the interpreting angel to throw her down into the middle of the ephah and secure its opening with a lead weight. This vision appears to be depicting the forced migration of a goddess whose origins are not in the land of Israel. While at first sight this appears to be an exilic forced migration in that it appears to be performed against the will of the figure and involves movement from one land to another, from a Yahwistic perspective it is actually a depiction of restoration as the goddess returns to her place of origin, that is, the land of Shinar.[48]

---

47. MT has "their eye," while LXX suggests "their iniquity."
48. Helpful for this connection to exile/restoration may be the link between this vision in Zech 5:5–11 and the second night vision in 2:1–4 [Eng. 1:18–21] argued by

Exile of Yahweh

It is this forced migration of the female deity in Zech 5 that raises awareness of another exile in the book, that of Yahweh.[49] In some of the first words of the book Yahweh reveals his desire to "return" (1:3), and this is repeated in his promise in the first night vision in 1:16 (I will return to Jerusalem with compassion) and in the third night vision in 2:9 (Eng. 5) (I will be a wall of fire around her and I will be the glory in her midst).[50] This promise of return is declared in the oracles of 2:10–17 (Eng. 6–13) as Yahweh promises to come and dwell in the midst of Daughter Zion (2:14–15 [Eng. 10–11]). The depiction of Yahweh's future possession (נחל) of Judah as his portion (חֵלֶק) in the Holy Land in 2:16 (Eng. 12) reveals a God separated from his ancestral property and desirous to return and repossess it.[51] Zechariah 2:17 (Eng. 13) confirms this with the declaration that Yahweh is presently in "his holy habitation," that is, his heavenly lair.[52] According to Zech 4, the temple will serve as a portal through which Yahweh will examine the world (the eyes of Yahweh). However, the final night vision depicts Yahweh in exile in Mesopotamia. The imagery found in 6:1, with the portal to the divine council set between two bronze

---

Meyers and Meyers, *Haggai, Zechariah 1–8*, 312–16. In the earlier vision the agents of Yahweh remove the figures symbolic of the foreign nations. Also there is a focus in both on exile and restoration.

49. See also ibid., 314, who note: "The movement toward the 'Holy Land' (Zech 2:16 [RSV v 12]) had to be balanced by a movement in the opposite direction, the direction from which Yahweh and his people had come: 'the land of Shinar.' The carrying of Wickedness away to Babylon serves as the counterpart to the return of Yahweh to the land he had chosen and to his rightful temple in Jerusalem."

50. The mission of the riders on the steeds in the first night vision suggests that of a reconnaissance mission spying out the land. Notice how similar language of "resting" is part of the observations of the Benjaminite spies in Judg 18:7.

51. It is possible that "Judah" here refers to the people (so Meyers and Meyers, *Haggai, Zechariah 1–8*, 169), esp. in light of Deut 32:8–9, where Yahweh's portion is identified as his people; so also Exod 34:9, where Moses asks Yahweh to come into the midst of the people to inherit them. In any case, this portion is specifically denoted as being "in the holy land."

52. As per ibid., 171, which cites the close affinity to Zech 1:7 with its eschatological portrait of Yahweh, although noting Karl Elliger, *Die Propheten Nahum, Habakuk, Zephanja, Haggai, Sacharja, Maleachi*, vol. 2 of *Das Buch der zwölf kleinen Propheten*, 7th ed., ATD 25.2 (Göttingen: Vandenhoeck & Ruprecht, 1975), who sees it as the earthly temple as per Ps 26:8.

mountains, is suggestive of Mesopotamian iconography related to the sun God Shamash.[53] Yahweh's promise in 8:3 to return to Zion and dwell in the midst of Jerusalem echoes the language of chapters 1 and 2, revealing that the enduring struggle for restoration evident on the human plane is paralleled by a struggle for restoration on the divine plane. Such a return is clearly part of the preferred future according to 8:20–23, as foreigners seek to accompany Jews back to Jerusalem because they have heard about Yahweh's presence. The depiction of the path of the divine warrior Yahweh in 9:1–8, a return that ends with him encamped at his house, that is, his temple in Jerusalem, confirms that Yahweh was in exile. Even in the future vision of chapter 14 it appears that Yahweh approaches Jerusalem from a distance, mustering the armies of the nations against Jerusalem[54] before he turns and then fights against those same nations on behalf of Jerusalem, with his feet positioned on the Mount of Olives, accompanied by his heavenly forces.

Summary

This divine dimension thus reveals that the deities of both Babylon and Judah had experienced exile/forced migration from their homelands. This exile/forced migration was to come to an end in the early Persian period.

Conclusion

The exile continues to leave its mark on the literature of Judah even as the prophetic witness shifts focus to restoration. Its indelible mark can be seen in all the major compositional layers and rhetorical phases of the book of Zechariah.

Various images are used for exile on the human plane throughout the book of Zechariah. Not surprisingly, various types of scattering within an agricultural context are employed, ranging from the scattering of (possibly) a flock of sheep by unruly oxen, scattering of chaff by a powerful wind, to scattering of seed by sowing. While the first two of these images are completely negative, the third image does suggest a hopeful future, as unlike chaff, seed has the potential to create new life. Another type

---

53. Petersen, *Zechariah 9–14 and Malachi*, 267–68.
54. For אסף *qal* as mustering warriors, an army, or armies, see Judg 3:13; 11:20; 1 Sam 17:1; 2 Sam 6:1; 10:17; 12:28, 29; 1 Kgs 10:26; 1 Chr 19:17; 2 Chr 1:14; Dan 11:10.

of scattering, that of a defeated army, can be discerned in chapter 2, and this scattering is followed by pillaging, violence, rape, and servitude. This provides a transition from the focus on movement inherent in the scattering motif to that of confinement seen in the servitude. Such confinement is evident in the image of imprisonment in a waterless pit in chapter 9. In addition, chapter 8 utilizes two further motifs, those of remnant and curse, to speak of the condition of exile. In the former, there is a sense of that which is left over, the other the stigma of those who have been judged by God.

Surprisingly, the exilic community is not narrowly defined in the book of Zechariah. Indeed, the focus is on Zion in 2:10–17 (Eng. 6–13) and on Judah in 2:4 (Eng. 1:21) and chapter 7 (Jerusalem, Negev, Shephelah), but elsewhere one can see the inclusion of those beyond Judah and Jerusalem in the terms Israel in 2:2, the house of Israel in 8:13, Ephraim in 9:13, and the house of Joseph and Ephraim in 10:6–11.[55] One can discern in the book an initial focus on Judah, which expands to include Israel before constricting in the final phase of chapters 12–14. Although not always explicitly stated, the identification of the one(s) who exiled this community ranges from Yahweh to the nations. This matches the revelation provided in the first night vision that, although Yahweh was angry with the people, the nations had taken judgment beyond divine design. The destination of exile is also not always stated. While in 2:10–17 (Eng. 6–13) Babylon is explicitly stated (something also seen in 6:9–15), the more generic terms like "land of the north" and even possibly "the four winds of heaven" suggest a broader geographical range. This more generic and broad approach is actually the rule rather than the exception in Zechariah, with reference to "all the nations" in 7:14, "the nations" and "distant east"/"distant west" in 8:7, "the peoples" and "distant places" in 10:9, and even the lands of Egypt and Assyria in 10:10. The book of Zechariah is nearly silent on the timing of exile and reason for exile, with these aspects only slipping through in the prophetic sermon of 7:1–14, which implicitly links the exile to the seventy-year motif (suggesting an exile that began ca. 588 BCE), and explicitly traces the exile to the refusal of Judah to pay attention to God's word through the prophets.

---

55. Kessler, "Diaspora and Homeland," 158–60, 165, who also adds gentile inclusion in the community (cf. Zech 2:15).

Although at the core of the Zecharian tradition one can see a focus on the exilic experience, which began with the fall of Jerusalem, included Judah and Jerusalem, and entailed exile to Babylon, one can discern a broader vision that expanded this community to include exiles from the former kingdom of Israel and those exiles dispersed throughout the ancient Near East, from east to west, from Egypt to Assyria. This broader perspective reaches a climax in the compositional phase, which saw the inclusion of chapters 9–10 into the Zecharian literary complex, and it is probably this broadening process that prompted the expansion of what was originally a night vision focused on Judah in 2:1–4 (Eng. 1:18–21) to one that included Israel as well. In the development of the Zecharian corpus, however, a crisis is reached at some point that leads to an abandonment of hope for the exiled house of Joseph (as seen in ch. 11) as well as abandonment of focus on the enduring Judean exilic community. But even then exile endures as a motif connected with the future cataclysmic day of Yahweh, which will see the defeat and submission of the nations after an initial defeat and exile of Jerusalem.

But exile is also a reality for characters on the heavenly plane. As a Babylonian deity is exiled from her homeland and must be returned, so Yahweh is exiled from his homeland and must return. The difference between these two divine figures, however, is that the Babylonian goddess shows signs of reticence while Yahweh is eager.

The development of exile on these two planes, human and divine, should not be considered separately. Examining their parallel development, one can discern a key strategy in the overall flow of the book of Zechariah. At the core of Zech 1–8 (the night visions and supplements in 1:7–6:15), the endurance of Yahweh's exilic sojourn is dependent on the endurance of the exilic sojourn of the community in Jerusalem and Judah, that is, the people are invited to return to the land (2:10–13 [Eng. 6–9]) and then Yahweh promises to return (2:14–17 [Eng. 10–13]). The prose sermon bracket surrounding the night visions, however, recognizes the exilic condition of the community and deity and also makes the endurance of Yahweh's exilic sojourn dependent on the endurance of the exilic sojourn of the community, but recasts this in covenantal terms, calling for a penitence rather than mere physical return. In this, one can see the interlinking of exile and apostasy, of restoration and repentance.

As one crosses into Zech 9–14, there is a clear shift in order as it is Yahweh's return in 9:1–8 that makes possible the return of Judah and Israel in chapters 9–10. This same divine priority of return is evident in chapters 12–14 as Yahweh returns in 14:1–2. However, this final return does not precipitate a return of the people, who are now depicted as embedded within their ancestral homeland. Instead, the outcome is a new exile as Yahweh musters the nations against Jerusalem. This shift in visions of exile in the book of Zechariah suggests the agenda of its overall shape. The community is challenged to take up Yahweh's exhortation to return: both physically to journey to the land but also covenantally to repent, so that Yahweh might return to the land. Failure to respond leads to a new phase typified by Yahweh's unilateral initiative to return to the land and inaugurate the restoration of both Judah and Israel to the land. In a final phase Yahweh threatens to return from exile, but this time to bring judgment on Jerusalem, which would experience exile again, even as Yahweh unilaterally purifies the community.

Exile is thus another motif that drives the rhetorical agenda of the book of Zechariah as a whole. It speaks to a community for whom exile has powerful rhetorical force, a motif that would continue to exercise its power over the Jewish community throughout the Second Temple period.

Bibliography

Ackroyd, Peter R. *Exile and Restoration: A Study of Hebrew Thought of the Sixth Century B.C.* OTL. Philadelphia: Westminster, 1968.

Adams, Jim W. *The Performative Nature and Function of Isaiah 40–55.* LHBOTS 448. London: T&T Clark, 2006.

Ahn, John J. *Exile as Forced Migrations: A Sociological, Literary, and Theological Approach on the Displacement and Resettlement of the Southern Kingdom of Judah.* BZAW 417. Berlin: de Gruyter, 2011.

———. "Psalm 137: Complex Communal Laments." *JBL* 127 (2008): 267–89.

Ahn John J., and Jill Middlemas, eds. *By the Irrigation Canals of Babylon: Approaches to the Study of the Exile.* LHBOTS 526. New York: Bloomsbury T&T Clark, 2012.

Albani, Matthias. *Der eine Gott und die himmlichen Heerscharen: Zur Begründung des Monotheismus bei Deuterojesaja im Horizont der Astralisierung des Gottesverständisses im Alten Orient.* ABIG 1. Leipzig: Evangelische Verlagsanstalt, 2000.

Alberto R. W. Green. "The Fate of Jehoiakim." *AUSS* 20 (1982): 103–9.

Albertz, Rainer. *Israel in Exile: The History and Literature of the Sixth Century B.C.E.* Translated by David Green. Biblical Encyclopedia 7. Atlanta: Society of Biblical Literature, 2003.

Alfrink, Bernardus. "L'expression שָׁכַב עִם אֲבוֹתָיו." *OtSt* 2 (1943): 106–18.

Allen, Leslie. *Ezekiel 1–19.* WBC 28. Dallas: Word, 1994.

Amit, Yairah. "Creation and the Calendar of Holiness." [In Hebrew.] Pages 13*–29* in *Tehillah le-Moshe: Biblical and Judaic Studies in Honor of Moshe Greenberg.* Edited by Mordechai Cogan, Barry L. Eichler, and Jeffrey H. Tigay. Winona Lake, IN: Eisenbrauns, 1997.

Anderson, Gary A. *Sin: A History.* New Haven: Yale University Press, 2009.

Baltzer, Dieter. *Ezechiel und Deuterojesaja: Berührungen in der Heilserwartung der beiden großen Exilspropheten.* BZAW 121. Berlin: de Gruyter, 1971.

Baltzer, Klaus. *Deutero-Isaiah*. Translated by Margaret Kohl. Hermeneia. Minneapolis: Fortress, 2001.
Barstad, Hans M. "Lebte Deuterojesaja in Judäa?" *NTT* 83 (1982): 77–87.
———. *A Way in the Wilderness: The "Second Exodus" in the Message of Second Isaiah*. Manchester: University of Manchester Press, 1989.
Becker, Uwe. "Die Entstehung der Schriftprophetie." Pages 3–20 in *Die unwiderstehliche Wahrheit: Studien zur alttestamentlichen Prophetie: Festschrift für Arndt Meinhold*. Edited by Rüdiger Lux and Ernst-Joachim Waschke. ABIG 23. Leipzig: Evangelische Verlagsanstalt, 2006.
Becking, Bob. *The Fall of Samaria: An Historical and Archaeological Study*. SHANE 2. Leiden: Brill, 1992.
Bedford, Peter R. "Diaspora: Homeland Relations in Ezra-Nehemiah." *VT* 52 (2002): 147–65.
Begg, Christopher T. "Jehoahaz, Jehoiakim, and Jehoiachin (10,81–102 + 229–230)." Pages 499–534 in *Josephus' Story of the Later Monarchy (AJ 9,1–10,185)*. BETL 145. Leuven: Peeters, 2000.
Ben-Dov, Jonathan. "Writing as Oracle and Law: New Context for the Book-Find of King Josiah." *JBL* 127 (2008): 223–39.
Benson, J. E. "Households, Migration, and Community Context." *Urban Anthropology* 19 (1990): 9–29.
Berges, Ulrich. *Das Buch Jesaja: Komposition und Endgestalt*. Herders biblische Studien 16. Freiburg im Breisgau: Herder, 1998.
———. "Farewell to Deutero-Isaiah or Prophecy without a Prophet." Pages 575–95 in *Congress Volume Ljubljana 2007*. Edited by André Lemaire. VTSup 133. Leiden: Brill, 2010.
———. "'Ich gebe Jerusalem einen Freudenboten': Synchrone und Diachrone Beobachtungen zu Jes 41,27." *Bib* 87 (2006): 319–37.
———. *Jesaja 40–48*. HTKAT. Freiburg: Herder, 2008.
———. "The Literary Construction of the Servant in Isaiah 40–55: A Discussion about Individual and Collective Identities." *SJOT* 24 (2010): 28–38.
Berlin, Adele. "Jeremiah 29:5–7: A Deuteronomic Allusion?" *HAR* 8 (1984): 3–11.
Berry, Donald K. "Malachi's Dual Design: The Close of the Canon and What Comes Afterward." Pages 269–302 in *Forming Prophetic Literature: Essays on Isaiah and the Twelve in Honor of John D. W. Watts*. Edited by James W. Watts and Paul R. House. JSOTSup 235. Sheffield: Sheffield Academic, 1996.

Beuken, Willem. "The Main Theme of Trito-Isaiah, 'The Servants of YHWH.'" *JSOT* 47 (1990): 67–87.
Blank, Sheldon H. *Prophetic Faith in Isaiah*. Detroit: Wayne State University Press, 1967.
Blenkinsopp, Joseph. *Ezekiel*. IBC. Louisville: Westminster John Knox, 1990.
———. *Isaiah 1–39: A New Translation with Introduction and Commentary*. AB 19. New York: Doubleday, 2000.
———. *Isaiah 40–55: A New Translation with Introduction and Commentary*. AB 19A. New York: Doubleday, 2002.
———. *Isaiah 56–66: A New Translation with Introduction and Commentary*. AB 19B. New York: Doubleday, 2003.
———. *Judaism: The First Phase*. Grand Rapids: Eerdmans, 2009.
Block, Daniel. *The Book of Ezekiel: Chapters 1–24*. NICOT. Grand Rapids: Eerdmans, 1997.
Boadt, Lawrence. "The Poetry of Prophetic Persuasion: Preserving the Prophet's Persona." *CBQ* 59 (1997): 1–21.
Boda, Mark J. "From Fasts to Feasts: The Literary Function of Zechariah 7–8." *CBQ* 65 (2003): 390–407.
———. *Haggai-Zechariah Research: A Bibliographic Survey*. Tools for Biblical Studies 5. Leiden: Deo, 2003.
———. "In Order to Fulfill the Word of the Lord: The Impact of Haggai and Zechariah on Post-Exilic Historiography." Paper presented at the annual international meeting of the Society of Biblical Literature. St. Andrews, Scotland, July 8, 2013.
———. "Legitimizing the Temple: The Chronicler's Temple Building Account." Pages 303–18 in *From the Foundations to the Crenellations: Essays on Temple Building in the Ancient Near East and Hebrew Bible*. Edited by Mark J. Boda and Jamie Novotny. AOAT 366. Munster: Ugarit-Verlag, 2010.
———. "Messengers of Hope in Haggai-Malachi." *JSOT* 32 (2007): 113–31.
———. "Reading between the Lines: Zechariah 11:4–16 in Its Literary Contexts." Pages 277–91 in *Bringing out the Treasure: Inner Biblical Allusion and Zechariah 9–14*. Edited by Mark J. Boda and Michael H. Floyd. JSOTSup 304. Sheffield: Sheffield Academic, 2003.
———. "Terrifying the Horns: Persia and Babylon in Zechariah 1:7–6:15." *CBQ* 67 (2005): 22–41.
———. *Zechariah*. NICOT. Grand Rapids: Eerdmans, forthcoming.

Boling, Robert G. "Levitical History and the Role of Joshua." Pages 241–61 in *The Word of the Lord Shall God Forth: Essays in Honor of David Noel Freedman in Celebration of His Sixtieth Birthday*. Edited by Carol L. Meyers and M. O'Connor. Winona Lake, IN: Eisenbrauns, 1983.

Borger, Riekele. *Die Inschriften Asarhaddons Königs von Assyrien*. AfO 9. Graz: Biblio-Verlag, 1967.

Botterweck, G. Johannes, Helmer Ringgren, and Heinz-Josef Fabry, eds. *Theological Dictionary of the Old Testament*. Translated by John T. Willis, Geoffrey W. Bromiley, David E. Green, and Douglas W. Stott. 15 vols. Grand Rapids, 1974–2006.

Brown, Raymond. *The Gospel according to John (XIII–XXI)*. AB 29A. Garden City, NY: Doubleday, 1970.

Brown, William P. *The Ethos of the Cosmos: The Genesis of Moral Imagination in the Bible*. Grand Rapids: Eerdmans, 1998.

Brownlee, William H. *Ezekiel 1–19*. WBC 28. Waco, TX: Word, 1986.

Brueggemann, Walter, and Hans Walter Wolff. *The Vitality of Old Testament Traditions*. 2nd ed. Atlanta: John Knox, 1982.

Buber, Martin. *I and Thou*. 2nd ed. Edinburgh: T&T Clark, 1958.

Calvin, John. *Commentary on the Book of the Prophet Isaiah*. Translated by William Pringle. 4 vols. Edinburgh: Constable, 1850.

Carr, David M. *The Formation of the Hebrew Bible: A New Reconstruction*. Oxford: Oxford University Press, 2011.

———. *Writing on the Tablet of the Heart: Origins of Scripture and Literature*. Oxford: Oxford University Press, 2005.

Carroll, Robert P. "Deportation and Diasporic Discourses in the Prophetic Literature." Pages 63–85 in *Exile: Old Testament, Jewish, and Christian Conceptions*. Edited by James Scott. JSJSup 56. Leiden: Brill, 1997.

———. *Jeremiah: A Commentary*. OTL. Philadelphia: Westminster, 1986.

Centers for Disease Control and Prevention. "Famine-Affected, Refugee, and Displaced Populations: Recommendations for Public Health Issues." *MMWR* 41.13 (1992). Online: http://www.cdc.gov/mmwr/preview/mmwrhtml/00019261.htm.

———. "Mortality during a Famine—Gode District, Ethiopia, July 2000." *MMWR* 50 (2001): 285–88. Online: http://www.cdc.gov/mmwr/PDF/wk/mm5015.pdf.

Childs, Brevard S. *Biblical Theology of the Old and New Testaments*. Minneapolis: Fortress, 1992.

———. *The Church's Guide for Reading Paul: The Canonical Shaping of the Pauline Corpus*. Grand Rapids: Eerdmans, 2008.

———. *Introduction to the Old Testament as Scripture.* Philadelphia: Fortress, 1979.
———. *Isaiah.* OTL. Louisville: Westminster John Knox, 2001.
———. *New Testament as Canon: An Introduction.* Philadelphia: Fortress, 1984.
Christian, Patricia B. "Family, Extended." Pages 943–44 in vol. 3 of *Encyclopedia of Anthropology.* Edited by H. James Birx. 5 vols. Thousand Oaks, CA: Sage, 2006.
Clements, Ronald E. *Abraham and David: Genesis XV and Its Meaning for Israelite Tradition.* SBT 2/2. Naperville, IL: Allenson, 1967.
———. "Beyond Tradition-History: Deutero-Isaianic Development of First Isaiah's Themes." *JSOT* 31 (1985): 95–113.
———. "The Chronology of Redaction in Ezekiel 1–24." Pages 283–94 in *Ezekiel and His Book: Textual and Literary Criticism and Their Interrelation.* Edited by Johan Lust. BETL 74. Leuven: Leuven University Press, 1986.
———. "The Ezekiel Tradition: Prophecy in a Time of Crisis." Pages 118–36 in *Israel's Prophetic Tradition: Essays in Honour of Peter R. Ackroyd.* Edited by R. J. Coggins, Anthony Phillips, and Michael A. Knibb. Cambridge: Cambridge University Press, 1982.
Cogan, Mordechai. "Omens and Ideology in the Babylon Inscription of Esarhaddon." Pages 76–87 in *History, Historiography, and Interpretation: Studies in Biblical and Cuneiform Literatures.* Edited by Hayim Tadmor and Moshe Weinfeld. Jerusalem: Magnes, 1983.
Cohen, Shaye J. D. "The Judaean Legal Tradition and the Halakhah of the Mishnah." Pages 121–43 in *The Cambridge Companion to the Talmud and Rabbinic Literature.* Edited by Charlotte Fonrobert and Martin S. Jaffee. Cambridge: Cambridge University Press, 2007.
Colic-Peisker, V., and I. Walker. "Human Capital, Acculturation and Social Identity: Bosnian Refugees in Australia." *Journal of Community and Applied Social Psychology* 13 (2003): 337–60.
Collins, Terence. "The Scroll of the Twelve." Pages 59–84 in *The Mantle of Elijah: The Redaction Criticism of the Prophetic Books.* Edited by Terence Collins. BibSem 20. Sheffield: JSOT Press, 1993.
Cook, Stephen L. *Conversations with Scripture: 2 Isaiah.* Anglican Association of Biblical Scholars Study Series. Harrisburg, PA: Morehouse, 2008.
———. Review of *Missing Priests: The Zadokites in Tradition and History,* by Alice Hunt. *CBQ* 71 (2009): 372–73.

———. *The Social Roots of Biblical Yahwism*. SBLStBL 8. Atlanta: Society of Biblical Literature, 2004.

Cook, Stephen L., and Corrine L. Patton. "Introduction: Hierarchical Thinking and Theology in Ezekiel's Book." Pages 1–26 in *Ezekiel's Hierarchical World: Wrestling with a Tiered Reality*. Edited by Stephen L. Cook and Corrine L. Patton. SymS 31. Atlanta: Society of Biblical Literature, 2004.

Cooke, G. A. *A Critical and Exegetical Commentary on the Book of Ezekiel*. ICC. New York: Scribner's Sons, 1937.

Craigie, Peter C. *Ezekiel*. Daily Study Bible. Philadelphia: Westminster, 1983.

Cross, Frank M. *Canaanite Myth and Hebrew Epic*. Cambridge: Harvard University Press, 1973.

Curtis, Byron G. *Up the Steep and Stony Road: The Book of Zechariah in Social Location Trajectory Analysis*. Academia Biblica 25. Atlanta: Scholars Press, 2006.

Delitzsch, Franz. *Bible Commentary on the Prophecies of Isaiah*. Translated by James Kennedy, William Hastie, Thomas A. Bickerton, and J. S. Banks. 4th ed. 2 vols. Edinburgh: T&T Clark, 1889–1910.

Dietrich, Manfried, Oswald Loretz, and Joaquín Sanmartín, eds. *Die keilalphabetischen Texte aus Ugarit*. AOAT 24.1. Neukirchen-Vluyn: Neukirchener Verlag, 1976. 2nd enlarged ed. of *KTU: The Cuneiform Alphabetic Texts from Ugarit, Ras Ibn Hani, and Other Places*. Edited by Manfried Dietrich, Oswald Loretz, and Joaquín Sanmartín. Münster: Ugarit-Verlag, 1995.

Donner, Herbert. *Von der Königszeit bis zu Alexander dem Großen: Mit einem Ausblick auf die Geschichte des Judentums bis Bar Kochba*. Part 2 of *Geschichte des Volkes Israel und seiner Nachbarn in Grundzügen*. 2nd ed. ATD Ergänzungsreihe 4/2. Göttingen: Vandenhoeck & Ruprecht, 1995.

Driver, G. R. "Studies in the Vocabulary of the Old Testament: II." *JTS* 32 (1931): 250–56.

Driver, S. R. *The Book of Exodus*. Cambridge Bible for Schools and Colleges. Cambridge: Cambridge University Press, 1953.

Duhm, Bernhard. *Das Buch Jesaja*. HKAT 3.1. Göttingen: Vandenhoeck & Ruprecht, 1892.

Durlesser, James A. *The Metaphorical Narratives in the Book of Ezekiel*. Lewiston, NY: Mellen, 2006.

Eichhorn, J. G. *Einleitung in das Alte Testament.* 3rd rev. and enl. ed. 5 vols. Leipzig: Weidmann, 1803.
Eichrodt, Walther. *Ezekiel: A Commentary.* Translated by Cosslett Quin. OTL. Philadelphia: Westminster, 1970.
Eitz, Andreas. *Studien zum Verhältnis von Priesterschrift und Deuterojesaja.* Heidelberg: Evangelisch Theologische Fakultät, 1969.
Elliger, Karl. *Die Propheten Nahum, Habakuk, Zephanja, Haggai, Sacharja, Maleachi.* Vol. 2 of *Das Buch der zwölf kleinen Propheten.* 7th ed. ATD 25.2. Göttingen: Vandenhoeck & Ruprecht, 1975.
Ellis, Richard S. *Foundation Deposits in Ancient Mesopotamia.* New Haven: Yale University Press, 1968.
Eshel, Esther. "Isaiah 11:15: A New Interpretation Based on the Genesis Apocryphon." *DSD* 13 (2006): 38–45.
Etherington, Norman. "War, Demographic Consequences of." Pages 963–66 in vol. 2 of *Encyclopedia of Population.* Edited by Paul Demeny and Geoffrey McNicoll. 2 vols. New York: Macmillan, 2003.
Feuerstein, Rüdiger. "Weshalb gibt es 'Deuterojesaja'?" Pages 93–134 in *Ich bewirke das Heil und erschaffe das Unheil (Jesaja 45,7): Studien zur Botschaft der Propheten—Festschrift für Lothar Ruppert zum 65. Geburtstag.* Edited by Friedrich Diedrich and Bernd Willmes. FB 88. Würzburg: Echter, 1998.
Firmage, Edwin B. "Genesis 1 and the Priestly Agenda." *JSOT* 82 (1999): 97–114.
Fishbane, Michael A. *Biblical Interpretation in Ancient Israel.* Oxford: Clarendon, 1985.
Flannery, K. V. "The Origins of the Village Revisited: From Nuclear to Extended Households." *American Antiquity* 67 (2002): 417–33.
Floyd, Michael H. *Minor Prophets, Part 2.* FOTL 22. Grand Rapids: Eerdmans, 2000.
Fohrer, Georg. *Studien zu alttestamentlichen Texten und Themen.* BZAW 155. Berlin: de Gruyter, 1981.
Ford, D. Y., and J. J. Harris. "The Extended African-American Family." *Urban League Review* 14 (1991): 71–83.
Freedman, David Noel, ed. *The Anchor Bible Dictionary.* 6 vols. New York: Doubleday, 1992.
———. *The Unity of the Bible.* Distinguished Senior Faculty Lecture Series. Ann Arbor: University of Michigan Press, 1993.

Friedman, Richard Elliott. *The Exile and Biblical Narrative: The Formation of the Deuteronomistic and Priestly Works*. HSM 22. Missoula, MT: Scholars Press, 1981.

———. *Who Wrote the Bible?* 2nd ed. San Francisco: HarperSanFrancisco, 1997.

Galil, Gershon. "Israelite Exiles in Media: A New Look at ND 2443+." *VT* 59 (2009): 71–79.

Garber, David G., Jr. "Trauma, History and Survival in Ezekiel 1–24." Ph.D. diss. Emory University, 2005.

———. "Traumatizing Ezekiel, the Exilic Prophet." Pages 215–35 in *From Genesis to Apocalyptic Vision*. Vol. 2 of *Psychology and the Bible: A New Way to Read the Scriptures*. Edited by J. Harold Ellens and Wayne G. Rollins. Praeger Perspectives: Psychology, Religion, and Spirituality. Westport, CT: Praeger, 2004.

Garfield, Richard M., and Alfred I. Neugut. "The Human Consequences of War." Pages 27–38 in *War and Public Health*. Edited by Barry S. Levy and Victor W. Sidel. Washington, DC: American Public Health Association, 2000.

Gerstenberger, Erhard S. *Israel in der Perserzeit: 5. und 4. Jahrhundert v. Chr.* Biblische Enzyklopädie 8. Stuttgart: Kohlhammer, 2005.

Gesenius, Wilhelm. *Philologisch-kritischer und historischer Commentar über den Jesaia*. 2 vols. Leipzig: Vogel, 1821.

Glick, J. E. "Nativity, Duration of Residence and the Life Course Pattern of Extended Family Living in the USA." *Population Research and Policy Review* 19 (2000): 179–98.

Glick, J. E., F. D. Bean, and J. V. W. Van Hook. "Immigration and Changing Patterns of Extended Household Structure in the United States: 1970–1990." *Journal of Marriage and Family* 59 (1997): 177–91.

Gowan, Donald E. *Theology of the Prophetic Books: The Death and Resurrection of Israel*. Louisville: Westminster John Knox, 1998.

Graham, J. N. "'Vinedressers and Plowmen': 2 Kings 25:12 and Jeremiah 52:16." *BA* 47 (1984): 55–58.

Gray, George Buchanan. *A Critical and Exegetical Commentary on Numbers*. ICC. Edinburgh: T&T Clark, 1903.

Grayson, Albert K. *Assyrian and Babylonian Chronicles*. 1975. Repr., Winona Lake, IN: Eisenbrauns, 2000.

Green, Alberto R. W. "The Fate of Jehoiakim." *AUSS* 20 (1982): 103–9.

Greenberg, Moshe. *Ezekiel 1–20*. AB 22. Garden City, NY: Doubleday 1983.

———. *Ezekiel 21–37*. AB 22A. New York: Doubleday, 1997.

Grünwaldt, Klaus. *Das Heiligkeitsgesetz Leviticus 17–26: Ursprüngliche Gestalt, Tradition und Theologie*. BZAW 271. Berlin: de Gruyter, 1999.
Haarmann, Volker. *JHWH—Verehrer der Völker: Die Hinwendung von Nichtisraeliten zum Gott Israels in alttestamentlichen Überlieferungen*. AThANT 91. Zurich: TVZ, 2008.
Halpern, Baruch. *David's Secret Demons: Messiah, Murderer, Traitor, King*. Grand Rapids: Eerdmans, 2001.
Hals, Ronald M. *Ezekiel*. FOTL 19. Grand Rapids: Eerdmans, 1989.
Haran, Menahem. "Behind the Scenes of History: Determining the Date of the Priestly Source." *JBL* 100 (1981): 321–33.
———. "Observations on Ezekiel as a Book Prophet." Pages 3–10 in *Seeking out the Wisdom of the Ancients: Essays Offered to Honor Michael V. Fox on the Occasion of His Sixty-Fifth Birthday*. Edited by Ronald Troxel, Kelvin G. Friebel, and Dennis Robert Magary. Winona Lake, IN: Eisenbrauns, 2005.
Hardmeier, Christof. "Zur schriftgestützten Expertentätigkeit Jeremias im Milieu der Jerusalemer Führungseliten (Jeremia 36): Prophetische Literaturbildung und die Neuinterpretation älterer Expertisen in Jeremia 21–23*." Pages 105–49 in *Die Textualisierung der Religion*. Edited by Joachim Schaper. FAT 62. Tübingen: Mohr Siebeck, 2009.
Hasel, Gerhard F. *The Remnant: The History and Theology of the Remnant Idea from Genesis to Isaiah*. 3rd ed. AUMSR 5. Berrien Springs, MI: Andrews University Press, 1980.
Heller, Steven. "War Is Not Healthy: The True Story." *AIGA Design Archives*. n.p. Cited September 20, 2005. Online: http://www.aiga.org/content.cfm/war-is-not-healthy-the-true-story.
Herman, Judith. *Trauma and Recovery*. New York: Basic Books, 1992.
Herrmann, Johannes. *Ezechielstudien*. BZAW 2. Leipzig: Hinrichs, 1908.
Hermisson, Hans-Jürgen. "Deuterojesaja." Pages 684–88 in vol. 2 of *Religion in Geschichte und Gegenwart: Handwörterbuch für Theologie und Religionswissenschaft*. Edited by Hans Dieter Betz, Don S. Browning, Bernd Janowski, and Eberhard Jüngel. 4th ed. 8 vols. Tübingen: Mohr Siebeck, 1999.
———. "Jakob und Zion, Schöpfung und Heil." *Zeichen der Zeit* 44 (1990): 262–68.
Heschel, Abraham Joshua. *The Prophets*. New York: Harper & Row, 1963.
Hibbard, James T. *Intertextuality in Isaiah 24–27: The Reuse and Evocation of Earlier Texts and Traditions*. FAT 2/16. Tübingen: Mohr Siebeck, 2006.

Hoffman, Yair. "Aetiology, Redaction and Historicity in Jeremiah XXXVI." *VT* 46 (1996): 179–89.
Hogland, Kenneth G. *Achaemenid Imperial Administration in Syria-Palestine and the Missions of Ezra and Nehemiah.* SBLDS 125. Atlanta: Scholars Press, 1992.
Holladay, William L. *Jeremiah 1: A Commentary on the Prophet Jeremiah, Chapters 1–25.* Hermeneia. Philadelphia: Fortress, 1986.
———. *Jeremiah 2: A Commentary on the Prophet Jeremiah, Chapters 26–52.* Hermeneia. Philadelphia: Fortress, 1989.
Hölscher, Gustav. *Die Profeten: Untersuchungen zur Religionsgeschichte Israels.* Leipzig: Hinrichs, 1914.
Hourani, Albert. *A History of the Arab Peoples.* New York: Warner, 1991.
Hurowitz, Victor A. *I Have Built for You an Exalted House: Temple Building in the Bible in Light of Mesopotamian and Northwest Semitic Writings.* JSOTSup 115. Sheffield: Sheffield Academic, 1992.
Hurvitz, Avi. "The Evidence of Language in Dating the Priestly Code: A Linguistic Study in Technical Idioms and Terminology." *RB* 81 (1974): 24–56.
———. *A Linguistic Study of the Relationship between the Priestly Source and the Book of Ezekiel: A New Approach to an Old Problem.* CahRB 20. Paris: Gabalda, 1982.
Huston, Phil. *Martin Buber's Journey to Presence.* New York: Fordham University Press, 2007.
Hutton, Jeremy M. *The Transjordanian Palimpsest: The Overwritten Texts of Personal Exile and Transformation in the Deuteronomistic History.* BZAW 396. Berlin: de Gruyter, 2009.
Irwin, W. A. *The Problem of Ezekiel: An Inductive Study.* Chicago: University of Chicago Press, 1943.
Jacob, Irene, and Walter Jacob. "Flora." *ABD* 2:803–17.
Jenni, Ernst, and Claus Westermann, eds. *Theological Lexicon of the Old Testament.* Translated by Mark E. Biddle. 3 vols. Peabody, MA: Hendrickson, 1997.
Jong, Matthijs J. de. "Ezekiel as a Literary Figure and the Quest for the Historical Prophet." Pages 1–16 in *The Book of Ezekiel and Its Influence.* Edited by Henk Jan de Jonge and Johannes Tromp. Aldershot: Ashgate, 2007.
Joosten, Jan. *People and Land in the Holiness Code: An Exegetical Study of the Ideational Framework of the Law in Leviticus 17–26.* VTSup 67. Leiden: Brill, 1996.

Joyce, Paul M. *Ezekiel: A Commentary.* LHBOTS 482. New York: T&T Clark, 2007.
Kaminsky, Joel S. *Corporate Responsibility in the Hebrew Bible.* JSOTSup 196. Sheffield: Sheffield Academic, 1995.
Karrer-Grube, Christiane. "Scrutinizing the Conceptual Unity of Ezra-Nehemiah." Pages 136–59 in *Unity and Disunity in Ezra-Nehemiah: Redaction, Rhetoric, and Reader.* Edited by Mark J. Boda and Paul L. Redditt. HBM 17. Sheffield: Sheffield Phoenix, 2008.
Katz, Ruth, and Yoav Lavee. "Families in Israel." Pages 486–506 of *Handbook of World Familes.* Edited by Bert N. Adams and Jan Trost. London: Sage, 2005.
Katz, Ruth, and Yochanan Peres. "The Sociology of the Family in Israel: An Outline of Its Development from the 1950s to the 1980s." *European Sociological Review* 2 (1986): 148–59.
Keel, Othmar. *Die Geschichte Jerusalems und die Entstehung des Monotheismus.* Part 2. Vol. 4 of *Orte und Landschaften der Bibel: Ein Handbuch und Studien-Reiseführer zum Heiligen Land.* Göttingen: Vandenhoeck & Ruprecht, 2007.
Kessler, John. "Diaspora and Homeland in the Early Achaemenid Period: Community, Geography and Demography in Zech 1–8." Pages 137–66 in *Approaching Yehud: New Approaches to the Persian Period.* Edited by Jon L. Berquist. SemeiaSt 50. Atlanta: Society of Biblical Literature, 2007.
Khalil, Karim. "Political Stalemates and Deepening Humanitarian Crises: Internal Displacement in the Middle East." Pages 53–64 in *Internal Displacement: Global Overview of Trends and Developments in 2007.* Edited by Edmund Jennings. Geneva: Internal Displacement Monitoring Centre, 2008.
Kiesow, Klaus. *Exodustexte im Jesajabuch: Literarkritische und motivgeschichtlichen Analysen.* OBO 24. Göttingen: Vandenhoeck & Ruprecht, 1979.
Kira, Ibrahim Aref. "Taxonomy of Trauma and Trauma Assessment." *Traumatology* 7, no. 2 (2001): 73–86.
Klein, Ralph W. "Ezekiel at the Dawn of the Twenty-First Century." Pages 1–14 in *The Book of Ezekiel: Theological and Anthropological Perspectives.* Edited by Margaret S. Odell and John T. Strong. SymS 9. Atlanta: Society of Biblical Literature, 2000.
———. *Israel in Exile: A Theological Interpretation.* OBT. Philadelphia: Fortress, 1979.

———. "The Message of P." Pages 57–66 in *Die Botschaft und die Boten: Festschrift für Hans Walter Wolff zum 70. Geburtstag*. Edited by Jörg Jeremias and Lothar Perlitt. Neukirchen-Vluyn: Neukirchener Verlag, 1981.

Knohl, Israel. *The Divine Symphony: The Bible's Many Voices*. Philadelphia: Jewish Publication Society, 2003.

———. *The Sanctuary of Silence: The Priestly Torah and the Holiness School*. Minneapolis: Fortress, 1995.

Kohn, Risa Levitt. "Ezekiel at the Turn of the Century." *CurBR* 2 (2003): 9–31.

———. *A New Heart and a New Soul: Ezekiel, the Exile and Torah*. JSOTSup 358. Sheffield: Sheffield Academic, 2002.

Kratz, Reinhard G. *Kyros im Deuterojesaja-Buch: Redaktionsgeschichtliche Untersuchungen zu Entstehung und Theologie von Jesaja 40–55*. FAT 1. Tübingen: Mohr Siebeck, 1991.

———. *Translatio Imperii*. WMANT 63. Neukirchen-Vluyn: Neukirchener Verlag, 1991.

Kutsko, John F. *Between Heaven and Earth: Divine Presence and Absence in the Book of Ezekiel*. Winona Lake, IN: Eisenbrauns, 2000.

Labahn, Antje. *Wort Gottes und Schuld Israels: Untersuchungen zu Motiven Deuteronomistischer Theologie im Deuterojesajabuch mit einem Ausblick auf das Verhältnis von Jes 40–55 zum Deuteronomismus*. BWANT 143. Stuttgart: Kohlhammer, 1999.

Lang, Bernhard. *Ezechiel: Der Prophet und das Buch*. EdF 153. Darmstadt: Wissenschaftliche Buchgesellschaft, 1981.

Lau, Wolfgang. *Schriftgelehrte Prophetie in Jes 56–66: Eine Untersuchung zu den Literarischen Bezügen in den Letzten elf Kapiteln des Jesajabuches*. Beihefte zur Zeitschrift für die alttestamentliche Wissenschaft 225. Berlin: de Gruyter, 1994.

Leene, Henk. "History and Eschatology in Deutero-Isaiah." Pages 221–49 in *Studies in the Book of Isaiah: Festschrift Willem A. M. Beuken*. Edited by Jacques van Ruiten and Marc Vervenne. BETL 132. Leuven: Leuven University Press, 1997.

———. *De vroegere en de nieuwe dingen bij Deuterojesaja*. Amsterdam: VU Uitgeverij, 1987.

Leuchter, Mark. "Eisodus as Exodus: The Song of the Sea (Exod 15) Reconsidered." *Bib* 93 (2011): 333–46.

———. "The Fightin' Mushites." *VT* 62 (2012): 479–500.

———. "Inter-Levitical Polemics in the Late 6th Century B.C.E.: The Evidence from Nehemiah 9." *Bib* 95 (2014): 269–79.

———. "Jeremiah's 70-Year Prophecy and the לב קמי/ששך *Atbash* Codes." *Bib* 85 (2004): 503–22.

———. "Personal Missives and National History: The Relationship between Jeremiah 29 and 36." Pages 275–93 in *Prophets, Prophecy, and Ancient Israelite Historiography*. Edited by Mark J. Boda and Lissa M. Wray Beal. Winona Lake, IN: Eisenbrauns, 2013.

———. *The Polemics of Exile in Jeremiah 26–45*. Cambridge: Cambridge University Press, 2008.

Levin, Christoph. *Das Alte Testament*. 2nd ed. Beck'sche Reihe 2160. Munich: Beck, 2003.

Leys, Ruth. *Trauma: A Genealogy*. Chicago: University of Chicago Press, 2000.

Lidstone, Robert. "Health and Mortality of Internally Displaced Persons: Reviewing the Data and Defining Directions for Research." Washington, DC: Brookings-Bern Project on Internal Displacement, 2007.

Lindars, Barnabas. "Ezekiel and Individual Responsibility." *VT* 15 (1965): 452–67.

Lipschits, Oded. "'Jehoiakim Slept with His Fathers' (II Kings 24.6)—Did He?" Pages 405–28 in vol. 4 of *Perspectives on Hebrew Scriptures. Vol. 1: Comprising the Contents of Journal of Hebrew Scriptures Volumes 1–4*. Edited by Ehud Ben Zvi. Piscataway, NJ: Gorgias, 2006.

Lohfink, Norbert. "Die Gattung der 'Historischen Kurzgeschichte' in den letzten Jahren von Juda und in der Zeit des Babylonischen Exils." *ZAW* 90 (1978): 319–47. Repr., pages 55–86 in *Studien zum Deuteronomium und zur deuteronomistischen Literatur II*. SBAB 12. Stuttgart: Katholisches Bibelwerk, 1991.

———. *Theology of the Pentateuch: Themes of the Priestly Narrative and Deuteronomy*. Translated by Linda M. Maloney. Minneapolis: Fortress, 1994.

Long, Michael H. "Maturational Constraints on Language Development." *Studies in Second Language Acquisition* 12 (1990): 251–85.

Luckenbill, D. D. *The Annals of Sennacherib*. Chicago: Oriental Institute, 1924.

Luhmann, Niklas. *Die Religion der Gesellschaft*. Frankfurt am Main: Suhrkamp, 2000. English translation: *A Systems Theory of Religion*. Translated by David A. Brenner with Adrian Hermann. Edited by André Kieserling. Stanford: Stanford University Press, 2013.

Lundbom, Jack R. "Baruch, Seraiah and Expanded Colophons in the Book of Jeremiah." *JSOT* 36 (1986): 89–114.

———. *Jeremiah: A Study in Ancient Hebrew Rhetoric*. SBLDS 18. Missoula, MT: Scholars Press, 1975.

———. *Jeremiah 37–52*. AB 21C. New York: Doubleday, 2004.

Maier, Christl. *Jeremia als Lehrer der Tora: Soziale Gebote des Deuteronomiums in Fortschreibungen des Jeremiabuches*. FRLANT 196. Göttingen: Vandenhoeck & Ruprecht, 2002.

Matties, Gordon H. *Ezekiel 18 and the Rhetoric of Moral Discourse*. SBLDS 126. Atlanta: Scholars Press, 1990.

McBride, S. Dean Jr. "Jeremiah and the Levitical Priests of Anathoth." Pages 179–96 in *Thus Says the Lord: Essays on the Former and Latter Prophets in Honor of Robert R. Wilson*. Edited by John J. Ahn and Stephen L. Cook. LHBOTS 502. New York: T&T Clark, 2009.

McEwan, Ian. *Atonement*. New York: Anchor, 2003.

McKane, William. *Commentary on Jeremiah XXVI–LII*. Vol. 2 of *A Critical and Exegetical Commentary on Jeremiah*. ICC. Edinburgh: T&T Clark, 1996.

McKeating, Henry. *Ezekiel*. OTG. Sheffield: Sheffield Academic, 1993.

Mein, Andrew. *Ezekiel and the Ethics of Exile*. OTM. Oxford: Oxford University Press, 2001.

Melugin, Roy F. *The Formation of Isaiah 40–55*. BZAW 141. Berlin: de Gruyter, 1976.

Merwe, Christo H. J. van der, Jackie A. Naudé, and Jan H. Kroeze. *A Biblical Hebrew Reference Grammar*. Biblical Languages: Hebrew 3. Sheffield: Sheffield Academic, 1999.

Meyer, Ivo. "Die Klagelieder." In *Einleitung in das Alte Testament*. Edited by Erich Zenger. 7th ed. Studienbücher Theologie 1.1. Stuttgart: Kohlhammer, 2008.

Meyer, Lester V. "Remnant." *ABD* 5:669–71.

Meyers, Carol L. "The Family in Early Israel." Pages 1–47 in *Families in Ancient Israel*. Edited by Leo G. Perdue, Joseph Blenkinsopp, John J. Collins, and Carol Meyers. Family, Religion, and Culture. Louisville: Westminster John Knox, 1997.

Meyers, Carol L., and Eric M. Meyers. *Haggai, Zechariah 1–8: A New Translation with Introduction and Commentary*. AB 25B. Garden City, NY: Doubleday, 1987.

———. *Zechariah 9–14: A New Translation with Introduction and Commentary*. AB 25C. New York: Doubleday, 1993.

Milgrom, Jacob. "Day of Atonement." *EncJud* 5:1384–87.
———. "HR in Leviticus and Elsewhere in the Torah." Pages 24–40 in *The Book of Leviticus: Composition and Reception*. Edited by Rolf Rendtorff and Robert A. Kugler. VTSup 93. Leiden: Brill, 2003.
———. "Israel's Sanctuary: The Priestly Picture of Dorian Gray." *RB* 83 (1976): 390–99.
———. "Kipper." *EncJud* 10:1039–44.
———. *Leviticus 1–16: A New Translation with Introduction and Commentary*. AB 3. New York: Doubleday, 1991.
———. *Leviticus 17–22: A New Translation with Introduction and Commentary*. AB 3A. New York: Doubleday, 2000.
———. "Sin Offering or Purification Offering?" *VT* 21 (1971): 237–39.
Minette de Tilesse, Caetano. "Joiaqim, repoussoir du 'pieux' Josias: Parallélismes entre II Reg 22 et Jer 36." *ZAW* 105 (1993): 353–76.
Monroe, Lauren A. S. *Josiah's Reign and the Dynamics of Defilement: Israelite Rites of Violence and the Making of a Biblical Text*. Oxford: Oxford University Press, 2011.
Mosis, Rudolf. "Ez 14:1–11—ein Ruf zur Umkehr." *BZ* 19 (1975): 161–94.
Motyer, J. Alec. *The Prophecy of Isaiah: An Introduction and Commentary*. Downers Grove, IL: InterVarsity Press, 1993.
Muilenburg, James. "The Book of Isaiah: Chapters 40–66." Pages 381–773 in vol. 5 of *The Interpreter's Bible*. Edited by George A. Buttrick. 12 vols. Nashville: Abingdon, 1956.
Mutawalli, Nawala al-. "A New Foundation Cylinder from the Temple of Nabû Ša Ḫare." *Iraq* 61 (1999): 191–94.
Na'aman, Nadav. "Death Formulae and the Burial Place of the Kings of the House of David." *Bib* 85 (2004): 245–54.
Nicholson, Ernest W. *Preaching to the Exiles: A Study of the Prose Tradition in the Book of Jeremiah*. New York: Schocken, 1971.
Nihan, Christophe. *From Priestly Torah to Pentateuch*. FAT 2/25. Tübingen: Mohr Siebeck, 2007.
Nissinen, Martti. "How Prophecy Became Literature." *SJOT* 19 (2005): 153–72.
Nogalski, James D. *Literary Precursors to the Book of the Twelve*. BZAW 217. Berlin: de Gruyter, 1993.
———. *Redactional Processes in the Book of the Twelve*. BZAW 218. Berlin: de Gruyter, 1993.

Nogalski, James D., and Marvin A. Sweeney, eds. *Reading and Hearing the Book of the Twelve*. SymS 15. Atlanta: Society of Biblical Literature, 2000.

North, Christopher R. *The Second Isaiah: Introduction, Translation, and Commentary to Chapters XL–LV*. Oxford: Clarendon, 1964.

Norwegian Refugee Council. *Iraq: A Displacement Crisis*. Geneva: Internal Displacement Monitoring Centre, 2007.

Noth, Martin. "Das Geschichtsverständnis der alttestamentlichen Apokalyptik." Pages 248–73 in *Gesammelte Studien zum Alten Testament*. ThB 6. Munich: Kaiser, 1957. English translation: "The Understanding of History in Old Testament Apocalyptic." Pages 194–214 in *The Laws in the Pentateuch and Other Studies*. Translated by D. R. Ap-Thomas. Edinburgh: Oliver & Boyd, 1966.

———. *The History of Israel*. Translated by Stanley Godman. New York: Harper & Row, 1960.

Novotny, Jamie. "Temple Building in Assyria: Evidence from Royal Inscriptions." Pages 109–39 in *From the Foundations to the Crenellations: Essays on Temple Building in the Ancient Near East and Hebrew Bible*. Edited by Mark J. Boda and Jamie Novotny. AOAT 366. Munster: Ugarit-Verlag, 2010.

Obaid, T. A. "Introduction." *Forced Migration* 27 (2007): 5–6.

Oded, Bustenay. *Mass Deportations and Deportees in the Neo-Assyrian Empire*. Wiesbaden: Reichert, 1979.

Odell, Margaret S. *Ezekiel*. SHBC. Macon, GA: Smyth & Helwys, 2005.

Odell, Margaret S., and John T. Strong, eds. *The Book of Ezekiel: Theological and Anthropological Perspectives*. SymS 9. Atlanta: Society of Biblical Literature, 2000.

Olyan, Saul M. "Exodus 31:12–17: The Sabbath according to H, or the Sabbath according to P and H?" *JBL* 124 (2005): 201–9.

Oorschot, Jürgen van. *Von Babel zum Zion*. BZAW 206. Berlin: de Gruyter, 1993.

Oswalt, John N. *The Book of Isaiah: Chapters 40–66*. NICOT. Grand Rapids: Eerdmans, 1998.

Patton, Corrine L. "Priest, Prophet, and Exile: Ezekiel as a Literary Construct." Pages 73–89 in *Ezekiel's Hierarchical World: Wrestling with a Tiered Reality*. Edited by Stephen L. Cook and Corrine L. Patton. SymS 31. Atlanta: Society of Biblical Literature, 2004.

Pearce, Laurie. "New Evidence for Judeans in Babylon." Pages 399–411 in

Judah and the Judeans in the Persian Period. Edited by Oded Lipschits and Manfred Oeming. Winona Lake, IN: Eisenbrauns, 2006.

Pearson, J. L., A. G. Hunter, M. E. Ensminger, and S. G. Kellam. "Black Grandmothers in Multigenerational Households: Diversity in Family Structure and Parenting Involvement in the Woodlawn Community." *Child Development* 61 (1990): 434–42.

Petersen, David L. *Haggai and Zechariah 1–8: A Commentary.* OTL. Philadelphia: Westminster, 1984.

———. *Zechariah 9–14 and Malachi: A Commentary.* OTL. Louisville: Westminster John Knox, 1995.

———. "Zechariah's Visions: A Theological Perspective." *VT* 34 (1984): 195–206.

Pierce, Ronald W. "A Thematic Development of the Haggai/Zechariah/Malachi Corpus." *JETS* 27 (1984): 401–11.

Pohlmann, Karl-Friedrich. *Das Buch des Propheten Hesekiel (Ezechiel): Kapitel 1–19.* ATD 22.1. Göttingen: Vandenhoeck & Ruprecht, 1996.

———. *Ezechiel: Der Stand der theologischen Diskussion.* Darmstadt: Wissenschaftliche Buchgesellschaft, 2008.

———. *Die Ferne Gottes—Studien zum Jeremiabuch: Beiträge zu den "Konfessionen" im Jeremiabuch und ein Versuch zur Frage nach den Anfängen der Jeremiatradition.* BZAW 179. Berlin: de Gruyter, 1989.

Polliack, Meira. "Deutero-Isaiah's Typological Use of Jacob in the Portrayal of Israel's National Renewal." Pages 72–110 in *Creation in Jewish and Christian Tradition.* Edited by Henning Graf Reventlow and Yair Hoffman. JSOTSup 319. Sheffield: Sheffield Academic, 2002.

Porter, Barbara N. *Images, Power, and Politics: Figurative Aspects of Esarhaddon's Babylonian Policy.* Philadelphia: American Philosophical Society, 1993.

Redditt, Paul L. "Zechariah 9–14, Malachi, and the Redaction of the Book of the Twelve." Pages 245–68 in *Forming Prophetic Literature: Essays on Isaiah and the Twelve in Honor of John D. W. Watts.* Edited by James W. Watts and Paul R. House. JSOTSup 235. Sheffield: Sheffield Academic, 1996.

Rehn, Elisabeth, and Ellen Johnson-Sirleaf. *Women, War, Peace: The Independent Experts' Assessment on the Impact of Armed Conflict on Women and Women's Role in Peace-Building.* Progress of the World's Women 1. New York: United Nations Development Fund for Women, 2002.

Reinmuth, Titus. *Der Bericht Nehemias: Zur literatischen Eigenart, traditionsgeschichtlichen Prägung und innerbiblischen Rezeption des Ich-Berichts Nehemias.* OBO 183. Freiburg: Universitätsverlag, 2002.

Renz, Thomas. *The Rhetorical Function of the Book of Ezekiel.* VTSup 76. Leiden: Brill, 1999.

Richter, Sandra Lynn. *The Deuteronomistic History and the Name Theology: lešakkēn šemô šām in the Bible and the Ancient Near East.* BZAW 318. Berlin: de Gruyter, 2002.

Rom-Shiloni, Dalit. *Exclusive Inclusivity: Identity Conflicts between the Exiles and the People Who Remained (6th–5th Centuries BCE).* LHBOTS 543. New York: Bloomsbury T&T Clark, 2013.

———. "Ezekiel as the Voice of the Exiles and Constructor of Exilic Ideology." *HUCA* 76 (2005): 1–45.

———. "Facing Destruction and Exile: Inner-Biblical Exegesis in Jeremiah and Ezekiel." *ZAW* 117 (2005): 189–205.

Römer, Thomas. "La conversion du prophète Jérémie à la théologie deutéronomiste." Pages 27–50 in *The Book of Jeremiah and Its Reception: Le livre de Jérémie et sa réception.* Edited by A. H. W. Curtis and Thomas Römer. BETL 128. Leuven: Peeters, 1997.

Roth, Cecil, and Geoffrey Wigoder, eds. *Encyclopaedia Judaica.* 16 vols. Jerusalem: Keter, 1971–1972.

Rudolph, Wilhelm. *Jeremia.* 3rd ed. HAT 1/12. Tübingen: Mohr, 1968.

Ruwe, Andreas. *"Heiligkeitsgesetz" und "Priesterschrift": Literaturgeschichtliche und rechtssystematische Untersuchungen zu Leviticus 17,1–26,2.* FAT 26. Tübingen: Mohr Siebeck, 1999.

Schaper, Joachim. "Numismatik, Epigraphik, alttestamentliche Exegese und die Frage nach der politischen Verfassung des achämenidischen Juda." *ZDPV* 118 (2002): 150–68.

Schart, Aaron. "Putting the Eschatological Visions of Zechariah in Their Place: Malachi as a Hermeneutical Guide for the Last Section of the Book of the Twelve." Pages 333–43 in *Bringing out the Treasure: Inner Biblical Allusion in Zechariah 9–13.* Edited by Mark J. Boda and Michael H. Floyd. JSOTSup 370. London: Sheffield Academic, 2003.

Schmid, Konrad. "L'Accession de Nabuchodonosor à l'hégémonie mondiale et la fin de la dynastie davidique: Exégèse intrabiblique et construction de l'histoire universelle dans le livre de Jérémie." *ETR* 81 (2006): 211–27.

———. *Buchgestalten des Jeremiabuches: Untersuchungen zur Redak-*

tions- und Rezeptionsgeschichte von Jer 30–33 im Kontext des Buches. WMANT 72. Neukirchen-Vluyn: Neukirchener Verlag, 1996.

——. "Kollektivschuld? Der Gedanke übergreifender Schuldzusammenhänge im Alten Testament und im Alten Orient." *ZABR* 5 (1999): 193–222.

——. *Literaturgeschichte des Alten Testaments*. Darmstadt: Wissenschaftliche Buchgesellschaft, 2008.

——. "Nebukadnezars Antritt der Weltherrschaft und der Abbruch der Davidsdynastie: Innerbiblische Schriftauslegung und universalgeschichtliche Konstruktion im Jeremiabuch." Pages 150–66 in *Die Textualisierung der Religion*. Edited by Joachim Schaper. FAT 62. Tübingen: Mohr Siebeck, 2009.

Schöpflin, Karin. "The Composition of Metaphorical Oracles within the Book of Ezekiel." *VT* 55 (2005): 101–20.

——. *Theologie als Biographie im Ezechielbuch: Ein Beitrag zur Konzeption alttestamentlicher Prophetie*. FAT 36. Tübingen: Mohr, 2002.

Schramm, Brooks. *The Opponents of Third Isaiah: Reconstructing the Cultic History of the Restoration*. JSOTSup 193. Sheffield: Sheffield Academic, 1995.

Schwartz, Baruch J. "The Bearing of Sin in the Priestly Literature." Pages 3–21 in *Pomegranates and Golden Bells: Studies in Biblical, Jewish, and Near Eastern Ritual, Law, and Literature in Honor of Jacob Milgrom*. Edited by David P. Wright, David Noel Freedman, and Avi Hurvitz. Winona Lake, IN: Eisenbrauns, 1995.

——. *The Holiness Legislation: Studies in the Priestly Code*. Jerusalem: Magnes, 1999.

——. "A Priest out of Place: Reconsidering Ezekiel's Role in the History of the Israelite Priesthood." Pages 61–71 in *Ezekiel's Hierarchical World: Wrestling with a Tiered Reality*. Edited by Stephen L. Cook and Corrine L. Patton. SymS 31. Atlanta: Society of Biblical Literature, 2004.

——. "The Priestly Account of the Theophany and the Lawgiving at Sinai." Pages 103–34 in *Texts, Temples, and Traditions: A Tribute to Menahem Haran*. Edited by Michael V. Fox, Victor Hurowitz, and Avi Hurvitz. Winona Lake, IN: Eisenbrauns, 1996.

Seitz, Christopher R. "Isaiah, Book of (First Isaiah)." *ABD* 3:472–88.

——. "The Book of Isaiah 40–66." Pages 309–552 in vol. 6 of *The New Interpreter's Bible*. Edited by Leader E. Keck. 12 vols. Nashville: Abingdon, 2001.

———. "Reconciliation and the Plain Sense Witness of Scripture." Pages 25–42 in *The Redemption: An Interdisciplinary Symposium on Christ as Redeemer*. Edited by Stephen T. Davis, Daniel Kendall, and Gerald O'Collins. Oxford: Oxford University Press, 2004.

———. *Zion's Final Destiny: The Development of the Book of Isaiah: A Reassessment of Isaiah 36–39*. Minneapolis: Fortress, 1991.

Shepherd, David. "Is the Governor Also among the Prophets? Parsing the Purpose of Jeremiah in the Memory of Nehemiah." Pages 209–28 in *Prophets, Prophecy, and Ancient Israelite Historiography*. Edited by Mark J. Boda and Lissa M. Wray Beal. Winona Lake, IN: Eisenbrauns, 2013.

Smart, James D. *History and Theology in Second Isaiah: A Commentary on Isaiah 35, 40–66*. Philadelphia: Westminster, 1965.

Smend, Rudolph. *Der Prophet Ezechiel*. Leipzig: Hirzel, 1880.

Smith, Daniel L. "The Politics of Ezra: Sociological Indicators of Postexilic Judaean Society." Pages 73–97 in *Persian Period*. Vol. 1 of *Second Temple Studies*. Edited by Philip R. Davies. JSOTSup 117. Sheffield: JSOT Press, 1991.

Smith, Mark S. *The Origins of Biblical Monotheism*. New York: Oxford University Press, 2001.

———. *The Priestly Vision of Genesis 1*. Minneapolis: Augsburg Fortress, 2010.

Smith-Christopher, Daniel L. *A Biblical Theology of Exile*. OBT. Minneapolis: Fortress, 2002.

———. "Ezekiel on Fanon's Couch: A Postcolonialist Dialogue with David Halperin's *Seeking Ezekiel*." Pages 108–44 in *Peace and Justice Shall Embrace: Power and Theopolitics in the Bible: Essays in Honor of Millard Lind*. Edited by Ted Grimsrud and Loren L. Johns. Telford, PA: Pandora, 1999.

———. "Reassessing the Historical and Sociological Impact of the Babylonian Exile (597/587–539 B.C.E.)." Pages 7–36 in *Exile: Old Testament, Jewish, and Christian Conceptions*. Edited by James M. Scott. JSJSup 56. Leiden: Brill, 1997.

Sommer, Benjamin D. *A Prophet Reads Scripture: Allusion in Isaiah 40–66*. Stanford, CA: Stanford University Press, 1998.

Stackert, Jeffrey. *Rewriting the Torah: Literary Revision in Deuteronomy and the Holiness Legislation*. FAT 52. Tübingen: Mohr Siebeck, 2007.

Stead, Michael R. *The Intertextuality of Zechariah 1–8*. LHBOTS 506. New York: T&T Clark, 2009.

Steiner, Richard C. "The Two Sons of Neriah and the Two Editions of Jeremiah in the Light of Two Atbash Code-Words for Babylon." *VT* 46 (1996): 74–84.

Stipp, Hermann-Josef. "Baruchs Erben: Die Schriftprophetie im Spiegel von Jer 36." Pages 145–70 in *"Wer darf hinaufsteigen zum Berg JHWHs?" Beiträge zu Prophetie und Poesie des Alten Testaments: Festschrift für Sigurdur Örn Steingrímsson*. Edited by Hubert Irsigler. Arbeiten zu Text und Sprache im Alten Testament 72. St. Ottilien: EOS, 2002.

———. *Jeremia im Parteienstreit: Studien zur Textentwicklung von Jer 26, 36–43 und 45 als Beitrag zur Geschichte Jeremias, seines Buches und judäischer Parteien im 6. Jahrhundert*. BBB 82. Frankfurt am Main: Hain, 1992.

———. "Sprachliche Kennzeichen jeremianischer Autorschaft." Pages 148–86 in *Prophecy in the Book of Jeremiah*. Edited by Hans M. Barstad and Reinhard G. Kratz. BZAW 388. Berlin: de Gruyter, 2009.

———. "Zur aktuellen Diskussion um das Verhältnis der Textformen des Jeremiabuches." Pages in 630–53 in *Die Septuaginta—Texte, Kontexte, Lebenswelten*. Edited by Martin Karrer and Wolfgang Kraus. WUNT 219. Tübingen: Mohr Siebeck, 2008.

Strine, Casey A. *Sworn Enemies: The Divine Oath, the Book of Ezekiel, and the Polemic of Exile*. BZAW 436. Berlin: de Gruyter, 2013.

Stuhlmueller, Carroll. *Creative Redemption in Deutero-Isaiah*. AnBib 43. Rome: Biblical Institute, 1970.

Stulman, Louis. "Reading the Prophets as Meaning-Making Literature for Communities under Siege." *HBT* 29 (2007): 153–75.

Stulman, Louis, and Hyun Chul Paul Kim, *You Are My People: An Introduction to Prophetic Literature*. Nashville: Abingdon, 2010.

Sweeney, Marvin A. *The Twelve Prophets*. 2 vols. Berit Olam. Collegeville, MN: Liturgical Press, 2000.

Tångberg, K. Arvid. *Die prophetische Mahnrede: Form- und traditionsgeschichtliche Studien zum prophetischen Umkehrruf*. FRLANT 143. Göttingen: Vandenheock & Ruprecht, 1987.

Taschner, Johannes. "Zusammenhalt trotz inhaltlicher Differenzen: Jer 36 als Selbstvergewisserung der Beamten und Schreiber in frühnachexilischer Zeit." *EvT* 69 (2009): 366–81.

Terrien, Samuel L. *The Elusive Presence: Toward a New Biblical Theology*. Religious Perspectives. San Francisco: Harper & Row, 1978.

Tiemeyer, Lena-Sofia. "Through a Glass Darkly: Zechariah's Unprocessed Visionary Experience." *V* 58 (2008): 573–94.

Tooman, William A. "Ezekiel's Radical Challenge to Inviolability." *ZAW* 121 (2009): 498–511.
Toorn, Karel van der. *Scribal Culture and the Making of the Hebrew Bible.* Cambridge: Harvard University Press, 2007.
Torrey, C. C. *The Second Isaiah: A New Interpretation.* Edinburgh: T&T Clark, 1928.
Trobisch, David. *Paul's Letter Collection: Tracing the Origins.* Minneapolis: Fortress, 1994.
Tuell, Steven Shawn. "Contemporary Studies of Ezekiel: A New Tide Rising." Pages 241–54 in *Ezekiel's Hierarchical World: Wrestling with a Tiered Reality.* Edited by Stephen L. Cook and Corrine L. Patton. SymS 31. Atlanta: Society of Biblical Literature, 2004.
———. *The Law of the Temple in Ezekiel 40–48.* HSM 49. Atlanta: Scholars Press, 1992.
United Nations High Commissioner for Refugees. "Total Population of Concern to UNHCR: Refugees, Asylum-Seekers, IDPs, Returnees, Stateless Persons, and Others of Concern to UNHCR by Country/Territory of Asylum, End-2009." Online: http://www.unhcr.org/globaltrends/2009-Global-Tends-annex.zip.
United Nations Population Fund. *Report on the International Symposium on Sexual Violence in Conflict and Beyond, 21–23 June 2006.* Brussels: UNFPA, 2006.
Vanderhooft, David. "Babylonian Strategies of Imperial Control in the West." Pages 235–62 in *Judah and the Judeans in the Persian Period.* Edited by Oded Lipschits and Manfred Oeming. Winona Lake, IN: Eisenbrauns, 2006.
———. *The Neo-Babylonian Empire and Babylon in the Latter Prophets.* HSM 59. Atlanta: Scholars Press, 1999.
———. "New Evidence Pertaining to the Transition from Neo-Babylonian to Achaemenid Administration in Palestine." Pages 219–35 in *Yahwism after the Exile: Perspectives on Israelite Religion in the Persian Era.* Edited by Rainer Albertz and Bob Becking. STAR 5. Assen: Van Gorcum, 2003.
Venema, G. J. *Reading Scripture in the Old Testament: Deuteronomy 9–10, 31; 2 Kings 22–23; Jeremiah 36; Nehemiah 8.* OtSt 48. Leiden: Brill, 2004.
Vogt, Peter T. *Deuteronomic Theology and the Significance of Torah: A Reappraisal.* Winona Lake, IN: Eisenbrauns, 2006.

Wagner, Amy E. "Extended Families." Pages 536–41 in vol. 2 of *International Encyclopedia of Marriage and Family*. Edited by James J. Ponzetti. 4 vols. New York: Macmillan, 2002.
Wahl, Harald-Martin. "Die Entstehung der Schriftprophetie nach Jer 36." *ZAW* 110 (1998): 365–89.
Wanke, Gunther. *Jeremia 25, 15–52, 34*. Vol. 2 of *Jeremia*. ZBK 20.2. Zurich: TVZ, 2003.
Weinfeld, Moshe. "God the Creator in Genesis 1 and in the Prophecy of Second Isaiah." [In Hebrew.] *Tarbiz* 37 (1968): 105–32.
Wellhausen, Julius. *Israelitische und jüdische Geschichte*. 9th ed. 1958. Repr., Berlin: de Gruyter, 1981.
Werlitz, Jürgen. "Vom Gottesknecht der Lieder zum Gottesknecht des Buches." *BK* 61 (2006): 208–11.
———. *Redaktion und Komposition: Zur Rückfrage hinter die Endgestalt von Jes 40–55*. BBB 122. Bodenheim: Philo, 1999.
Whybray, R. N. *Isaiah 40–66*. NCB. London: Oliphants, 1975.
Willey, Patricia Tull. *Remember the Former Things: The Recollection of Previous Texts in Second Isaiah*. SBLDS 161. Atlanta: Scholars Press, 1997.
Williamson, H. G. M. *Ezra, Nehemiah*. WBC 16. Waco, TX: Word, 1985.
Williamson, Paul R. *Abraham, Israel and the Nations: The Patriarchal Promise and Its Covenantal Development in Genesis*. JSOTSup 315. Sheffield: Sheffield Academic, 2000.
Wolters, Al. "'The Whole World Remains at Rest' (Zechariah 1:11): The Problem and an Intertextual Clue." Pages 128–43 in *Tradition in Transition: Haggai and Zechariah 1–8 in the Trajectory of Hebrew Theology*. Edited by Mark J. Boda and Michael H. Floyd. LHBOTS 475. New York: T&T Clark, 2008.
Wood, William P. "The Congregation of Yahweh: A Study of the Theology and Purpose of the Priestly Document." ThD diss., Union Theological Seminary in Virginia, 1974.
Worschech, Udo. "War Nebukadnezar im Jahre 605 v.Chr. vor Jerusalem?" *BN* 36 (1987): 57–63.
Wright, David P. "Holiness in Leviticus and Beyond: Differing Perspectives." *Int* 53 (1999): 351–64.
Zevit, Ziony. *The Religions of Ancient Israel: A Synthesis of Parallactic Approaches*. London: Bloomsbury, 2001.
Zimmerli, Walther. "Die Eigenart der prophetischen Rede des Ezechiel: Ein Beitrag zum Problem an Hand von Ez. 14 1–11." *ZAW* 66 (1954): 1–26.

———. *Ezekiel: A Commentary on the Book of the Prophet Ezekiel.* Vol. 1 translated by Ronald E. Clements; vol. 2 translated by James D. Martin. 2 vols. Hermeneia. Philadelphia: Fortress, 1979–1983.

Contributors

John Ahn, PhD (Yale), Assistant Professor of Religious Studies, St. Edward's University, Austin, Texas, USA

Frank Ritchel Ames, PhD (University of Denver/Iliff School of Theology), Professor of Medical Informatics, Rocky Vista University, Denver, Colorado, USA

Ulrich Berges, PhD (Gregorian University), Professor of Old Testament, University of Bonn, Bonn, Germany

Mark J. Boda, PhD (Cambridge), Professor of Old Testament, McMaster Divinity College; Professor, Faculty of Theology, McMaster University, Hamilton, Ontario, Canada

Stephen L. Cook, PhD (Yale), Catherine N. McBurney Professor of Old Testament Language and Literature at Virginia Theological Seminary, Alexandria, Virginia, USA

Corinna Körting, PhD (Hamburg), Professor of Old Testament Studies, University of Hamburg, Hamburg, Germany

Mark Leuchter, PhD (Toronto), Associate Professor of Hebrew Bible and Ancient Judaism, Director of Jewish Studies—Department of Religion, Temple University, Philadelphia, Pennsylvania, USA

David L. Petersen, Ph.D. (Yale), Franklin N. Parker Professor of Old Testament Emeritus, Candler School of Theology, Emory University; Atlanta, Georgia, USA

Konrad Schmid, PhD (Zurich), Professor of Hebrew Bible and Ancient Judaism at the University of Zurich, Zurich, Switzerland

Christopher R. Seitz, PhD (Yale), Senior Research Professor of Biblical Interpretation, Wycliffe College, University of Toronto

Louis Stulman, PhD (Drew), Professor of Religious Studies, University of Findlay, Findlay, Ohio, USA

Index of Primary Sources

Hebrew Bible / Old Testament

Genesis

1	2, 59 n. 18
1:1	56 n. 15, 57 n. 15
1:22	59
1:26	56 n. 15, 59 n. 18
1:27	59
1:28	59
2:2–3	56 n. 15, 57 n. 15
3:24	142
4:16	142
8:17	59
9:1	59
9:6	59 n. 18
9:7	59
9:8–17	52
10:8–12	164 n. 10
11	2
11:30	57
12	10
15:18	88
16:3	57
17	51 n. 6, 52, 58, 59–60
17:2	60
17:4	60
17:5	59
17:6	59
17:7	52, 58, 60
17:7–8	52 n. 8
17:8	60
17:16	60
17:17	57
17:20	59
20:6	167 n. 23
21:5	57
25–36	41
25:24–34	42
26	10
26:11	167 nn. 23–24
26:12	173
27:35–36	42
28:3	59
28:14	99
32:26	167 n. 24
32:33	167 n. 24
35:11	59
37:20	172
37:22	172
37:24	172
37:28–29	172
39:20	172
40:15	172
41:14	172
46	10
47:27	59
49	107

Exodus

Reference	Page
1:7	59
1:14	57
2:22	148
6:9	57
9:29	166 n. 20
9:33	166 n. 20
12:15	175
15	78
16	57
16:8	57 n. 16
16:11–12	57 n. 16

Exodus (cont.)

16:19–20	57
16:22–30	57 n. 16
24:15–18	54
24:17	55
25:8	54
25:20	166 n. 18
25:22	54, 55
28:38	123 n. 8, 130
28:43	123 n. 9
29:45–46	54
30:6	54–55
30:9	55
30:36	54
31:12–17	56 n. 14, 57 n. 15
31:13–17	57 n. 15
31:14	124 n. 15
31:17	56, 56 n. 15
34:7	123
34:9	176 n. 51
35:1–3	57 n. 15
37:9	166 n. 18

Leviticus

5:1	123 n. 9
5:2–3	128
5:14	50
5:15–16	50
5:17	123 n. 9
5:17–19	50
7:18	123 n. 9
9:23–24	54–55
10:2	54–55
10:10–11	126
10:11	97
10:17	123 n. 8, 130
11:44	54
14:6–10	57
16:2	55
16:22	130
16:22–26	123 n. 8
17	122, 125 n. 16, 131
17:3	125 n. 16
17:8	125 n. 16
17:10	125 n. 16
17:13	125 n. 16
17:16	123 n. 9
18:25–28	81 n. 12
19:1–2	54
19:8	123 n. 9
20:2	124 n. 15
20:7–8	54
20:17	123 n. 9, 124
20:19	123 n. 9, 124
20:20	124
22:16	123 n. 9
22:32	54
23:40	43 n. 36
24:8–9	55
24:15	124
25:25	53
25:47–49	53
26	80
26:33	163 n. 8
26:38–39	81 n. 12
26:44	81 n. 12

Numbers

5:3	54
5:31	123 n. 9
13:23	106
13:28	172 n. 39
14	58 n. 17
14:18	123
18:1	123 n. 8
19:20	175
28:2	55
30:16	123 n. 9
35:34	54

Deuteronomy

1:7	88
1:28	172 n. 39
3:5	172 n. 39
4:27	174 n. 45
4:27–28	113
9:1	172 n. 39
10:1–5	86, 87
11:26	170
18:1–8	48 n. 3

INDEX OF PRIMARY SOURCES

22:10	163	4:3–4	53
24	53		
24:3	53	1 Samuel	
27	92 n. 41	3	92
28	80	15:1–23	129 n. 35
28:15	170	17:1	177 n. 54
28:26	163		
28:36	113	2 Samuel	
28:45	170	6:1	177 n. 54
28:52	172 n. 39	7:18	126
28:63–64	81 n. 12	10:17	177 n. 54
28:64	113, 174 n. 45	12	106
29:16	113	12:28	177 n. 54
30:1	170	12:29	177 n. 54
30:3–4	173 n. 42	14:10	167 n. 24
31:9–13	79, 86	20:6	172 n. 39
31:11–12	95		
31:15	42	1 Kings	
31:19	95	3:6	58
31:22	95	4:21	89
31:26	86, 87, 95	4:33	106
32:8–9	176 n. 51	6:11–13	87–88
32:10	167 n. 25	6:27	166 n. 18
32:11	166 n. 18	8:7	166 n. 18
32:45	95	8:11	144
33:5	42	8:22	166 n. 20
33:17	163 n. 6	8:38	166 n. 20
33:26	42	8:54	166 n. 20
		9:4	58
Joshua		10:26	177 n. 54
1:4	88	14:15	89, 163 n. 8
9:19	167 n. 24	19	163 n. 6
14:12	172 n. 39	19:19	163
		19:19–20	163 n. 6
Judges		22:17	174 n. 45
3:13	177 n. 54	22:19–23	128 n. 32
9:12	106		
11:20	177 n. 54	2 Kings	
14:18	163 n. 6	6:32	126
16:21	172	15:1–4	108
16:25	172	17:13	125
18:7	176 n. 50	17:20	12
		18:13	172 n. 39
Ruth		19:18	113
3:2	163 n. 8	19:25	172 n. 39

2 Kings (cont.)
21:18	65
21:26	65
22	64 n. 2, 66
22:8	86, 87
24	109
24:6	65, 67
24:8	65
24:14, 16–17	13, 65
25:12	108 n. 25
25:22–26	108

1 Chronicles
3:17–18	67
9:24	167
16:8–36	37
16:13	38
16:35	173 n. 42
17:16	126
19:17	177 n. 54
22:2	166 n. 18
25:2	37
25:3	37
28:18	166 n. 18

2 Chronicles
1:14	177 n. 54
3:13	166 n. 18
5:8	166 n. 18
5:14	144
6:12	166 n. 20
6:13	166 n. 20
6:29	166 n. 20
7:2	144
17:2	172 n. 39
19:5	172 n. 39
20:7	52
32:1	172 n. 39
33:14	172 n. 39
36:14	50

Ezra
7:1	126 n. 23
7:11	126 n. 23
9:5	166 n. 20
10	126 n. 23
10:9	126 n. 23
10:19	50

Nehemiah
1:8	174 n. 45
1:8–9	173 n. 42
7:26	9 n. 1
9:25	172 n. 39
12:44	166 n. 18

Esther
4:16	166 n. 18

Job
1:14	163 n. 6
1:19	167 n. 24
3:13	172
11:13	166 n. 20
39:26	166 n. 18
40:22	43 n. 36

Psalms
17:8	167 n. 25
22:6	54
22:7 MT	54
26:8	176 n. 52
33:7	166 n. 18
44:12	163
44:21	166 n. 20
46:2	52
47:9	58–59
51:1	167
51:3 MT	167
68:1	166
68:2 MT	166
68:6	172
68:7 MT	172
68:14	166
68:15 MT	166
68:30	166
68:31 MT	166
69:31	163 n. 6
69:32 MT	163 n. 6
69:33	172

INDEX OF PRIMARY SOURCES 211

69:34 MT	172	5	104
79:11	172	5:1	104
83:17	169 n. 30	5:3	104
96	34, 37	5:4	104
98	34	5:7	104
102:20	172	5:10	104
102:21 MT	172	5:13	15
104:32	167 n. 24	6	92
105	37	6:1	59 n. 18
105:6	38	8:16	23
106:27	163 n. 8	8:18	23
106:47	173 n. 42	10:6	167
107:3	173 n. 42	10:20–23	15
107:10	172	11:11	15
135:4	42	11:12	173 n. 42
137	17, 23, 131	11:16	15
137:1	92 n. 43	13–23	28
137:1–6	109	13:9	169 n. 31
137:2	43	14:1	42
137:7–8	116	14:1–2	15
137:7–9	109	14:4b–12	18 n. 19
143:6	166	15:7	43 n. 36
144:5	167 n. 24	17:2	163
		24–27	37
Proverbs		25:2	172 n. 39
6:29	167 n. 23	25:11	166
7:2	167 n. 25	27:2	104
20:26	163	27:10	172 n. 39
31:20	166 n. 20	28:24–28	163 n. 6
		28:26	106
Ecclesiastes		30:24	163 n. 8
2:8	166 n. 18	33:10	59 n. 18
2:26	166 n. 18	33:13	165 n. 17
3:5	166 n. 18	35:6–7	25 n. 22
		36–39	15, 22, 28
Isaiah		36:1	172 n. 39
1–39	21–22	36:17	15
1:1	38	37:19	113
1:8	104	37:26	172 n. 39
1:10–17	50	38:3	58
1:11–14	55 n. 13	39	28, 37–38
1:15	166	40	23, 28, 38
2:6	142	40–48	25, 33
2:15	172 n. 39	40–50	4
3:14	104	40–55	24–28, 33–40, 51

Isaiah (cont.)

40–66	22, 48	43:10 Vg	39 n. 19
40:1	33	43:18	51
40:1–11	39	43:19	43 n. 35, 45
40:6	35, 43	43:22–38	49
40:8	54	43:24	50, 55
40:15	28	43:25	50
40:18	55, 56 n. 15	43:27	42
40:18–20	37	44	113
40:22	55	44:1	38, 42, 44 n. 41
40:24	169 n. 30	44:1–2	42, 44
40:25	56 n. 15	44:1–5	60
40:27	51	44:1–8	44
40:28–29	55	44:2	38, 42, 44 n. 41
41–44	42	44:3–4	42
41–48	38, 42	44:5	42
41:1–7	44	44:6–8	44
41:1–10	52	44:8	44
41:6–7	37	44:9–20	37, 44, 113–14
41:8	38, 42	44:11	44
41:9	25 n. 21, 44 n. 41	44:14–17	105
41:14	54	44:15	113
41:15–16	169 n. 30	44:16	114
41:16	163 n. 8	44:16–20	115
41:21–29	44	44:17	113, 170
41:27	38–39, 39 n. 18, 45	44:21	38, 44 n. 41
42	38, 43	44:22	50
42:1	44 n. 41	44:23	33, 46
42:1–4	38–39	44:26	39, 44 n. 41
42:1–9	29	44:28	48, 75
42:4	59 n. 18	45:1	75
42:9	39, 43 n. 35, 45	45:1–7	70
42:10	45	45:4	38, 44 n. 41
42:10–11	25 n. 21	45:8	33
42:10–12	33	45:13	48, 53
43	49	45:22–23	60
43:5	173 n. 42	46:5	56 n. 15
43:5–6	25 n. 21	46:5–7	37
43:5–7	28	46–47	29
43:6	165 n. 17	48:6	45
43:7	42	48:6–21	29
43:8	43	48:7	29
43:9	44	48:8	42
43:9–10	43	48:10	39, 45
43:10	3, 39, 43–44	48:11	34
		48:16	35

INDEX OF PRIMARY SOURCES

48:16b	39	53:10	48, 50
48:16c	38	53:11	123 n. 8
48:20	38	54	28
48:20–21	33	54–55	28
49	38	54:4–8	53
49–55	25, 28, 45	54:5	53
49:1–6	35, 38–39	54:7	173 n. 42
49:1–13	29	54:8	53
49:2	54	54:9	52
49:3	38	54:9–10	52
49:5	38	54:9–17	30
49:5–6	50	54:10	51–52
49:6	38	54:11	168–69
49:12	25 n. 21, 28, 165 n. 17	55:1–5	58
49:14	51	55:3	45, 58
49:14–23	28	55:3–5	34, 46 n. 45
49:26	45 n 44	55:4	45–46
50	38	55:5	46
50–66	55	55:10	43 n. 35
50:1	53, 53 n. 10	55:11	31
50:1–3	52	54:17	40, 40 n. 23, 44 n. 41
50:4	39	56–66	24, 27, 30, 37
50:4–9	35, 39, 40	56:3	116
50:5	39	56:6	40 n. 23
50:7	39	56:7	48
50:9	39	56:8	173 n. 42
50:10a	59 n. 18	57:15	54–55, 59 n. 18
51	60	60:4	165 n. 17
51:1–2	60	60:7	48
51:1–8	60	60:9	25 n. 21, 165 n. 17
51:1–17	28	60:13	48
51:2	51 n. 6	61:11	43 n. 35
51:11	50	62:9	48
51:15	34	62:12	48
52–53	130	63:17	40 n. 23
52:1	48	64:11	48
52:3	53, 53 n. 10	65:2	166
52:7	45	65:8–9	40 n. 23
52:8	48	65:13–17	40 n. 23
52:9–10	33	66:1	55
52:13	29, 59 n. 18	66:2	54
52:13–15	54	66:6	48
52:15	59 n. 18	66:14	40 n. 23
53	28, 35, 38		
53:3	125 n. 16		

Jeremiah		22:18–19	66–68, 75, 75 n. 21
1–25	94, 96	22:22	17
2:15	169 n. 31	22:23	110
2:21	107	22:29–30	66
2:23	128	22:30	67–68, 75, 75 n. 21
2:27	113	23:1	174 n. 45
3:1–8	52	23:2	174 n. 45
3:18	168	23:3	173 n. 42
4:7	169 n. 31	23:8	168
4:11	163 n. 8	23:19	169 n. 30
4:31	166	24:9	170
6:14	82 n. 15	25	69
6:20	55 n. 13	25:1	69, 75
6:22	168	25:10–11	69
7: 21–22	55 n. 13	25:11–12	73
7:24	125	25:18	170
7:33	163	25:32	169 n. 30
8:11	82 n. 15	26–45	82, 94, 95 n. 54, 96–97, 119
9	79	27	72–73, 75, 92
9:3	42	27–28 LXX	83
9:11–12	79, 95	27–29	82–83, 105
9:13	126	27:1	72–73, 73 n. 17
9:15 MT	174 n. 45	27:1–6	72
9:16	174 n. 45	27:3	72
9:20	79, 95	27:6	72
10:17–18	17	27:7	84
10:21	174 n. 45	27:12	72
10:22	168	27:22	84
12:10	104	28	85
12:14	167 n. 24	29	81–82, 92, 96, 104
13:10	126	29:1–3	84
13:17	17	29:5–7	81, 84–85, 159
13:19	17 n. 17	29:7	82, 84
13:24	17, 174 n. 45	29:10	81
14:16	66 n. 7	29:10–11	84
15:2	17	29:14	173 n. 42, 81
15:7	163 n. 8	29:21–32	82
15:20	172 n. 39	30:10	17, 38, 165 n. 17
16:1–9	139	30:23	169 n. 30
16:15	168	31:8	168, 173 n. 42
17:5	125	31:10	163, 163 n. 8, 173 n. 42
18:16	171	31:29	104
19:8	171	31:35	34
22	75 n. 21	32:6–15	98
22:18	67	32:37	173 n. 42

33:1	48 n. 3	50:3	169 n. 31
33:17-22	49 n. 4	50:10	167
33:21	48 n. 3	50:13	171
33:22	48 n. 3	50:14	163
35	63	50:17	18 n. 19
36	66, 70-71, 75, 93, 97	50:17-18	164 n. 10
36:1	68	51 LXX	83
36:1-3	70	51:29	169 n. 31
36:1-8	98	51:50	165 n. 17
36:9	68	51:53	169 n. 31
36:20	93	51:58	93
36:22	68	51:59	5, 84
36:30	5, 64-68, 65 n. 4, 66 n. 7, 71, 74, 75 n. 21	51:59-64a	83
		51:60	95
36:32	97	51:61	84
38:6	172	51:62	84
39:1-18	113	51:62-63	85
40-44	116, 119	51:63	85, 95
40:7	108	51:64	85, 93
40:13	115	51:64a	85, 93
42	10	51:64b	85
42-43	110	52	22, 109
42:13	116	52:16	108 n. 25
42:18	170	52:31	10
43	109	52:28-30	10, 13
43:6-7	111	59:9	168
43:8	108		
44	99 n. 63	Lamentations	
44:8	170	1:10	166 n. 20
44:12	170	2:18	167 n. 25
44:22	170	3	40
45:5	98	3:53	163
46-51	83, 85 n. 24	4:4	166 n. 20
46:10	168	5:20	51
46:19	169 n. 31	28:25	38
46:27-28	38 n. 17	37:25	38
48:9	169 n. 31		
48:40	166 n. 18	Ezekiel	
48:45-47	10 n. 2	1	92
48:46	10	1-3	141
49:13	171	1:1	12, 92
49:22	166 n. 18	1:1-3	121
49:32	163, 163 n. 8	1:2	17
49:36	163, 167	1:3	92
50-51	83, 84 n. 22	1:4	169 n. 30

Ezekiel (cont.)

1:26	59 n. 18
2:8	140
2:9–31	97 n. 56
2:10	138
3:14	139–40
3:15	92
3:22–26	139
4–24	138
4:4–6	124 n. 15, 130
4:4–8	139
4:4–17	123 n. 8
4:9–17	129, 139
5:1–4	139
5:2–4	174
5:2	163 n. 8
5:10	163, 163 n. 8
5:12	108, 163, 163 n. 8, 174
6	113
6:1	35
6:8	163 n. 8
7:1	35
7:26	128
8	112
8–11	92
8:1	110, 126 n. 22, 141–42
8:9	144
8:10	144
8:12	140
9:3	142
9:8	140
9:9	141
10:3–4	142
10:15	92
10:18–22	54, 142
10:20	92
10:22	92
11:1–25	142
11:3	141
11:13	140
11:16	97, 144, 174 n. 45
11:17	173 n. 42, 174 n. 45
11:19	125 n. 19
11:20–21	131
11:22–24	143
12	17, 105–6, 113
12:1	35, 106
12:1–6	139
12:2–5	106
12:3–6	105
12:4	108
12:6	139
12:6–8	106
12:8–9	105
12:10	106
12:12c	106
12:14	163 n. 8
12:14–15	163
12:14–16	106
12:15	106, 163 n. 8
12:17–20	139
12:21–25	141
13	113
13:11	169 n. 30
13:13	169 n. 30
13:23	143
14	112–15, 122–24, 126, 128, 130–31
14:1	126
14:1–5	112
14:1–11	6, 122, 126–27, 127 n. 24
14:3	125, 128
14:4	125, 125 n. 6, 128
14:6	125
14:6–10	112
14:7	112, 125, 125 n. 16, 128
14:8	112
14:8–9	124
14:10	123 n. 9
14:11	126, 129, 131
14:12	123 n. 9
14:16	113
14:20	115
14:22	113
14:22–23	77, 98
15	6, 103–6, 109–11, 111 n. 34, 115, 119
15–19	103–4, 107–6, 110
15:1–4	116
15:1–8	101
15:2–5	105

15:4	116, 118	26:12	167
15:4 LXX	116	28:25	173 n. 42
15:5	104, 118	29:1	110
15:5 LXX	117	29:13	173 n. 42
15:5 MT	117	29:17	110
15:5–6	116	29:19	167
15:6 MT	117	33:10	141
15:6–8	105	33:17	140
15:7 LXX	118	33:21	17
15:7–8	116–18	33:23–29	61, 108
16	82	33:24	51 n. 6
17	107, 110–11, 111 n. 34	33:31	126
17–19	104	34	82
17:7	104	34:5	174 n. 45
17:10	167 n. 24	34:6	174 n. 45
17:17	104	34:12	166 n. 19, 174 n. 45
17:21	166–67	34:13	173 n. 42
18	107, 110–11, 111 n. 34, 128, 130	35:7	169 n. 31
18:2	104, 140	36–37	82
18:25	140	36:19	163 n. 8
19	107, 110–11, 111 n. 34	36:24	173 n. 42
19:4	110	36:25	128
19:10	104	36:26–27	125 n. 19
20	110, 112–15	36:26–29	131
20:1	126	36:35	172 n. 39
20:9	34	37:1–14	139
20:12	54	37:11	140
20:14	34	37:21	173 n. 42
20:22	34	37:23	131
20:23	163 n. 8	37:27	54
20:25	140	38:12	167
20:32	112, 115	39:10	167
20:41	173 n. 42	39:27	173 n. 42
20:45–49	113	40–48	132 n. 44, 144
20:47	115	40:1	17
21:1–5 MT	113	40:44–46	49 n. 3
22:15	163 n. 8	42:20	167
22:26	127	43:5	144
22:20–22	113	43:6–9	144
23	82	43:7	54
24:15–27	139	43:9	54
24:24	139	44:4	144
25–32	108	44:23	127
25:4	142	48:35	144
25:10	142		

Daniel	
6:10	109
9	7
9:7	165 n. 17
11:4	167
11:10	177 n. 54

Hosea	
2:25	173
8:13	14
8:14	172 n. 39
9:3	14
9:17	15
10:1	107
10:2	126
10:11	163 n. 6
11:5	14
12:4	42
13:3	169
14:7	107

Joel	
1:11–12	107
2:22	107

Amos	
1:6	14
1:9	14
1:14	169 n. 30
4:11	165
5:5	14
5:19	106
5:27	14
6:7	14
6:12	163 n. 6
7:11	14
9:5	167 n. 24

Jonah	
1:4	169 n. 30
1:12	169 n. 30
4:5	142
4:6	107

Micah	
1:16	16
2:12	173 n. 42
3:3	166 n. 20
4:4	107
4:6	16, 173 n. 42
4:10	18 n. 19
4:12	173
5:3	16
6:6–7	55 n. 13
7:6	125 n. 16

Nahum	
2:7	16
3:20	16

Habakkuk	
2:8	167
3:14	169 n. 30

Zephaniah	
1:16	172 n. 39
3:20	173 n. 42

Haggai	
1:1	165 n. 13
1:12	170
1:14	170
2:2	170
2:11	127
2:15–19	171
2:19	107

Zechariah	
1	177
1–2	162
1–6	156
1–8	7, 20, 20 n. 4, 148, 156–58, 170 n. 32, 179
1:1	156
1:1–6	156, 168
1:3	176
1:4	158
1:7	156, 162, 176 n. 52, 179
1:7–17	156, 162

1:12	73, 73 n. 18, 74	4:6b–10a	164
1:12–17	164	4:10b	162
1:14–17	157	5	176
1:16	176	5:5–11	175, 175 n. 48
1:17	157	5:6	175
1:18–21	157, 162–63, 175 n. 48, 179	5:8	175
1:18–2:1	157	6:1	176
1:18–2:13	168, 177–78	6:1–8	162, 168 n. 28
1:19	164, 164 n. 9, 178	6:9–15	164–65, 178
1:21	158, 164, 164 n. 9, 178	6:10	165
2 MT	168, 177–78	6:10–17	168 n. 28
2:1–4 MT	162–63, 175 n. 48, 179	7	20, 178
2:1–5	162	7–8	21, 168–69
2:1–5 MT	157	7:1	156
2:2 MT	164, 164 n. 9, 178	7:1–14	168, 178
2:4 MT	158, 164, 164 n. 9, 178	7:7	157, 169
2:5	176	7:9–10	158
2:5–9 MT	162	7:14	168–69, 169 n. 31, 178
2:6	164, 168	8:1–13	168–71
2:6–9	161, 165, 167, 174, 179	8:3	158, 177
2:6–13	164–65, 168, 176, 178	8:4	158
2:7	168	8:6–8	169–70
2:9	167	8:7	170–71, 178
2:9 MT	176	8:9–13	169
2:10 MT	164, 168	8:10–12	157
2:10–11	176	8:11	171
2:10–13	179	8:11–13	169–70
2:10–13 MT	161, 165, 167, 174, 179	8:12	107
2:10–17 MT	164–65, 168, 176, 178	8:13	170, 171, 178
2:11	178 n. 55	8:14–23	168
2:11 MT	168	8:15	157
2:12	176, 176 n. 49	8:17–20	158
2:13	176	8:20–23	29, 158, 177
2:13 MT	167	8:23	158
2:14–15 MT	176	9–10	171, 173, 179
2:14–17 MT	179	9–14	20, 24, 156, 159 n. 39, 171, 174, 179
2:15 MT	178 n. 55		
2:16 MT	176, 176 n. 49	9:1	171
2:17 MT	176	9:1–8	177, 179
3	164	9:9–15	159 n. 39
3:8	126 n. 23	9:11–13	171–72
3:10	107	9:13	178
4	176	9:17	159 n. 39
4–6	162	10	172–73
4:1–6a	162	10:1	159 n. 39

Zechariah (cont.)

10:1–3a	174		
10:3a–5	172	Yoma	8:8
10:6	173	124	
10:6–11	171–72, 178		
10:7	173	Septuagint	
10:8	173 n. 42		
10:9	173, 178	Jeremiah	
10:10	173, 173 n. 42, 178	27–28	83
11	179	51	83
11:1–3	174		
11:4–16	174	Ezekiel	
11:17	174	15:4	116
12	174	15:5	117
12–14	173, 178, 180	15:7	118
12:1	173		
13:7–9	174–75	Deuterocanonical Works	
14	173–74, 177		
14:1	174	Sirach	
14:1–2	180	37:25	42
14:2	159 n. 39, 174–75	48:24	30

Malachi

2:2–10	127	Dead Sea Scrolls	
2:3	127		
2:4	49 n. 4	1QIsa[a]	60
2:7	127		
3:6	42	Ancient Near Eastern Texts	

KTU

1.6.8–25   79

New Testament

John
- 2   107
- 15   107

Acts
- 19   114 n. 39

Hebrews
- 2:13   23

Josephus

Jewish Antiquities
- 10.180–185   110

Index of Modern Authors

Ackroyd, Peter R. 165, 171
Adams, Jim W. 44 n. 40
Ahn, John J. 101–3, 109, 115
Ahn, John 1, 6
Albani, Matthias 73 n. 19
Albertz, Rainer 35 n. 6
Alfrink, Bernardus 65 n. 3
Allen, Leslie 109, 134
Al-Mutawalli, Nawala 90 n. 38
Ames, Frank 1, 7
Amit, Yaira 57 n. 15
Anderson, Gary A. 124
Baltzer, Dieter 34 n. 3
Baltzer, Klaus 25, 25 n. 24, 28 n. 31
Barstad, Hans 24 n. 20, 26, 26 n. 26, 28 n. 31
Bean, F. D. 154
Becker, Uwe 64 n. 2
Becking, Bob 12 n. 10
Bedford, Peter 98 n. 62
Begg, Christopher T. 65 n. 4
Ben-Dov, Jonathan 97 n. 57
Benson, J. E. 154
Berges, Ulrich 4–5, 33, 33 n. 1, 39 n. 21, 42 n. 33, 43 n. 35, 44 n. 38, 46 n. 46
Berlin, Adele 81 n. 13
Berry, Donald K. 21 n. 8
Beuken, Willem 28 n. 33
Blank, Sheldon H. 40 n. 24, 40 n. 27
Blenkinsopp, Joseph 25, 26 n. 25, 28 n. 31, 78 n. 31 25, 134
Block, Daniel 106–7
Boadt, Lawrence 103
Boda, Mark 7, 21 n. 6, 21 n. 7, 87 n. 29, 98 n. 61, 156, 161–64, 170, 174
Boling, R. G. 49 n. 4
Borger, Riekele 89 n. 35
Breugemann, Walter 51 n. 6
Brown, Raymond 107
Brown, William P. 57 n. 15
Brownlee, William 106, 108, 127–28, 134
Buber, Martin 136
Calvin, John 22 n. 13
Carley, Keith W. 109
Carr, David M. 80–81 n. 11, 93 n. 47, 97 n. 57
Carroll, R. P. 13 n. 14, 67 n. 8
Childs, Brevard S. 19 n. 2, 26, 26 n. 29, 27 n. 30
Childs, Brevard 104, 111
Christian, Patricia B. 154
Clements, R. E. 109, 123, 132, 134
Clements, R. E. 29 n. 34, 51–52 n. 7
Cogan, Mordechai 73 n. 19
Cohen, Shaye J. D. 94 n. 50
Colic-Peisker, V. 155
Cook, Stephen L. 4–5, 47, 48 n. 2, 49 n. 3, 54 n. 11, 55 n. 12, 57 n. 16, 81 n. 14
Cook, Stephen L. 48 n. 3
Cooke, G. A. 108–9
Craigie, Peter C. 145
Cross, Frank Moore 78 n. 5
Curtis, Byron G. 164
Delitzsch, Franz 22, 22 n. 14, 23
Donner, Herbert 69 n. 11
Driver, G. R. 165–66
Driver, S.R. 56 n. 15, 57 n. 16
Duhm, Bernhard 21, 21 n. 9, 22 n. 11, 24, 24 n. 20, 33, 38

Durlesser, James A. 109
Eichhorn, J. G. 21, 22, 22 n. 12,
Eichrodt, Walther 103, 108–9
Elitz, Andreas 51 n. 7
Elliger, Karl 176
Ellis, Richard S. 86 n. 27
Ensminger, Margaret E. 154
Eshel, Esther 89 n. 33
Etherington, Norman 147
Ewald, Heinrich 21
Fabry, H.-J. 125–26
Feuerstein, Rüdiger 37 n. 16
Firmage, Edwin B. 56–57 n. 15
Fishbane, Michael 51 n. 6, 56 n. 15, 59 n. 18, 60 n. 19
Flannery, K. V. 154–55
Floyd, Michael H. 165–66, 173
Fohrer, Georg 84 n. 22, 85 n. 24
Ford, D. Y. 154
Freedman, David Noel 148
Friedman, Richard E. 49 n. 4, 88 n. 31
Galil, Gershon 11 n. 6
Garber, David G., Jr. 112, 136, 139
Garfield, Richard M. 152
Gerstenberger, Erhard S. 36 n. 11
Gesenius, Wilhelm 21, 21 n. 9
Glick, J. E. 154
Gowan, Donald E. 134, 138
Graham, J. N. 108
Graupner, M. 125
Gray, George Buchanan 58 n. 17
Grayson, A.K. 12 n. 9, 69 n. 11, 69 n. 13, 71 n. 16
Green, Alberto R. W. 65 n. 3
Green, David 35 n. 6
Greenberg, Moshe 102, 105, 107–9, 122, 128, 134
Gründwaldt, Klaus 123, 125
Haarmann, Volker 41 n. 30
Halperin, David 136
Halpern, Baruch 89 n. 34
Hals, Ronald M. 127
Haran, Menahem 80 n. 11, 96 n. 56
Hardmeier, Christof 64 n. 2
Harris, J. J. 154
Hasel, Gerhard F. 124, 170
Heinisch, Paul 109
Heller, Steven 152
Herman, Judith 137
Hermisson, Hans-Jürgen 34 n. 5, 35 nn. 7–8, 40 n. 28, 46 n. 45
Herrmann, Johannes 103
Heschel, Abraham Joshua 139
Hibbard, James T. 37 n. 15
Hoffman, Yair 63 n. 2, 66 n. 6
Hoglund, Kenneth G. 172
Holladay, William L. 67 n. 8, 82 n. 16, 84 n. 22
Hölscher, Gustave 103
Hourani, Albert 133
Hunter, Andrea G. 154
Hurowitz, Victor A. 87 n. 28
Hurvitz, Avi 80 n. 11, 123
Huston, Phil 136
Hutton, Jeremy M. 78 n. 7
Irwin, W. A. 105
Jacob, Irene 107
Jacob, Walter 107
Johnson-Sirleaf, Ellen 151–52
Jong, Matthijs J. de 122
Joosten, Jan 123, 125
Joyce, Paul M. 125, 129, 134
Kaminsky, Joel S. 129–30
Karrer-Grube, Christiane 98 n. 61
Katz, Ruth 154–55
Keel, Othmar 41 n. 29
Kellam, Sheppard G. 154
Kessler, John 161, 163–65, 168, 170–71, 178
Khalil, Karim 150, 152
Kiesow, Klaus 25 n. 22
Kim, Hyun Chul Paul 111, 133
Kira, Ibrahim Aref 137
Klein, Ralph W. 52 n. 7, 53 n. 10
Klein, Ralph W. 102
Knohl, Israel 47 n. 1, 48, 48 n. 3, 53 n. 10, 55 n. 12, 56 nn. 14–15, 57 n. 15, 58 n. 17, 80 n. 11
Körting, Corrina 6
Kohn, Risa Levitt 102, 134

Kratz, Reinhard G. 39 n. 22, 73 n. 18
Kutsko, John F. 134, 143–45
Labahn, Antje 34 n. 4
Lang, Bernhard 121–22
Lau, Wolfgang 37 n. 14
Lavee, Yoav 154
Leene, Henk 34 n. 2, 39 n. 22, 45, 45 n. 42,
Leeuwen, Cees van 43 n. 37
Leuchter, Mark 5–6, 7 n. 3, 49 n. 4, 74 n. 19, 77, 78 n. 4, 81 n. 13, 86 n. 25, 89 n. 37, 94 nn. 48–49, 94 n. 51, 95 n. 53, 96 n. 55, 97 n. 57, 97 n. 60
Levin, Christophe 36 n. 10, 116
Ley, Ruth 136
Lidstone, Robert 153
Lindars, Barnabas 129, 132
Lipschits, Oded 65 n. 3
Lohfink, Norbert 57 n. 16, 64 n. 2
Long, Michael H. 155
Luckenbill, D.D. 90 n. 39
Luhmann, Niklas 3
Lundbom, Jack R. 83 nn.19–21, 84 n. 22, 85 n. 24, 86 n. 25, 93 nn. 45–46, 94 n. 51, 95 n. 52
Maier, Christl 67 n. 8
Matties, Gordon H. 129
McBride, S. Dean, Jr. 49 n. 4
McEwan, Ian 141
McKane, William M. 67 n. 8
McKeating, Henry 137
Mein, Andrew 124, 127, 130, 134
Melugin, Roy F. 44, 44 n. 39
Meyer, Ivo 40 n. 25
Meyer, Lester V. 170
Meyers, Carol L. 20, 20 n. 5, 149, 163–64, 167–68, 170–74, 176
Meyers, Eric M. 20, 20 n. 5, 163–64, 167–68, 170–74, 176
Middlemas, Jill 101–2
Milgrom, Jacob 47 n. 1, 50 n. 5, 56 n. 14, 57 n. 15, 124, 129
Monroe, Lauren A. S. 80 n. 11
Mosis, Rudolf 126, 131
Moyter, J. Alec 55 n. 13

Muilenberg, James 24, 24 n. 18, 25
Na'aman, Nadav 65 n. 3
Neugut, Alfred I. 152
Nicholson, Ernest W. 23 n. 16
Nihan, Christophe 52 n. 8
Nissinen, Martti 75 n. 23
Nogalski, James W. 21 n. 8
North, Christopher R. 55 n. 13
Noth, Martin 75 n. 22, 110
Novotny, Jamie 86–87 n. 27
Obaid, T. A. 152
Oded, Bestenay 10 n. 4, 11 n. 6
Odell, Margaret S. 112, 134, 142
Olyan, Saul M. 56 n. 14, 57 n. 15
Oorschot, Jürgen van 25, 25 n. 23
Oswalt, John 55 n. 13
Patton, Corrine L. 48 n. 3, 121–22, 127, 131
Pearce, Laurie 11 n. 8
Pearson, J. L. 154
Peres, Yochanan 155
Petersen, David L. 3–4, 9, 161, 168–69, 174, 177
Pierce, R.W. 21 n. 7
Pohlmann, Karl-Friedrich 40 n. 26, 121–22, 131
Polliack, Meria 41 n. 31, 42, 42 nn. 33–34
Porter, Barbara N. 86 n. 27, 89 n. 36
Redditt, Paul L. 21 n. 7
Rehn, Elisabeth 151–52
Reinmuth, Titus 98 n. 61
Renz, Thomas 111, 122, 130
Richter, Sandra L. 86 n. 27
Ringgren, Helmer 70 n. 15
Römer, Thomas 64 n. 2
Rom-Shiloni, Dalit 7 n. 3, 78 n. 2, 82 n. 17, 92 n. 42, 98 n. 61, 103, 113
Rudolph, Wilhelm 83–84 n. 22
Ruwe, Andreas 47 n. 1
Schaper, Joachim 68 n. 10
Schart, Aaron 21 n. 7, 24 n. 19
Schmid, Konrad 5, 63, 63 n. 1, 64 n. 2, 73 n. 18, 125, 129
Schöpflin, Karin 109, 122, 131

Schramm, Brooks	37 n. 14	Weinfeld, Moshe	56 n. 15
Schumpp, Meinrad	109	Welhausen, Julius	35, 36 n. 9
Schwartz, Baruch J.	47 n. 1, 124, 126–28	Werlitz, Jurgen	39 n. 18, 40 n. 27, 45 n. 43
Seitz, Christopher	4, 19, 19 n. 2, 22 n. 10, 25 n. 22, 28 nn. 31–33	Whybray, R. N.	55 n. 13
		Willey, Patricia Tull	52 n. 7, 52 n. 9
Shepherd, David	98 n. 61	Williamson, H. G. M.	126
Smart, James D.	25 n. 21, 26, 26 n. 28	Williamson, Paul R.	52 n. 7
Smend, Rudolf	103	Wolters, Al	20 n. 3
Smith, Daniel L.	148	Wood, William P.	53 n. 10
Smith, Mark S.	78 n. 6, 89 n. 32	Worschech, Udo	69 n. 11
Smith-Christopher, Daniel	134, 136	Wright, David P.	47 n. 1
Sommer, Benjamin D.	49 n. 3, 52, 52 n. 9, 56 n. 15, 59 n. 18	Wright, N.T.	30 n. 37
		Zevit, Ziony	79 n. 8
Stackert, Jeffrey R.	47 n. 1, 57 n. 15	Zimmerli, Walther	102, 109–10, 121–23, 130, 134
Stead, Michael R.	21 n. 6		
Steiner, Richard C.	83 n. 19		
Stipp, Hermann-Josef	63 n. 2, 66 n. 5, 73 n. 17		
Strine, Casez A.	102		
Strong, John T.	134		
Stuhlmuller, Carroll	51 n. 6, 53 n. 10		
Stulman, Louis	6, 111, 133, 156		
Sweeney, Marvin A.	21 n. 8, 163, 165, 168		
Tångberg, K. Arvid	127		
Taschner, Johannes	64 n. 2		
Terrien, Samuel L.	136		
Tilesse, Caetano Miette de	64 n. 2		
Tooman, William A.	93 n. 44, 97 n. 58		
Toorn, Karel van der	36 n. 12, 75 n. 23, 79 n. 10, 85 n. 25, 91 n. 40, 97 n. 56		
Torrey, C. C.	26, 26 n. 27		
Trobisch, David	19 n. 1		
Tuell, Steven Shawn	49 n. 3, 102		
Van Hook, J. V. W.	154		
Vanderhooft, David	10 n. 5, 11 n. 7, 12 n. 10, 18 n. 19		
Venema, G. J.	64 n. 2		
Vogt, Peter T.	49 n. 4		
Wagner, Amy E.	154		
Wahl, Martin	63 n. 2, 66 n. 6		
Walker, I.	155		
Wanke, Gunther	64 n. 2		

www.ingramcontent.com/pod-product-compliance
Lightning Source LLC
Chambersburg PA
CBHW031709230426
43668CB00006B/164